My People

Abba Eban's History of the Jews

ADAPTED BY DAVID BAMBERGER

My People

Abba Eban's
History of the Jews

VOLUME II

BEHRMAN HOUSE, INC., PUBLISHERS
NEW YORK, NEW YORK

To my family

DESIGNER: *Betty Binns*
ARTIST: *Alice D'Onofrio*
PROJECT EDITOR: *Geoffrey Horn*

© Copyright 1979 by Abba Eban and David Bamberger

Published by Behrman House, Inc.
1261 Broadway
New York, N.Y. 10001
MANUFACTURED IN THE UNITED STATES OF AMERICA

Levi Yitzhok of Berdichev, "Kaddish." From *The Golden
Peacock*, translated by Joseph Leftwich. 1969. Thomas
Yoseloff. Used by permission.
Children's poems from Terezin. From . . . *I NEVER SAW
ANOTHER BUTTERFLY* . . . edited by H. Volavokova.
1964. McGraw-Hill Book Company. Used with permission
of the publisher.

Library of Congress Cataloging in Publication Data
Bamberger, David.
  My people.

  Includes index.
  SUMMARY: A two-volume history of the Jewish people.
  1. Jews—History—Juvenile literature. [1. Jews—
History] I. Eban, Abba Solomon, 1915–   My people.
II. Title.
DS118.B344   909'.04'924   77-10667
ISBN 0-87441-263-3 (v. 1)
ISBN 0-87441-280-3 (v. 2)

Contents

A WORD OF THANKS

I would like to express my gratitude to Jacob Behrman for entrusting me
with the responsibility of preparing these volumes. I have found that
immersing myself in the history of the Jewish people has been one of the
most exciting experiences of my life. I am also grateful to his staff, and
especially editor Geoffrey Horn, for their wonderful preparation and
illustrating of the text.

It has been my good fortune to have a family which could make extraordinary contributions to the project. My wife, Carola, has always been both
my greatest support and my most incisive critic. My son, Steven, offered
useful suggestions from the student viewpoint. My brother, Rabbi Henry
Bamberger, provided thorough notes on every draft. My father, Rabbi
Bernard J. Bamberger, brought his encyclopedic knowledge to bear on every
page; yet, even more than from his specific suggestions, this book has been
inspired by a lifetime of experiencing his learning, his wisdom, and his love
for Judaism.

A special word of appreciation is due to the men and women of Beth
Israel–The West Temple, Cleveland, Ohio (and especially to the congregation's all-volunteer library committee) for creating a research facility of
extraordinary quality. If I had not had access to this library, this book could
never have been completed on schedule.

D.B.

Thanks are once again due to Morrison D. Bial, Neal Kozodoy, and Myron
E. Schoen, who contributed as significantly to this second volume of
My People as they did to the first. In addition, I am grateful to Seymour
Rossel of Behrman House, who helped with the Hebrew and the special
topics, particularly "The Making of Modern Hebrew" (pages 122–123).

The sources of some of the quotations in text are as follows: page 96,
"A Shtetl Marriage Contract," freely adapted from *The Autobiography of
Solomon Maimon*, translated by J. Clark Murray (East and West Library,
1954); page 103, "The Cantonists," quoted in S. M. Dubnow, *History of the
Jews in Russia and Poland*, translated by I. Friedlander (Jewish Publication
Society, 1918); page 142, "The Banner of the Jew," in *Poems of Emma
Lazarus* (Boston: Houghton Mifflin, 1899); page 157, quoted in William L.
Shirer, *The Rise and Fall of the Third Reich* (Simon and Schuster, 1960).
The data used in the map on pages 174–175 come from Lucy S. Dawidowicz,
The War Against the Jews, 1933–1945; the data for the map on pages
220–221 are based on population estimates in the *American Jewish Year Book,
1978*. The source for the "American Jewish Firsts" cited on page 230 is
Tina Levitan's *The Firsts of American Jewish History* (Charuth Press,
1957).

Finally, I should like to express my gratitude to Abba Eban, whose
anecdotes and seasoned judgments (appearing under the heading "Abba
Eban Remembers") so greatly enrich this second volume.

G.M.H.

The Great Tradition

The history of the Jews is the story of the impossible. Time after time, the Jewish people has challenged ideas and practices that seemed easy, obvious, and "normal." We have opposed mighty nations and empires when we thought their beliefs were false. Yet we have survived and prospered for forty centuries, while many powerful empires have collapsed and disappeared.

Our willingness to stand alone in the search for truth can be traced back to our very beginnings as a people. Four thousand years ago, the tribe of Abraham became convinced that God had given it a special destiny, a special role in the life of humanity. It was to inherit the land of Canaan, and to change the religious life of the world.

Wishful thinking. Wild ideas. Yet today the descendants of this people are living in the Promised Land, and nearly half the peoples of the earth trace their religious history back to the moment when Abraham felt himself called to the service of the One God.

The birth of an idea

Faith in a single God was our people's most basic belief, and the one that at first seemed the most ridiculous to others. Today, though we realize there can be no scientific proof that God exists, we do know that there is one basic structure to all matter and energy. But to the ancients, the idea that there was any basic unity in the world seemed absurd. How could there be one common force in such differing elements as earth and air, fire and water? Nearly everyone believed that these were separate powers, each with its own god represented by a special idol.

"No," said our ancestors. "If everyone believes this, then everyone is wrong. There is one single Force which is the source of all life, a Force which is present in each part of the universe and yet which cannot be portrayed in any form."

Our ancestors went much further. "This Force — our God — is also the source of law," they said, "We need no longer fear that while the

Facing page: a wall painting shows
slaves making bricks in ancient Egypt,
just as the Hebrews did before Moses
led them to freedom. Right: a
3000-year-old incense-burning altar
found at Megiddo, a Canaanite city
rebuilt by our ancestors during the reign
of King Solomon.

spirit of the sun wants us to act one way, the spirit of the moon may
command the opposite. With One God there is one standard — one
principle of right and wrong."

What a revolutionary idea this was! God's law code required that all
people be treated as equals. There was one set of laws for king and
commoner alike. Everyone was expected to face the challenging
command to "Love your neighbor as yourself." Every human
being — indeed, every living thing — was to have a weekly day of rest.

Of course, these ideas did not all develop at the same time.
Abraham and his tribe came to believe that there is only one God
about the year 2000 B.C.E. It took 800 years before the Hebrews,
having been led by Moses out of slavery in Egypt, adopted God's
law as the constitution of the people of Israel.

A struggle for survival in the Ancient World

The conditions under which the ancient Hebrews lived often distracted them from their noble aims. As our ancestors took control of Canaan, they often thought more of survival and success than of God and Torah. By the year 1000 B.C.E. they had become masters of the area we now know as Eretz Yisrael – the land of Israel – and had formed an important empire under King David. Already the Prophets, spokesmen for God, were warning that if the Hebrews continued to disobey God's commandments, disaster would result.

Their prophecies were correct. After the reign of King David's son Solomon, the nation plunged into civil war. When the fighting ended, the nation was split. The northern half – the Kingdom of Israel – was later overrun by the armies of Assyria. Then the southern portion – the Kingdom of Judah – was conquered by the Babylonians. The beautiful Temple that had been built by King Solomon was destroyed, and the Judeans were exiled to Babylon.

Yet the Hebrews – now called Jews (the name comes from "Judah") – did not lose heart. Prophets had warned the people that God would punish them for failing to obey His commandments. Now other Prophets assured the exiles that God would forgive them and return His people to Eretz Yisrael. Within a generation this promise came true. The Persians conquered Babylonia and allowed the Jews to return to Zion, and to build the Second Temple.

Ancient peoples generally believed that separate gods ruled the many parts of nature, and made idols like this Assyrian idol to represent their gods.

During the centuries that they were again in the Holy Land, our ancestors produced much of lasting value. Their greatest triumph was the decision to join to the Torah the words of the Prophets and works of poetry, fiction, and history, in order to create a permanent collection of sacred texts. This became the most important and influential of all books — the Hebrew Bible.

The development of the Bible was only one expression of the creative spirit of our people. The Torah provided a firm basis for Jewish life, but even its simplest commandments needed interpretation. "You shall not murder" seems clear enough, but what does it really mean? If one kills in self-defense, is that murder? What if one kills in a sudden burst of anger? What if the killer is insane? Questions like these were discussed, examined, considered, and reconsidered in order to establish a detailed guide for every phase of human life. In time, the records of the discussions among Jewish sages were written down in a work called the Talmud, which then became second only to the Bible as a sacred text of Judaism.

Above: an enameled lion from Babylon. Right: a model of the Second Temple, now on display at the Holyland Hotel in Jerusalem.

Under Greece and Rome

While the Jewish religion was developing, Jewish political life was becoming more and more difficult. Persia was conquered by Greece, and soon the Greek rulers tried to force their Jewish subjects to worship idols. Revolt broke out under the leadership of the priest Mattathias and his son Judah Maccabee. The Greeks were defeated, and for a time the Jewish people had an independent state. It did not last long.

From across the Mediterranean Sea came the all-conquering armies of Rome, and the land of Israel was soon part of the Roman Empire. The Romans assigned cruel and greedy men to rule in Eretz Yisrael, which led to a new revolt. For several years the Jews of Jerusalem managed to hold off the might of Rome, but finally they were defeated, and in 70 C.E. the Second Temple was destroyed. A later Jewish revolt was also crushed. From 135 C.E. until the twentieth century, no Jewish force took up arms to fight for freedom in the Holy Land.

Thus Jewish life in Israel faded. Fortunately, Jewish life in other countries remained strong. In fact, it was the scholars of Babylonia who became the leading authorities on Jewish law. People traveled hundreds, even thousands, of miles to bring the Babylonian scholars religious and legal questions that needed to be answered. The answers (responsa), set down in writing, added to the growing body of material on Jewish law.

Scenes from Jewish life in Greek and Roman times.
From left to right: Mattathias, the father of
Judah Maccabee, kills a Jew who is about to offer
a sacrifice to a Greek god; styles of Jewish art
during the Roman period; the Arch of Titus, honoring
the Roman conquest of Jerusalem and the destruction
of the Second Temple.

Ashkenazim and Sephardim

For a period of four centuries, the Babylonian community ruled much of the intellectual and spiritual life of world Jewry. Its customs and traditions were adopted by Jews as far away as Spain, and those who followed these traditions became known as Sephardim. The Jews of Central and Eastern Europe, on the other hand, generally preserved the traditions of Palestine through their own practices and customs. These Jews were called Ashkenazim.

There was no disagreement between these groups concerning the basic principles of Judaism. However, because of their different political situations, the Sephardim and Ashkenazim developed very different life-styles.

The Sephardim lived in the Muslim Empire — a huge territory which enjoyed a magnificent culture. Daily life was busy, varied, and fascinating. In this "Golden Age," the Sephardim rose to the highest ranks of government, participated at all levels of society, prospered in business, and gained fame in the professions, particularly in medicine. At the same time, they produced outstanding Jewish literature, including the finest Hebrew poetry since the days of the Bible, and one of the greatest of all Jewish philosophers, Moses Maimonides.

Life for the Ashkenazim of Central Europe was very different. After the fall of the Roman Empire, the area in which they lived became a battleground for roving Germanic tribes. City life collapsed, schools closed, and education was all but unknown.

This seder plate, made in Spain about 1450, is a beautiful example of Sephardic craftsmanship.

This menorah, an eighteenth century masterpiece, was created by German Ashkenazim.

Unknown, that is, except among Jews. The Ashkenazim, like Jews everywhere, believed that every male should learn to read the Bible, Talmud, and siddur. So the Jews handled their own education and remained literate and learned. In fact, the Jews were one of the few connecting links between the Christians of Central Europe and the Muslim Empire which controlled much of the ancient world. Hebrew was for a time the international language between points as distant as Paris and Jerusalem.

Christian Europe versus the Jews

With some exceptions, the rulers of the Muslim Empire were tolerant of the Sephardim. But the Ashkenazim had a powerful and persistent enemy: the Roman Catholic Church. The Catholics falsely accused the Jews of all sorts of crimes — even of murdering Christian children to use their blood in Passover matzah. Jews were massacred because of such foolish accusations, or sometimes simply because they were Jews. Our people were exiled from England, from France, and from many parts of Germany.

For many years, Spanish Jews escaped the worst of these horrors. Then the Catholics gained control of Spain and promptly expelled the entire Jewish population — more than 250,000 people. Jews who had been forced to convert could not leave and had to live as Catholics, though many continued to practice Judaism in secret. These secret Jews were called Marranos. Those who were caught were ruthlessly tortured, then burned at the stake.

Early in the 1500's, the Christian oppression of the Jews took a new turn. Jews who were living in Germany and Italy were required to move into special walled sections of the towns in which they lived. These "locked-in" communities became known as ghettos. For a time, an active and productive Jewish life continued within the ghetto walls. But as the ghetto became more and more crowded, and as Christian rulers imposed heavier and heavier taxes, our people were reduced to poverty and near despair.

The Jews of Eastern Europe were not locked in ghettos, but they too lived in isolation. Their Christian neighbors were frequently Jew-haters, and the Jews had little sympathy for these Gentiles who ate pig and worked on the Sabbath. Moreover, since the Jews spoke and wrote in Yiddish — which uses Hebrew letters — they did not even share a common alphabet with the Christian world. Nevertheless, for a long time the Eastern European Jews were reasonably secure. Then, beginning in 1648, they became the victims of a series of ghastly massacres. To many it seemed that the world could not be worse.

There were a few bright spots in this generally gloomy picture. At the beginning of the sixteenth century the Turks, who had welcomed the Jewish exiles from Spain, conquered the Holy Land and permitted Jewish settlement there. In the seventeenth century, small Jewish communities in Holland, England, and the New World began to enjoy increasing amounts of freedom. But the vast majority of world Jewry lived in Central and Eastern Europe under harsh rulers who kept Jews isolated from the culture developing around them.

This was still the pattern of society as 1776 began. No one realized that the world — and the Jewish people — would soon experience the most explosive and far-reaching changes of any two centuries in human history.

PART ONE

The World in 1776

At the Dawn of the Modern Era

This is the second volume of **My People**. In the first, we emphasized the full sweep of Jewish history. Here we concentrate on the last two centuries—only a tiny fragment of our 4000-year-old story, yet a period filled with momentous events, and one that is particularly our story, in the sense that it has influenced our own lives.

We pick as our starting point the signing of the American Declaration of Independence, because that event marked a key change in human thought. Almost all previous societies believed that God (or the gods) had appointed earthly kings to rule the world. From ancient Egypt, where the Pharaohs were thought to be the children of the sun, to seventeenth century Europe, where kings were said to govern by "divine right," God was seen as the direct source of state power. The Declaration of Independence, on the other hand, said that governments received their power only by the consent of the people they ruled.

Similarly, it had been thought that nothing could be true unless it agreed with the teachings of Holy Scripture. The Roman Catholic Church forced the scientist Galileo to deny the truth of his own experiments because they contradicted the official Christian view of the Bible. Now we recognize that there are many sources of truth. There is no single answer to the problems of nature or of man.

All this has led to differing ideas about humanity and God. Many of our new ideas are valuable; but, as we shall see, many of the old ones are as valuable as ever. The State of Israel treasures the ideals of the New World. Its own Declaration of Independence is, in spirit, much like that of the United States. Yet Israel exists, at least in part, because the Bible tells us that God promised the tribe of Abraham a special destiny among the peoples of the earth.

ABBA EBAN

1

INTRODUCTION TO PART ONE:

The World in 1776

The city of Philadelphia was in a frenzy of excitement. On July 4, 1776, the Continental Congress approved a Declaration of Independence from Great Britain. After more than ten years of protests, appeals, and battles, the great step was taken. The Americans told the world that these thirteen colonies of England were now free and independent.

Free and independent of unjust British rule—and of the old ideas of Europe as well. The New World colonies refused to believe that kings and nobles were chosen by God to rule the common people. "We hold these Truths to be self-evident," wrote Thomas Jefferson in the Declaration, "that all Men are created equal, that they are endowed by their Creator with certain unalienable Rights, that among these are Life, Liberty, and the Pursuit of Happiness."

Never before had a nation been established by men who claimed the right to make their own laws and decide their own future. No wonder the people of Philadelphia, the first citizens of the first modern nation, celebrated far into the night. Although gunpowder was scarce, and would be needed for the battles ahead, they fired a massive twenty-one-gun salute to welcome the new era.

Gershom Seixas in America

When the news from Philadelphia reached him, Gershom Seixas was filled with relief and delight. Just a few months before, as religious leader of New York's only synagogue, he had asked his fellow Jews to risk their property—and their lives—in support of American independence. The British forces were about to invade New York, and there was no doubt their attack would be successful. Seixas had asked the members of his synagogue to flee from the city, so that no Jew could be forced to use his business to help the armies of King George III.

Some Jews did not want to follow

American patriots sign the Declaration of Independence.

Seixas. They had done well under British rule, and though they did not yet have full legal rights in the colonies, they were far better off than Jews in Europe. If peace with Great Britain could be restored, they thought, the English might one day give Jews full equality.

But most members of Seixas' congregation were unwilling to wait and hope for such a change. To them, King George was just one in the line of tyrants that began with Pharaoh, Haman, and Antiochus. At long last, they thought, Jews could strike a blow against tyranny. They voted to close their lovely little synagogue and escape from New York before the British arrived.

Packing whatever they could, the New Yorkers traveled through hard winter weather to safety in Pennsylvania and Connecticut. Some were forced to leave behind businesses and fortunes. Many faced serious dangers. The thirty-one-year-old Seixas had risked his life to save the Torah scrolls of the congregation. Hearing the news of the Declaration of Independence, he felt that all the struggle, all the risk, had been worthwhile. What words could express his emotions?

Reason and Revolution

The planet Uranus
was first sighted
through this eighteenth
century telescope.

Two revolutions rocked the Western world in the late eighteenth century. The first one came to America in 1776, the second to France in 1789. But neither rebellion could have occurred without an earlier, quieter revolution—a revolution in ideas. This revolution is called the Enlightenment. (Some historians call this period the Age of Reason.)

More than anything else, the Enlightenment was an age of science. Before the Enlightenment, scientists felt the need to make sure that their findings did not conflict with the Bible or Church teachings. But the scientists of the Enlightenment believed that only careful experiments could prove or disprove their theories about the world. The invention of the steam engine, the discovery of oxygen, the beginnings of modern chemistry and geology, the first sighting of the planet Uranus—all these we owe to the astronomers, physicists, chemists, physicians, and other scientists and inventors who lived in Western Europe during the eighteenth century.

The new scientists believed that they were sweeping away superstition and clearing new paths for progress and human reason. Soon, Enlightenment thinkers were applying the "scientific method" to other fields. If reason could discover how gravity worked, or how the earth revolved around the sun, couldn't reason discover the principles of history, government, and economics? For centuries, kings had claimed to rule by divine right—they were kings, they said, because God meant them to be kings. But human reason said that people had a right to choose their own leaders. An American revolutionary, Tom Paine, did not need the words of Scripture to prove that the Thirteen Colonies should be free from England: "common sense" (the title of a booklet he published in 1776) would prove it for him.

Thus, even before America declared its independence, the ideas of the Enlightenment had swept through the Western world with revolutionary power. In later chapters you will learn how these same ideas had an equally revolutionary impact on the Jews of the West and in the ghettos of Eastern Europe.

בָּרוּךְ אַתָּה יְיָ. אֱלֹהֵינוּ
מֶלֶךְ הָעוֹלָם. שֶׁהֶחֱיָנוּ.
וְקִיְּמָנוּ. וְהִגִּיעָנוּ לַזְּמַן הַזֶּה:

Blessed art Thou, O Lord our God, King
of the Universe, who has given us life, sustained us, and brought us to this time.

Moses Mendelssohn in Germany

Months passed before word of the
Declaration of Independence crossed the
Atlantic Ocean and reached a world-
famous Jew living in the city of Berlin.
But when he heard this great statement of
human rights, Moses Mendelssohn must
have been almost as excited as were the
Jews of the New World.

Mendelssohn had enjoyed great success
during his lifetime. Thanks to his brilliant
mind, his charming personality, and his
forceful writings, he had risen from poverty to the heights of German society.

Yet he realized that his good fortune
was almost unique. Most German Jews
still lived in ghettos. For them the events
in America might be the signs of a new
age. The time of freedom was coming—
by revolution in America, and perhaps by
the gradual growth of justice and toleration in Europe. Mendelssohn looked forward to the day when the walls of the
ghettos would be torn down, when Jews
would be free to live as equals in the nations of Europe.

By 1776, Jews made their homes in the New
World, Africa, India, and (to a lesser
extent) in the Far East, but three-fourths
of our people were still concentrated in
Central and Eastern Europe. Compare this
map to the one on pages 220–221 to see how
far the Diaspora spread during the next two
centuries.

Newport
New York
Philadelphia
UNITED STATES
Charleston
Savannah

Gershom Seixas
1746-1816

Curaçao

The DIASPORA • 1776

Leading centers of Jewish life

Other major Jewish settlements

O Urban Jewish communities

△ Isolated Jewish sects

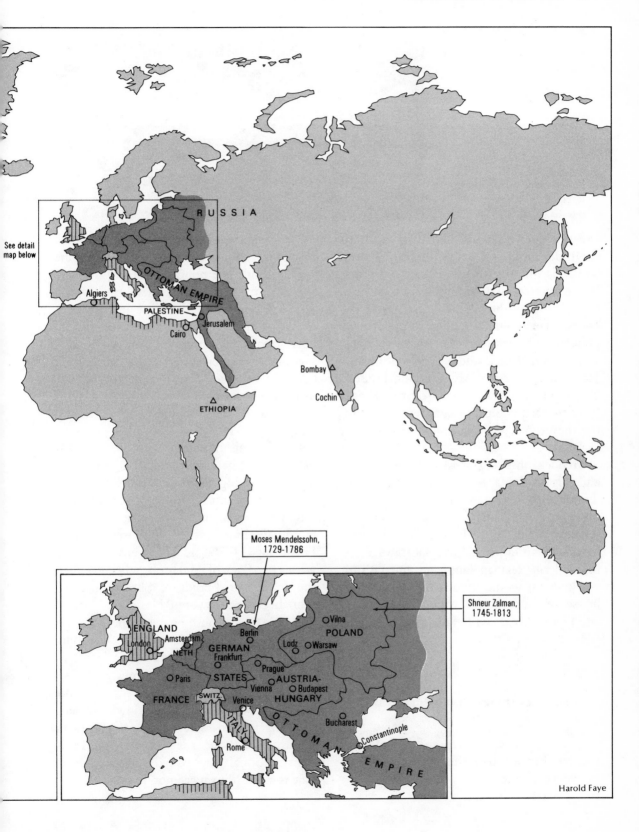

See detail map below

RUSSIA

OTTOMAN EMPIRE

Algiers

PALESTINE

Cairo

Jerusalem

Bombay

Cochin

ETHIOPIA

Moses Mendelssohn,
1729-1786

Shneur Zalman,
1745-1813

ENGLAND

London

Amsterdam

NETH.

GERMAN

Berlin

Vilna

POLAND

Frankfurt

Lodz

Warsaw

Prague

Paris

STATES

AUSTRIA-

Vienna

Budapest

FRANCE

SWITZ.

HUNGARY

Venice

ITALY

Bucharest

Rome

OTTOMAN

Constantinople

EMPIRE

Harold Faye

Two views of Shearith Israel, New York's first synagogue. Left, the synagogue (built in 1730) as Gershom Seixas knew it; right, as it was rebuilt in 1818.

But were the Jews of Germany ready to enter the modern world? They had been locked in ghettos for more than 200 years. In the ghettos, they had their own culture, but they knew little about changes in the outside world—the scientific discoveries of Galileo and Newton, the art of Michelangelo and Rembrandt, the writings of Jefferson or even of Mendelssohn himself. Worst of all, it was hard for the ghetto Jews to learn about the non-Jewish world, for they spoke and read only Yiddish and Hebrew.

Mendelssohn set out to change this. He and his students began to translate the Torah into German. They printed the German side-by-side with the Hebrew and wrote it in Hebrew letters. In this way, Mendelssohn hoped to give the Jews a key to modern German language and culture —a key that would unlock the great storehouse of European learning.

"The ghettos will fall," he thought. "My people must be made ready."

Shneur Zalman in Eastern Europe

The Jews in the towns and townlets of Eastern Europe had their own problems to worry about.

"How simple the world once seemed," thought Rabbi Shneur Zalman. When he was a child, the political lines of Europe were clear, and within them the Jewish world was united. Like most Jewish boys, he spent all his time in the study of the holy books, beginning at an early age. He had mastered them with astounding ease. By the age of twelve he was recognized as a young genius—an ILLUI—and was known far and near as a leading scholar.

Despite this, Shneur Zalman was dissatisfied. He felt he knew "a little about learning but nothing about prayer." At the age of twenty he left his home to study a new religious movement in Judaism, one which taught feelings rather than scholarship: HASIDISM (חֲסִידוּת). He went to study with Dov Baer of Mezirich, who was then the leader of Hasidism. Shneur Zalman soon became a devoted Hasid.

As he grew and changed he felt the world growing and changing around him. In 1772 the great empires of Eastern Europe each captured large pieces of Polish territory, placing many Jews under the heel of new and often anti-Jewish rulers. Dov Baer died that same year, leaving Hasidism without a leader. Also in 1772, the traditional Jews issued a decree stating that the Hasidim were not Jews at all, and that no true Jew should have anything to do with them. In 1776, Shneur Zalman was desperately searching for a way to bring the Ḥasidim and the traditionalists together again.

Did he ever hear of the Declaration of Independence? Perhaps not. But if he did, it would not have pleased him. He deeply feared what was going on in the West. Jews were receiving more freedom, true; but they were using that freedom to abandon their traditional duties. Zalman was opposed to any freedom that would distract a Jew from being religious.

Different paths

Thus Gershom Seixas, Moses Mendelssohn, and Shneur Zalman each reacted in his own way to the events of 1776—and each was right. The Declaration of Independence *did* mark the beginning of a new age for our people. The ghetto walls *would* fall. And these changes *would* be a threat to the traditional Jewish world.

As the Sabbath arrived, each of the three joined with his fellow Jews in prayer that his dream of the future would come speedily. For each of these men was a dedicated Jew. Each observed the rituals of Jewish tradition, studied and honored the ancient texts of our people, and led his fellow Jews in what he saw as the path of righteousness. Yet how different they were —an American revolutionary, a German thinker, and a Ḥasidic rabbi—and how difficult it would have been for any one of them to accept the ways of the others!

Even two centuries ago there was not perfect agreement on what makes "a good Jew." And today there are still other ways in which Jews worship and dedicate themselves to serving the Jewish people. One of the reasons for studying modern Jewish history is to learn how other Jews live, to discover the many ways of being "good Jews."

But we will find much more than that in the history of our people since 1776. There are exciting stories of men, women, and children whose dramatic lives make up the Jewish adventure. There is delight in understanding the world of our parents and grandparents. There is the tragedy of the Holocaust, but also the thrilling story of the State of Israel.

We will set the stage for these remarkable events as we discover our people AT THE DAWN OF THE MODERN ERA.

SUMMARY   *Jews lived in a great variety of ways in 1776. A few were involved in the American Revolution; others were emerging from the ghettos of Western Europe. Most were caught in the political and religious conflicts of Eastern Europe. Since 1776, the task of defining a "good Jew" has become even more complex.*

2

At the Ends
of the Earth

Today the largest and most important Jewish communities of the world are in the United States and Eretz Yisrael (אֶרֶץ יִשְׂרָאֵל). Jews lived in both places at the time of the American Revolution—but their way of life was very different from ours today.

To the New World

The first European to set foot in the New World was a man of Jewish birth—Luis de Torres. He was physician on the voyage led by Christopher Columbus, and was sent ashore to speak to the Indians because he knew several languages. (It is doubtful that his grasp of Spanish, Hebrew, Aramaic, and Arabic helped him very much in this first meeting with American Indians!) Jews also raised money for Columbus' voyage, and provided the star charts which played a part in the success of the voyage.

But Jews could not follow Columbus to the New World—the Spanish and Portuguese Catholics who made the first settlements in the Western Hemisphere executed every Jew who dared cross the ocean. The Catholic rulers of Spain and Portugal at the end of the fifteenth century were the worst oppressors the Jews had known in 1000 years. In fact, on the very day Columbus set sail for the West, a quarter of a million Jews were expelled from their Spanish homes by King Ferdinand and Queen Isabella.

Dutch colonies

For more than a century, no European nation would allow Jews to settle in the New World. Then Holland won its independence from Spain, and its Protestant rulers invited Jews to live there. And wherever the Dutch set up colonies our people were allowed to live and worship freely.

When the Dutch ruled the city of

Forced to leave Brazil, Dutch Jewish refugees were
at the mercy of Caribbean pirates and privateers.

Recife in Brazil, Jews settled there, making it the first Jewish community in the Americas. Between 1632 and 1654 the community prospered. But in 1654 the Portuguese Catholic armies recaptured Recife, and the Jews were forced to leave.

They scattered, many finding safety on islands in the Caribbean Sea, others returning to Holland. Sailing to the Netherlands, twenty-three Jews were captured by Spanish pirates. As luck would have it, they were rescued by a French ship, which towed them as far as the French West Indies. Stranded and almost penniless, the Jews found a vessel that was willing to take them north. This hair-raising adventure

finally ended in September 1654, when the poor refugees arrived in the one-year-old Dutch colony of New Amsterdam.

The local governor, peg-legged Peter Stuyvesant, was determined to get rid of them. He wrote to his employers, the Dutch West India Company, asking that "the deceitful race—such hateful enemies and blasphemers of Christ—be not allowed to infect and trouble this colony." But the Jews of Holland argued against Stuyvesant's request, and in the end, the governor was told to allow the newcomers to settle.

But the twenty-three Jews were not given full legal rights. For example, because Stuyvesant did not trust the Jews, he did not allow them to serve guard duty like the other colonists. A Jewish settler, Asser Levy, insisted that the Jews be allowed to obey exactly the same rules and perform precisely the same duties as Christians—including risking their lives as guards. After much argument his request was granted. By 1664, when England captured New Amsterdam and renamed it "New York," the Jews had gained almost total equality—an equality which was preserved under British rule.

Under British rule

Not all American colonies treated Jews this well. Most New World settlements were created by people with strong, and even bigoted, religious views. The Puritans of Massachusetts, for example, left Europe to escape persecution—but they saw nothing wrong in persecuting members of their own community who disagreed with official Puritan teachings. Members of other sects, Christian or Jewish, were simply not allowed to live in Massachusetts.

At the time of the American Revolution, there were organized Jewish congregations in only five North American cities. The first was established in New York by the refugees from Recife. (This was congregation Shearith Israel, whose members, led by Gershom Seixas, left New York in 1776.) The second was in Newport, Rhode Island, the third in Charleston, South Carolina. Next came Savannah, Georgia, and Philadelphia. These five were all ports. Most American Jews were involved in the sea trade which connected the various colonies with Great Britain.

This meant that, in 1776, much of Jewish economic life depended on peace between the colonies and Great Britain. Nevertheless, the vast majority of colonial Jews were in favor of the revolution. They knew too well what it meant to live under the rule of tyrants, and so placed the cause of liberty above their business needs.

Haym Salomon

During the revolution, Jews served General Washington as foot soldiers and as officers, risking—and often losing—their lives and fortunes to fight for freedom. But the Jew who was most important to the cause of the revolution was a man who probably never saw a battle: Haym Salomon.

Salomon agreed to raise the vast sums of money needed for the expenses of the young republic. To do this he needed to sell bonds—no simple task, since if the Americans were defeated by the British any American bond would be worthless. Neverthless, he did manage to raise the needed money, and he gave every penny of it to the American government. He did not follow the usual practice of taking some of the money from the sales for himself, because this immigrant from Poland felt that in serving his new country he was only performing his patriotic duty.

Freedom and Jewish ideals

The Jewish tradition also played a part in the early history of the United States. Some heroes of the revolution, including Benjamin Franklin and Thomas Jefferson, were Deists—men who believed in God but did not belong to any church. They,

Marriage contract (ketubah) drawn up for Haym Salomon and Rachel Franks in 1777.

May the children of the stock of Abraham who dwell in this land continue to merit and enjoy the good will of the other inhabitants, while every one shall sit in safety under his own vine and fig tree, and there shall be none to make him afraid.

It was, however, John Adams—the revolutionary patriot and America's second president—who praised the Jewish heritage most directly when he wrote: "The Hebrews have done more to civilize men than any other nation."

In Eretz Yisrael

No such praise was offered the Jews who lived in Eretz Yisrael.

To be sure, Zion was never far from the thoughts of Jews all over the world. Prayers were said facing Jerusalem. Harvest festivals were celebrated in every Jewish community at the time of harvests in the Holy Land. Each Passover seder concluded with the words:

לְשָׁנָה הַבָּאָה בִּירוּשָׁלַיִם

Next year in Jerusalem.

The dream of Eretz Yisrael was in the heart of world Jewry, but Palestine, the real land of Israel, was a minor outpost of the huge Ottoman (Turkish) Empire. Those Jews who lived in Palestine were very poor and often in great danger. In 1775, for example, the Jews of Hebron were falsely accused of having murdered a nobleman, and barely escaped massacre by paying a huge bribe.

Such conditions would have made it very difficult for the Jewish community of Palestine to support itself even if all its members had been businessmen. But most of the Jews who lived in Eretz Yisrael were there to study and worship, to

along with many Protestant leaders, were deeply influenced by our Bible, and felt that colonial Americans fighting the British were like the Jewish slaves in ancient Egypt struggling to win freedom from Pharaoh.

George Washington paid tribute to our traditions soon after he became president. Replying to the congratulations he received from members of the Newport synagogue, he used words from their letter to pen what has become a classic statement of American democracy: "Happily the Government of the United States . . . gives to bigotry no sanction, to persecution no assistance." Then, echoing the prophet Micah, he added:

Eretz Yisrael
Before 1740

What happened in Eretz Yisrael between the Age of the
Rabbis * and Ḥaim Abulafia's arrival in 1740?

Records are sketchy for much of this time. We do know
that the Jewish community in Palestine grew smaller in
numbers and less important from the fourth century to
the seventh century, reviving soon after the Muslim conquest.
It was during this period (about 650–750 C.E.) that the
standard version of the Hebrew Bible, the Masora (מָסוֹרָה),
was compiled. After the eighth century, however, the
number of Jews in Zion again declined, and Iraq
("Babylonia"), Spain, and Egypt became the major centers
of Jewish intellectual life.

The low point for Jewish life in Eretz Yisrael came in
1099, when Crusaders from Christian Europe sacked
Jerusalem and massacred all the Jews in the city. (The
Crusaders massacred the Jews of Haifa a year later.) Fighting
between Muslims and Christians lasted well over a century,
and Jerusalem was again destroyed in about 1260. When
Rabbi Moses ben Naḥman, also known as Naḥmanides,
reached Jerusalem in 1267, he found only two Jews still living
in the City of David.

Naḥmanides later traveled to Acre, where the Jewish
community was much larger and more active. Some 300
French and English rabbis had come to Acre in 1211,
and another 300 Jewish scholars arrived from France
about fifty years later. But Acre was sacked by Muslim
warriors in 1291, and did not revive until the Ottoman Turks
conquered Palestine in 1516.

After the Turkish conquest, Safed became the hub of
Jewish intellectual life in the Holy Land. Safed was a refuge
for famous rabbis and mystics, and it was here that
Joseph Karo wrote his "Shulchan Aruch" (שֻׁלְחָן עָרוּךְ).
Jerusalem, by contrast, played little part in the economic
or cultural affairs of Palestine until our own time—
though the City of David never lost its central place in the
thoughts and prayers of our people.

*Ending in the fifth century C. E. See Volume One, Part Two.

In 1740 the Muslim ruler of Northern Palestine asked Rabbi Ḥaim Abulafia to rebuild Tiberias. Two years later, the rabbi could point with pride at his achievement.

devote themselves to Judaism, hoping in this way to bring about the END OF DAYS (אַחֲרִית הַיָּמִים). Then the Messiah would come—the long-awaited ruler who would end the suffering of the Jews, reestablish the Kingdom of Israel, and bring peace to the world.

Since it did not have enough income of its own, the community had to rely on TZEDAKAH (צְדָקָה)—help from Jews in other countries—in order to survive. Fund-raisers traveled to Constantinople, Europe, and as far as Rhode Island in search of gifts to support Palestinian Jewry.

Small beginnings

There was a brighter side to the picture. In the early 1700's the Muslim sheik of Northern Palestine decided it would be useful to rebuild the city of Tiberias. This

city, on the western shore of the beautiful Sea of Galilee (כִּנֶּרֶת), had been very important in ancient times. The Jewish Supreme Court—the SANHEDRIN, סַנְהֶדְרִין— moved there after the Romans destroyed Jerusalem. Moreover, the Palestinian Talmud, though often called the "Jerusalem Talmud," was actually completed in Tiberias.

For centuries Tiberias had been in ruins; and it was to this dismal site that the sheik summoned Rabbi Ḥaim Abulafia from Turkey with the words: "Arise, come up and inherit the land of Tiberias which your forefathers possessed." Abulafia arrived in Eretz Yisrael in 1740. The sheik greeted him royally, dressed him in beautiful robes, and gave him everything he needed.

The rabbi plunged into his work with enthusiasm. In only two years, he had built houses and shops, restored the wall which had once protected the Jewish

At the Western Wall

Through the ages, Jewish pilgrims (such as those shown at upper left, right, and below) have stopped at the Western Wall to pray for the renewal of the Jewish people, or to weep in sadness at the thought of the ruined glory of the ancient Temple. Since 1967, when the Israeli army broke through the gates of the Old City and reunited Jerusalem (upper right), the Wall has become a symbol of hope for Israel's future.

quarter, begun construction of roads, planted fields and orchards, and even built a fine bathhouse. He did not forget religion, either. He built the most beautiful synagogue then in Eretz Yisrael.

Yet if any monument represented the Jews of Palestine during this period, it was not the new synagogue of Tiberias. It was a fragment of the ancient Temple of Jerusalem—the Western Wall. Its huge stones had refused to fall before either the soldiers of Rome or the assaults of time. The wall stood through the centuries as a symbol of hope that one day the Temple would be rebuilt and the entire people of Israel would return to Zion. Yet so grief-stricken were the Jews who came to pray there that the site was often called the "Wailing Wall."

The United States and Eretz Yisrael— the Bible had said our people would be scattered to the ends of the earth, and these communities seemed to prove it. And yet, how small they were! At the time of the American Revolution, there were only 2500 Jews in North America among a total population of about 4 million. Palestine was home to only 300,-000 people—less than the population of Jerusalem today. And of these, just 5000 were Jews.

Two tiny communities, differing from each other in language, life-style, and attitudes. Yet each represented a bold attempt to build a home where Jews could live safely in the future. In America, Jewish patriots helped build a country where, for the first time in this era, Jews were guaranteed freedom of religion. In Eretz Yisrael, men and women of the deepest piety kept Judaism alive in the land which had been promised to Abraham endless centuries before, and which would one day again hold an independent Jewish state.

SUMMARY *Jews and Judaism played important roles in the success of the American Revolution and in the growth of religious freedom in the United States. Eretz Yisrael remained central to the thoughts of Jewish people through centuries of exile. Only a small number of Jews lived in either of these lands during the 1700's, but their courage and dedication helped lay the foundations for the two most important Jewish communities in the world today.*

3

In the Heartland
of Our People

During the 1700's only a few thousand Jews lived in the United States and Eretz Yisrael, but some 2,500,000 Jews—80 percent of the world total—lived in the countries of Central and Eastern Europe.

Partitions of Poland

"Eastern Europe" is the 1000-mile-wide area between Berlin and Moscow. The center of this area is the large, fertile plain which is home to the Polish people. During the 1200's, the king of Poland opened his country to any German who wished to settle there and develop the nation's economy. A great many Germans, among them many German Jews, accepted this invitation, working to create a powerful country which at the end of the fourteenth century combined with Lithuania to form a huge empire.

By the 1700's, however, this empire had been hopelessly weakened by foolish kings and greedy nobles. Seeing that Poland now had no defenses, three neighboring nations —Russia, Austria-Hungary, and Prussia— agreed to snatch pieces of Polish territory for themselves. This first division or "Partition of Poland" took place in 1772; the Poles were so weak that more land was taken in 1793 and 1795. By the time the three "Partitions" were completed, Poland had disappeared from the map of Europe.

These events sent waves of shock and confusion through the Jewish community in Poland, which was then the world's largest. Suddenly some Jews found themselves under the rule of Austrians or Germans. By far the greatest number found themselves under the fiercely anti-Jewish rule of the Russian government. (Their story will be told in Part Three.)

False Messiahs

By 1776, only the first Partition of Poland had taken place. Yet the Jews of

Jacob Frank, a false Messiah, had an audience in 1775 with
Empress Maria Theresa and her son Joseph. Frank's anti-Jewish
ideas appealed to the Austrian monarch.

Eastern Europe were already deeply split by social and religious differences.

During the centuries of Polish rule, some Jews had become quite wealthy—but most were very poor indeed. The rich enjoyed comfort, power, and time to develop the Jewish knowledge which was widely respected and prized. The poor led very hard lives, had no political power, and had little time for Jewish studies.

The poor longed for an escape from the suffering of their daily lives, and found comfort in the belief that the Messiah would soon come. They were ready to follow men who claimed that God had sent them to free Jews from their misery. Such a man was Shabbetai Zevi, who during the 1600's posed as the Messiah until,

threatened with execution, he converted to Islam in order to save his life. (The story of Shabbetai Zevi is told in Volume One, Chapter 21.)

This betrayal of Judaism cured many Jews of their hope that one man would bring a miracle to end their troubles. Yet other false Messiahs continued to appear, and there were always some Jews ready to follow.

Of these false Messiahs, the worst was Jacob Frank. He taught the strange idea that God would not send a Messiah until the world had become as evil as it could possibly be. So, said Frank, it was his duty as a follower of Shabbetai Zevi to bring about a time of pure evil.

Thus, Frank and his followers spent

their days *breaking* the Ten Commandments! They spoke out against the sacred Jewish books, took part in the public burning of the Talmud, and converted to Christianity. The organized Jewish community condemned the Frankists, of course; but Church officials were also shocked to find that these supposed converts to Christianity worshipped Jacob Frank as their "Lord of Holiness." Frank was thrown into prison, where for thirteen years he was honored by his followers as "the suffering Messiah." He was released by the Russians after the first Partition of Poland—whereupon he promptly reestablished his court.*

Hasidim and Mitnagdim

With this sort of criminal pretending to be an inspired leader, it is not surprising that the rabbis of Eastern Europe were upset when they heard that another man was winning thousands of followers in southern Poland—the very area which had given strong support to Shabbetai Zevi and Jacob Frank. This new leader also had some unusual ideas. He taught that traditional forms of worship were unnecessary, even harmful. True Judaism, he said, meant worshipping God with a joyful heart, and reaching with one's thoughts and feelings to a special sense of nearness to Him.

This teacher was Israel ben Eliezer, the BAAL SHEM TOV (בַּעַל־שֵׁם־טוֹב); and the movement which he founded is called HASIDISM (חֲסִידוּת).

Today we know that Hasidism has contributed much in warmth and wisdom to Jewish life. We also know that Hasidism soon became old-fashioned in many ways. (For example, most Hasidic men still wear the heavy black coats which were the fashion in the cold weather of eighteenth century Poland.) But in the late 1700's the Hasidim appeared to be upstarts—revolutionaries—and the traditional rabbis strongly opposed them.

The traditionalists were led by a Lithuanian scholar, Elijah ben Solomon, known as the Vilna Gaon.** He and his followers, the MITNAGDIM (מִתְנַגְּדִים), were so set against the new movement that when Shneur Zalman traveled to Lithuania to explain that many Hasidim respected Jewish learning and Jewish law, the Vilna Gaon would not even speak with him.

More than that, the Mitnagdim issued decrees stating that true Jews could have nothing further to do with Hasidim. One decree of excommunication (חֵרֶם) said that the Hasidim "must leave our communities with their wives and children . . . they should not be given a night's lodging . . . It is forbidden to do business with them and to intermarry with them, or to assist at their burial." Not to be outdone, the Hasidim issued similar decrees against the Mitnagdim.

So, in the 1770's, Eastern European Jewry was in a state of civil war. This war of words and decrees continued for several generations—even today, Mitnagdim and Hasidim live in the same quarter of Jerusalem but send their children to different schools and pray in different buildings. By the mid-1800's, however, the fiercest battles had ended. A majority of Eastern European Jews became Hasidim but never

---

* Frank died in 1791. His daughter, appropriately named Eve, took over leadership of his group, but without success. She died in poverty in 1817, and the Frankists disappeared within a few decades.

** The Baal Shem Tov and the Vilna Gaon are discussed in Volume One, Chapter 22.

lost their love of traditional Jewish learning. And soon, Mitnagdim and Ḥasidim were forced to unite by a common enemy —the modern ideas seeping into their communities from Central Europe.

In Central Europe

Central Europe would later become the nations of Germany and Italy, but in the 1700's it was a great hodgepodge of small states, each with its own ruler. Most of the Jews in Central Europe lived in ghettos set up in the early 1500's.

Ghetto life had not, at first, been entirely bad, and Jewish art and scholarship had flourished. But repeated anti-Jewish legislation reduced ghetto communities to poverty and despair. Jews were turned into ragpickers who barely survived by peddling old clothes or other nearly worthless items.

The once great ghetto community of Venice dwindled to fewer than 2000 souls. The ghetto of Rome was only slightly larger—about 3000. Jews were kept there under the direct rule of the Popes, who wished to show the world that anyone who did not accept Christianity would have to endure frightful suffering.

In Italy, the misery was increased when Pius VI became Pope in 1775. Just as America was boiling over with the ideas of a new age, this Pope issued his "Edict Against the Jews," which brought back all the anti-Jewish laws of the thirteenth century. Jews were forced to wear yellow badges on their hats. Jewish books were censored. Jews were not permitted to have shops outside the ghetto, or to set up tombstones in their cemeteries. And they were forced to hear sermons in which preachers urged them to become Roman Catholics.

This lovingly detailed silver filigree spice box was handcrafted in Poland during the late eighteenth century.

Scenes from City Life

Most Polish Jews lived in small village communities called shtetls (see Chapter 10). Some Jews, however, lived in the Jewish sections of Poland's major cities. Above, an artist's view of some Jewish merchants on a Polish city street; upper right, a group of Talmudic scholars in Vilna; lower right, a street in Lublin's Jewish quarter in the early 1900's.

In the German lands, things were hardly better. King Frederick II of Prussia ("Frederick the Great") gave religious freedom to his Protestant and Catholic subjects, but not to the Jews. As for his Jewish subjects, Frederick wanted to take as much money as possible from them, while keeping the Jewish population from growing. One of his schemes was to tax every Jew who wished to cross a frontier or enter a city, and then force every Jewish boy (except an oldest son) to leave home and pay a tax to earn his living elsewhere.

Court Jew and shtadlan

Beginning in the mid-1600's, however, some Jews were freed from such harsh treatment. Those skilled in business could leave the ghetto to serve the nobles as "Court Jews." Almost every ruler of every small German state had a Jewish official in his service, even if he did not permit other Jews to live in his state. And many of the Court Jews enjoyed a great deal of influence and power. (See Volume One, Chapter 22.)

The Court Jews often used their positions to plead for those Jews still trapped within ghetto walls. A man who spoke for the Jewish community before Christian authorities was called a SHTADLAN (שְׁתַּדְלָן). Not every Court Jew was a shtadlan, nor was every shtadlan a Court Jew, but when the two roles were joined the local Jewish community often prospered. The Jewish leaders also worked in support of scholarship. The first printing of the Talmud in Germany was made possible by the generosity of a man who was both Court Jew and shtadlan.

The inside of Prague's Alt-Neu (Old-New) Synagogue, depicted by a nineteenth century engraver.

Mendelssohn and the Christian challenge

The escape route from the ghetto opened by the business-minded Court Jew was followed by Jews with other skills. Of these, far and away the most important was Moses Mendelssohn, whose scholarly and literary talents brought him fame in Gentile society.

It seemed odd to the Christian world that a brilliant man like Mendelssohn should remain a Jew—and a strictly observant Jew at that. A minister even printed a public challenge to Mendelssohn, asking him to accept Christianity or to explain to the world why it was not a true religion.

Mendelssohn understood the danger that he faced in answering. A public attack on

Christianity could only hurt the Jewish people. So instead of attacking the Christian religion, Mendelssohn replied by saying that he was convinced of the truth of Judaism. But since Judaism teaches that the righteous of all nations "have a share in the world to come," he did not wish to prove any other religion wrong. He only hoped that each Jew and Christian would pursue the highest ideals of his own faith.

Yet Mendelssohn was deeply shocked to think that even when a Jew reached his level of success, he might be asked to make a public defense of his religion—and by a Christian who claimed to be his friend. This was a turning point in his life, for it was after this challenge that he began to translate the Torah into German, to help his fellow Jews learn the German language so that they could meet the pressures of the Gentile world. Mendelssohn also helped establish the Jewish Free School, the first school to teach Jewish children both Hebrew and German literature.

If Christians did not really understand Mendelssohn, it was also true that the privileged Jews did not really understand Christianity. For example, one of the founders of the Jewish Free School, seeing that Christians believed in one God, suggested that he would be willing to become a Protestant as long as he did not have to worship Jesus! Needless to say, the Protestant officials refused this offer. Still, the incident shows how even an intelligent Jew could become confused when first discovering the common elements in Judaism and Christianity.

What would have happened if Jews and Christians had been given a bit more time to understand each other? We will never know. The breezes of change that had begun to stir by the 1770's were suddenly swelled to hurricane force by the events of the French Revolution.

SUMMARY   *The Partitions of Poland sent political shock waves through the Jews of Eastern Europe at the very time that Jewish society was split by the conflict of Ḥasidim and Mitnagdim. In the end, both sides combined to fight a common enemy—the modern ideas coming out of Central Europe. Though most Jews in the Italian and German states lived in ghettos as paupers, a few Jews, like Moses Mendelssohn, enjoyed special privileges and made the first major contacts between Judaism and the modern world.*

PART TWO

The Age of Revolution

Emancipation

Most revolutions are waged in the name of some unifying ideal, such as social justice, human rights, or freedom from tyranny. A truly successful revolution — for example, the American Revolution in 1776 — is able to transform its unifying ideal into a living reality.

A revolutionary situation develops when peaceful avenues of change have been exhausted. In America, only gradually and after a long political struggle did the conflict between the Thirteen Colonies and England turn into open warfare. The same can be said of the struggle for Israel in the late 1940's, a struggle in which I took part.

Until 1946, it had been our hope that diplomatic pressure and the power of public opinion would enable the Jewish people to realize the Zionist dream of establishing a homeland within at least part of Palestine. Eventually, however, we realized that with the combined opposition of the Arab world and of Great Britain, we would not be able to achieve our ends by diplomacy alone. I was among those who reached this conclusion reluctantly. But when it became clear that we had only two choices — either to give up our dream or to fight for its fulfillment — I was among those who recognized that we had passed from an era of peaceful persuasion to a revolutionary age.

Take a good look at the three synagogues on the facing page—how very different they appear! Yet the changes in building styles over the last two centuries are no more amazing than the changes in the Jewish community these synagogues were built to serve. In 1763, when the Judah Touro Synagogue (top left) was dedicated in Newport, Rhode Island, only a few thousand Jews were living in the New World. Not many more Jews were living in the Americas in 1833, when the Sephardic Synagogue (right) on the Caribbean island of St. Thomas was finished. However, in 1954, when the world-famous architect Frank Lloyd Wright built the Beth Shalom Synagogue (bottom left) at Elkins Park, near Philadelphia, the United States was home to the largest and most prosperous Jewish community in history. Nowhere else in the Diaspora have Jews played so powerful a role in public life, yet remained so firmly committed to their own heritage and institutions.

History teaches us that many revolutions end unhappily. The Terror that followed the French Revolution of 1789 was in some ways as horrible as the evils the revolution was meant to erase; the Russian Revolution in 1917 eventually brought to power a regime that proved far more cruel than the nineteenth century czars had been.

In the mid-1940's we too faced terrible risks. There were already about a half a million Jews in Palestine. By rebelling against Great Britain, we risked the possibility not only of failing to win our freedom, but also of losing everything we already had.

Our revolution was crowned by success in two stages: first, when the United Nations agreed in November 1947 that Israel's claim to statehood was legitimate; and second, when we proclaimed our independence on May 14, 1948, and secured the recognition of the world community. It was a moment that would linger and shine in the national memory forever.

ABBA EBAN

Left and below, an artist's vision of life around 1900 on Manhattan's Lower East Side; for more on this era in American Jewish history, see Chapter 15. The two photographs at right—a Brooklyn sukkah (top) and a New York tallis maker at work (bottom)—show that even in an ever-changing city, some vital traditions can be preserved.

What could be further from the
streets, slums, and sweatshops
of the Lower East Side than a
Jewish summer camp (above) in
the woodlands of California?
At right, a scene that might take
place in any city in America:
a Bar Mitzvah boy in his
moment of glory.

4

INTRODUCTION TO PART TWO:

The Age of Revolution

We often hear that our century is one of rapid change, and of course it is. Yet it is hard to think of any country that changed more rapidly than France between 1789 and 1871. If you were born in Paris in 1787, and lived to be eighty-five, you would have seen four revolutions, the birth and death of two French empires, the creation of three French republics, and two international wars.

Even more startling would be the changes in daily life. At your birth you would have been ruled by kings and nobles wearing fine wigs and living in elegant palaces. Not long after, you would have seen the nobles and kings give way to the new middle class. Toward the end of your life, you would see railroads criss-cross Europe, and you might even send a message to an American via the brand-new transatlantic cable.

Even the world of art changed. Painters stopped painting pictures of gods, goddesses, and nobles, and found beauty in ordinary life. Soon they would go beyond this, treating objects and light in a dazzling new manner. Art historians call this movement Impressionism. It was the beginning of modern art.

Revolution and class conflict

All this happened, in one way or another, because of the changes in thought which brought about the Declaration of Independence. The theories of liberty, equality, and scientific inquiry which inspired Jefferson to write the Declaration were first developed among the Germans, French, and English. After the success of the American Revolution, Europe was ready for these ideas to come home. The turning point came in 1789, with the outbreak of the French Revolution. Within four years the monarchy was overthrown, a new government was set up, and the king was beheaded.

Napoleon spurs on his troops against the British in the Battle of the Pyramids, a key victory in the French general's campaign in Egypt and Palestine.

The revolution in France seemed to be as successful as the revolution in America, but the two events were really quite different. George Washington and the American armies fought a king who was thousands of miles away. After the Revolutionary War, the defeated British were separated by an ocean from the victorious rebels, and the English nobles were not affected by the government in the New World.

Revolutions on the European mainland, however, meant a direct conflict between revolutionaries and nobility. The nobles who were overthrown did not accept defeat easily, and they schemed to regain power. (Even now there are Frenchmen who hope for the day when a king will again rule France.)

While revolution in America established a new and permanent government, revolution in Europe set off a lasting struggle between the rebels and the old upper classes. Often this struggle stopped only when a strong leader seized power.

Such a leader was Napoleon Bonaparte.

Napoleon Bonaparte

Napoleon was a short, temperamental man with coarse manners and a weakness for cheating at cards. He was also a masterful leader and, at his best, a brilliant general. He became a military hero by leading a French army across the Alps and driving the Austrians from northern Italy in 1797. He next outwitted the British fleet by landing an army at the mouth of the Nile, then marching into the Holy Land in an attempt to gain control of the Ottoman Empire and smash British trade in the Mediterranean. Though he was unable to conquer Palestine, he was able to take over Egypt. When the revolutionary government in France failed to rule successfully, he again slipped through the British fleet and used his French army to march on Paris. In 1799, at the age of thirty, Napoleon became absolute ruler of France.

But Napoleon's dream was to become emperor of Europe—and he nearly did! By 1810 almost the entire European continent had either been conquered by his soldiers, or had joined in alliance with him. Yet the leaders of Europe did not like being ruled by the French, and the rulers of the old empires hated the ideas of freedom and equality which Napoleon preached. When he weakened his army by battling Spain and Russia at the same time, the other nations of Europe (led by Great

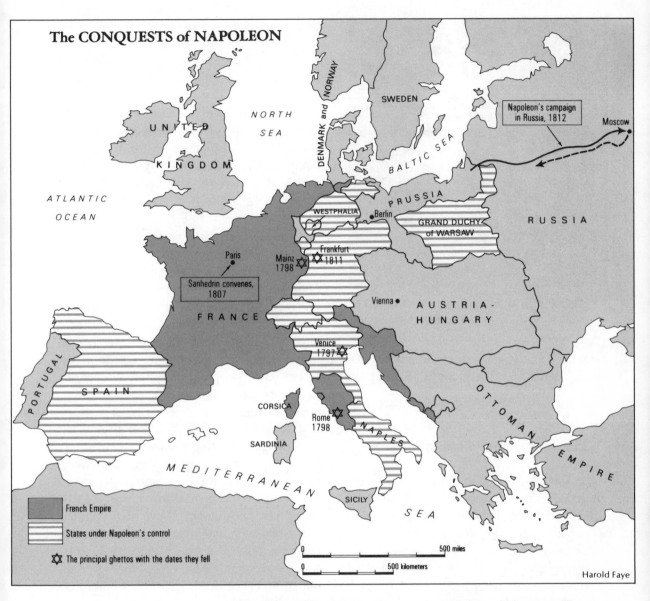

The CONQUESTS of NAPOLEON

By the end of 1810, Napoleon was at the height of his power. He ruled France, Belgium, the Netherlands, and parts of Spain, Germany, Italy, and southeastern Europe directly from Paris. His relatives occupied some of the major thrones of Western Europe, and Napoleon himself had divorced his first wife, Josephine, to marry the Austrian emperor's daughter. In 1812, Napoleon led an army through Poland into Russia, capturing Moscow by September. However, his troops proved no match for the severe Russian winter, and (as you can see from the map) Napoleon was forced to retreat.

British men of finance in the late 1800's. The man on the right wears Ashkenazi clothing.

Britain) joined against him. Bonaparte was finally defeated in Belgium in 1815, at the Battle of Waterloo.

The rise of nationalism

As soon as Napoleon's empire collapsed, there was a reaction against his dream of a united Europe. Bonaparte had spoken of a single European culture. Those who were now free of his rule praised their own special cultures. They stressed their differences, the special character of each nation's "spirit."

This new feeling was called NATIONAL-ISM.

Like a great wave, nationalism swept over Europe. Italy had been a jumble of small independent states ever since the fall of Rome. It now became a unified country. The Germans had been citizens of hundreds of separate states connected only by language. Now they began to think of themselves as one people with a destiny of national greatness.

To achieve this greatness, the German states began to unite under the powerful king of Prussia. Even before this was done, the Germans went to war with France, scored an easy victory, and declared the creation of the German Empire. Out of many small, weak states they had built the strongest nation on the European continent.

The struggle for power

The countries which had fallen to Napoleon now tried to turn back the clock of freedom. Napoleon had given land to the peasants and freed the Jews from their ghettos. The restored kings tried to reverse those changes. Feeling their freedom slip away, the peoples of these countries fought revolutions in 1830, most of them unsuccessful.

Adding fuel to the political fires were the changes affecting the lives of the common people. The early nineteenth century was the era of the INDUSTRIAL REVOLUTION, a time when machinery was used to make new and improved products. Skilled craftsmen who had always worked in their cottages now lost their jobs to factory workers, who made use of machines to turn out products far more quickly. The craftsmen and their families were forced to move from the countryside to the cities in a desperate search for jobs. In the new factories, they had to work long hours for pitifully low wages.

All these pressures exploded in 1848 in another flood of revolutions. The French government was overthrown, the Austrian Empire trembled, German states were swept with demands for reform, and war

*Capitalism, Socialism,
Communism,
Nationalism*

Four important "isms" help to explain the history of the nineteenth and twentieth centuries.

CAPITALISM is based on free trade. In a capitalist society, the means of producing and distributing goods—land, factories, railroads, and so forth—are privately owned and run for profit. The United States is a capitalist country, though the U.S. government tries to regulate industry for the good of society as a whole.

Some thinkers, blaming capitalism for the hardships suffered by workers during the Industrial Revolution, came up with new ideas of how society should be ordered. One such idea was **SOCIALISM**, in which the workers themselves control the means of producing and distributing goods. In practice, this means that the government runs the economy. Some socialist countries are democracies, others are dictatorships. England and Israel are two democracies based, in part, on socialist principles.

COMMUNISM is a special kind of socialism. The guiding ideal of Communism is supposed to be "from each according to his ability, to each according to his needs." But in fact, everyone in a Communist country must do whatever the Communist Party bosses demand. The Soviet Union and China are examples of this kind of dictatorship.

The 1800's also saw the rise of **NATIONALISM**, the belief that every people should have its own nation-state. Modern Zionism is a nationalist movement, as were the campaigns to unify Italy and Germany. There is nothing wrong with taking pride in one's homeland. Unfortunately, nationalism in some countries (such as Nazi Germany) led to the idea that other peoples were inferiors or outsiders, and to the blind belief that one's own nation could do no wrong.

Leon Trotsky (born Lev Bronstein), a Jew who helped lead the Communist revolution in Russia in 1917.

broke out in Italy. In large and small states the same cry went up: "Give us constitutional government."

But the forces of the kings and nobles stood firm; the revolutionaries were beaten back on every front. National liberty was no more advanced in 1850 than it had been early in 1848. Seeing that the call for free-

dom could be totally crushed by force, Europeans developed a new toughness of mind—a new way of thinking about power and how to get it. Showing this new attitude was a little book which happened to appear in the year of the great revolutions, 1848, and which called for workers everywhere to overthrow their political

Karl Marx, a founder of Communism and coauthor of the *Communist Manifesto*. To learn more about him, see Chapter 12.

felt that their only hope for freedom lay in the New World. So began the first great migration of Europeans to the United States.

These events of the early 1800's changed the lives of the Jews of Central and Western Europe. Those who lived in France, Holland, and England had been fairly well accepted into Christian society by the 1790's, and were able to enjoy the general increase in living and cultural standards during the next 100 years. The Jews in the Italian ghettos, and the far larger numbers in the ghettos of Germany, had a much more difficult task. They had to adjust not only to the changes going on around them, but also to the advances that society had made during the centuries they were shut behind ghetto walls.

and economic rulers. That book was the *Communist Manifesto*.

Most Europeans, however, were not interested in further fighting. Disappointed liberals, along with thousands of workers struggling under the burdens of poverty,

We will see how the Jewish people succeeded in entering the stormy modern world as we look at the era of EMANCIPATION.

SUMMARY   *From the beginning of the French Revolution in 1789 to the unification of Germany in 1871, Europe went through a great many revolts and political upheavals. The main results were that traditional governments became stronger, while the middle class became richer and the working class became poorer. During this era of rapid change, large numbers of Jews became part of the modern world.*

5

The Challenge
of Freedom

Freedom presents problems.

Does this idea seem strange? Living in a free country, perhaps you take your many rights and privileges for granted. But those who escape from dictatorships soon discover that freedom can be frightening as well as exciting. The freedom to choose for yourself opens many wonderful possibilities—but also creates the risk of making new mistakes.

Today this problem faces Jews who escape from the Soviet Union. They are happy to live without fear of oppression; but they are worried when they discover that many Western governments, unlike the Russian government, do not pay everybody's medical bills, or give each person a job.

In the 1770's the Jews of Europe did not have to worry about the problems of freedom. Their problem was how to survive without it! Ever since the Roman Empire had become Christian, nearly 1500 years before, Jews had been denied most human rights—even, at times, the right to live. As Europe turned to the modern era, our people could not know that many of them were about to encounter freedom for the first time, and that this would present them with new and difficult challenges.

Equality in France

The first to make this discovery were the Jews of France. At the time of the American Revolution, 50,000 Jews lived in French territory. They did not live in ghettos, but heavy taxes and strict laws kept most of them extremely poor. One of them, however—Herz Cerfberr—was so successful in providing supplies for the French army that he was given French citizenship.

He set up three factories and hired as many Jews as he could, showing them for the first time how modern industry works. Then, with the help of Moses Mendelssohn, he proved to a Gentile writer, Christian Dohm, that Jewish poverty was not the fault of the Jews, as was widely said. It was the result of anti-Jewish laws. Dohm was so moved that he wrote the first modern book calling for Jewish emancipation.

At the same time, a movement for giving equal rights to Jews was beginning. Among the leading spokesmen for liberty was the Count Mirabeau. His words sound like today's pleas for other peoples in need of equality:

> If you wish the Jews to become better . . . citizens, then banish every humiliating distinction, open to them every avenue of gaining a livelihood. . . . There is only one thing to be lamented, that so highly gifted a nation should so long have been kept in a state wherein it was impossible for its powers to develop.

The Count was attacked as a traitor to his class, but his words were heard. Partly because of the work of Mirabeau and Cerfberr, Jews were at last given the right to take the French oath of citizenship. The French Revolution was barely two years old when, in September 1791, the Jews of France received full equality —the first Jews in Europe to become legally equal members of a modern European state.

Napoleon and the Sanhedrin

New laws did not erase old prejudices. When Napoleon came to power, Christians began telling him that Jews were disloyal to France and that all anti-Jewish laws should be restored. The Emperor was proud of his ability to make rapid decisions, but in this case he decided to hear the other side of the story before taking action. He called an assembly of Jewish leaders to tell him how the Jews really felt about living on French soil.

These Jewish leaders saw that their new freedom had created a serious problem for them. How could they answer Napoleon? Jews had always thought of themselves— and been thought of by Gentiles—as a nation in exile, waiting for the chance to return to Eretz Yisrael. But the Emperor of France would not like it if they told him that the Jewish dream was to leave France and return to Palestine.

The Jewish leaders had a hard choice to make. Should they give up their long-held dream of a Jewish state? Or should they give up their newly won rights as Frenchmen?

They chose to be citizens of France. Judaism no longer meant loyalty to Palestine, they said—it was a religion of loyal French citizens. "We are no longer a nation within a nation," proclaimed one of the men who made this decision. "France is our country, Jews. Your obligations are outlined; your happiness is waiting."

Napoleon was so pleased that he called a new council of Jewish leaders to give formal approval to this decision. He arranged for the new council to meet with great pomp and ceremony, and named it after the court which had ruled Jewish life in Roman times—the Sanhedrin. He even promised the Jewish people "to find for them a new Jerusalem in France."

Much of this was just for show. The new "Sanhedrin" had no real authority, and never met again. Napoleon did not establish "a new Jerusalem." In fact, he issued new laws which seriously limited Jewish rights. (Full equality for the Jews of France did not come again until 1831.)

The Sanhedrin met with great pomp and
ceremony, but accomplished little.

Yet the meeting of the Sanhedrin was
still very important. It marked a turning
point in our history: the first official statement that the goal of our people was to be
fully accepted as citizens of Europe. Jews
would give up their hope of returning to
Zion in order to be loyal to their home
country. They felt sure that once they had
done this, Gentiles would discard their
anti-Jewish prejudices to welcome the
children of Abraham as citizens of the
modern world.

It was only when it became clear that,
no matter how Jews acted, the Christian
community would not accept them as
equals, that the idea of building a Jewish
state was reborn.

Freedom appears—
and vanishes

Napoleon did less for the Jews of France
than he had promised, but he left them
with far more freedom than the Jews of
Central Europe had ever known. Moreover, as the French armies swept across
the continent, Napoleon ordered that Jews
in the conquered lands also be given some
legal rights. The gates of the ghettos were
ripped from their hinges, and ghetto walls
were torn to the ground.

The rapid rise and fall of Napoleon's
empire led to confusion in the countries he
had conquered. The fact that a *foreign*
ruler had opened the ghettos sparked new

The Jewish quarter of Frankfurt, Germany, as it looked more than a century ago.

anti-Jewish feelings. After Napoleon was finally defeated, European rulers met to discuss the "Jewish problem." At first they agreed that "the rights already conceded the Jews in the . . . (German) states will be continued." But, at the last minute, the word *in* was changed to *by*. Only rights given *by* the states were to be protected. And since almost all the new rights had been given *in* the states but *by* the French, this change of a single word wiped out the freedom of many Jewish communities.

Jews also suffered on other fronts. Christians in many countries reacted against Napoleon's call for a united Europe by insisting on their own special cultural identity. Some German writers claimed that the Germans had a "unique national spirit" and that Jews would always be outsiders—even though Jews had been living in Germany for over 1000 years.

This nationalistic attitude gave rise to anti-Jewish riots all over Germany in 1819. Throughout this period, Jews found their professional and social lives strictly limited.

Holland was a rare exception to the European pattern. Dutch Jews had long been accepted by that nation's Gentile community, and suffered few restrictions. Amsterdam was, in fact, home to the single largest Jewish community in Western Europe—10,000 in number. After the fall of Napoleon, Holland was the only nation to allow the Jews full equal rights, and it was the first country in the modern world to let Jews serve in parliament and high public office.

Jews and Christian culture

The sudden gain of liberty, followed by its equally sudden loss, was a terrible shock for the Jewish people. But those who left the ghettos had a special problem—one that Jews never faced before, and would probably never face again.

For the first time in history, Jews found themselves part of a culture that seemed, in many ways, superior to their own. In earlier times, Jews had been isolated, rejected, and persecuted, but they felt that this was due to the primitive nature of Gentile society. At times when Christian kings could barely sign their own names, all Jewish males could read and write. For fun the Gentiles got drunk, cheered as animals killed each other, or watched the public torture of criminals—actions which Jews considered immoral and disgusting. All this helped convince our people that they were followers of the only true religion and members of the only truly civilized nation.

Jews continued to believe in the superiority of their culture during the centuries that they spent locked inside the ghettos. Perhaps it was true at first, but when the ghetto walls were torn down, Jews found a world shining with the art of the Renaissance and the machinery of the Industrial Revolution. Even more startling and confusing was the fact that some Gentiles were preaching ideals of universal justice and equality, beliefs as noble as any in our Bible.

Some Jews felt that the only way to end their confusion was by converting to Christianity. Even while Napoleon was still on his throne, fully one-tenth of the German Jewish population was baptized. As many as half the Jews of Berlin may have become Christians. The deserters included many of the best-educated Jews, who could not resist taking the "simple" step into Gentile society. Among them were four of the children of Moses Mendelssohn.

A large number of German Jews held to their old traditions, but the Judaism they practiced seemed old-fashioned to the younger generation. Most synagogues were dingy. The services held in them were routine and mechanical—dull and unclear at best, noisy and disorderly at worst. There was a real chance that within a generation Judaism in Germany might disappear.

The first to do something about this critical situation was Israel Jacobson.

Israel Jacobson

Jacobson came from a wealthy and important family. His father wanted him to become a rabbi, but Israel was too interested in studying German and French to devote himself entirely to rabbinic studies. He turned to banking, earning a small fortune by the time he was nineteen!

During his business travels he visited many Jewish communities. Everywhere he saw the need to improve Jewish education. In 1801 he opened, with his own money, a school for poor children.* There he began a weekly worship program at which Jewish prayers were said in German, hymns were sung, and a shortened service was conducted in a quiet and orderly fashion. In addition, there was a weekly sermon—something not heard in synagogues for centuries. (Rabbis had become used to preaching only two or three times a year.)

The children liked the changes—and so did some of Jacobson's adult friends. In fact, they enjoyed the new services so much that they came regularly to pray with the children.

By 1810 there was so much interest in his work that Jacobson opened a little "Temple" on the grounds of his school, dedicating it with the first public Reform service. After the fall of Napoleon, Jacobson was forced to move to Berlin, where he continued his new program. His services were so well attended that Berlin's traditional Jews became deeply worried. It was probably at their request that the German government ordered a halt to Jacobson's activities.

Why were German officials concerned

* Both Jews and Christians attended the school, which flourished until the Nazi era.

In this seventeenth century woodcut, a Dutch Jewish housewife lights candles for Shabbat. For centuries, Jews enjoyed more freedom in Holland than anywhere else in Europe.

were afraid that a modernized Judaism would keep Jews from converting to Christianity—which, in fact, it did. Reform produced a major revival of Jewish spirit and activity. Fine synagogues were built, and attracted large congregations. Jewish books and magazines appeared in increasing numbers, and attracted more and more readers. Even the opponents of Reform were affected, for they were forced to rethink and improve their own practices.

All this could not be foreseen when Jacobson opened his little Temple. Actually, he made very few changes. His services were more traditional than those of present-day American Conservative synagogues. Yet his work was highly important in proving that change could be a part of modern Judaism. He showed that the way for Jews to enter the modern world was not to desert our heritage (as those who converted to Christianity had done) nor to hide in the ways of the past (as the traditionalists were doing) but to *use* the newfound freedom to improve Jewish life. His work, which began as an experiment in a small school, was destined to stimulate every branch of the Jewish community.

with how Jewish services were conducted? Language was the problem. The Germans claimed that preaching in the language of the country was not in keeping with Jewish tradition. We shall see that they were wrong—but, in reality, they had no interest in preserving Jewish customs. They

SUMMARY   *The freedom that came to Jews at the time of the French Revolution brought opportunities, but also problems. The Jews of France had to give up, for a time, their dream of a Jewish homeland. The Jews of Germany won their civil rights from Napoleon, only to lose those same rights after his defeat. In this difficult and confusing situation, Israel Jacobson was one of those who saw that change could improve the quality of Jewish life, and so help our religion survive.*

6

The Making of Modern Judaism

Israel Jacobson tried to reform certain Jewish practices. Soon there was a movement trying to modernize all of Jewish thought and practice: REFORM JUDAISM.

At first, Reformers only wanted to improve forms of worship. They replaced confusion and hubbub during prayer services with beauty and order. Instrumental music, which had had no place in the synagogue since the destruction of the Jerusalem Temple, was used in the service. New rituals, such as confirmation, were created, and prayers and sermons in German were added.

While the traditionalists were basically opposed to change, they imitated some of the new practices, particularly the use of a weekly sermon. But when it came to Jewish law, they saw no possibility for change. A leading Orthodox rabbi spoke out against Reform, saying:

All commandments and prohibitions contained in the Books of Moses—in the very form given by Talmudic interpretation—are of divine origin, binding for all time upon the Jews. Not one of these commandments or prohibitions, whatever its character, can be abolished or modified by any human authority.

The Reformers took a totally opposite view. As one of their leaders said:

Judaism is not a finished tale; there is much in its present form that must be changed or abolished.

Problems in the Torah

The leaders of Reform loved Torah, but they found some things in it that they could not accept. Its laws dealing with the treatment of slaves were advanced for an-

The Case of the Disappearing Husband

An eighteenth century wedding ring.

From its beginnings, Reform Judaism has tried to solve some of the more difficult problems of traditional Jewish law. One such problem might be called the "case of the disappearing husband."

When a man and a woman marry according to Jewish law, a contract called a "ketubah" (כְּתֻבָּה) spells out the terms of the marriage. The ketubah gives the woman legal rights; and if the husband does not live up to his end of the bargain, a woman can sue for divorce. But the law also states that a divorce may only be given by the man. The husband must hand his wife a bill of divorce, called a "get" (גֵּט).

But what if the husband disappears? (Although this rarely happens today, it was fairly common in days when travel was dangerous.) And what if, after some time, the wife of a missing husband wishes to marry again? What can be done? According to traditional law, nothing.

Although the wife might have to live without her husband for the rest of her life, she cannot remarry. She cannot be divorced, since her husband cannot be found to present her with her get. And in Jewish law she is not a widow, because her husband is thought of as alive unless there are witnesses to his death or his body can be found. Such a woman is known as an "agunah" (עֲגוּנָה), a deserted or abandoned wife.

The Reformers felt that this was an unfair and unacceptable solution. Since government courts in most countries set standards by which a person who has been missing for a very long time can be declared "legally dead," the Reform Jews said a woman may accept the state's ruling as to when she is free to take a new husband.

cient times—but in modern times we learned that slavery itself is wrong. The Bible forbids the practice of witchcraft—yet it never doubts that witchcraft is powerful and real. But in modern times we know that witchcraft is false and its practice can be harmful. And Jewish law had clearly treated women as second-class citizens. This, too, called for change.

It is true that, throughout much of history, the Jewish woman enjoyed a position as good as or better than that of other women. She was respected as the cornerstone of the family, given the sacred task of making the home a "kosher" and "Jewish" one. Every Sabbath she would hear her husband recite words from the Book of Proverbs to pay tribute to her:

אֵשֶׁת חַיִל מִי יִמְצָא
וְרָחֹק מִפְּנִינִים מִכְרָהּ

A woman of valor, who can find?
For her worth is far above rubies.
(*Proverbs 31:10*)

Still, each day the man of the household thanked God "for making me a man." The Jewish woman could only praise God "for making me according to Your will." She could not take part in some synagogue rituals, and was forced to sit in a separate area divided from the rest of the synagogue. Moreover, Jewish law limited her rights in ways which could cause her severe hardship and grief.

The Reformers felt that these traditions needed changing. In changing them they created Reform Judaism.

Can Jewish law change?

But how did they show that what they were doing was Jewish? How could the Reformers declare that laws which had been practiced by Jews for thousands of years were no longer valid? The person who took the lead in answering these questions was Abraham Geiger.

Geiger was both a rabbi and the son of a rabbi, and was learned in Bible and Talmud. He had a great appreciation for tradition; and even when he became a leader of Reform he observed such rules as dietary laws, so that no one could accuse him of changing Judaism just to make his own life easier.

Yet he championed the basic principles of Reform. The Bible and Talmud record the moral history of humanity, said Geiger, but they were written by human beings. Therefore they contain both Divine and human elements. Modern Jews must de-cide which laws are Divine and therefore meaningful, and which laws should be discarded. The great challenge presented by Reform was to ask the house of Israel to study the past in order to find what is truly valuable for life in the present.

The Reformers believed that the basic moral laws of Judaism are eternal, but that much of Jewish practice has to change from generation to generation. And, said the Reformers, this is exactly what has been happening since earliest times.

To prove this, they turned to the work of a true hero of modern Judaism—the historian Leopold Zunz. To understand what Zunz accomplished, try to imagine what the study of Judaism was like in the days when Israel Jacobson was holding his first Reform services. There was not a single modern book written by a Jew on Jewish history. There were no Jewish encyclopedias, no Jewish bibliographies, no Jewish textbooks. The modern study of history had developed while the Jews were still in isolation, so Jewish scholarship was limited to the traditional study of Bible and Talmud.

New Jewish studies

In 1819, a small group of idealistic Jews decided to change all this. Among them were a businessman, Moses Moser; a brilliant law student, Eduard Gans; and Zunz himself. Joining these three was Heinrich Heine, an unsuccessful scholar who had shown a great gift for poetry. The goal of these young men was to explore the Jewish heritage using modern historical methods.

They started off with enthusiasm, giving lectures and publishing an excellent

היינריך היינע

Born a Jew, Heinrich Heine found that he could not earn a living as a writer unless he converted to Christianity.

magazine, but soon they faced a shocking reality. The Jews of Berlin were simply not interested in studying Judaism. Those who were "modern" wanted only to study European culture, while the traditionalists did not want to learn Judaism in a "new" way.

The young men saw that they could not make a living from their Jewish studies. Quite the contrary—Judaism was getting in their way. Gans discovered that as a Jew he would always be kept in the lowest teaching ranks at the University of Berlin. He promptly converted to Christianity and was promoted to the rank of professor.

Heine spoke out against Gans' conversion—but soon after, he too was baptized. He became Germany's greatest lyric poet, but never forgave himself for accepting what he called "the ticket of admission to European culture."

"If I could have made a living by stealing spoons without going to prison," he said, "I would never have been christened."

Leopold Zunz

Leopold Zunz soon realized that he was one of the few Jews in all of Germany deeply devoted to Jewish history. He dedicated his life to his studies, which he named the SCIENCE OF JUDAISM.

Zunz began with a question of immediate importance. He had been one of the preachers at Israel Jacobson's Reform services—services which, as we have seen, the German government outlawed on the grounds that preaching was a Christian, not a Jewish, practice. Through his work, Zunz was able to prove that the opposite was true: preaching was an ancient Jewish custom that had been taken over by the Church! Zunz called for rabbis to return to the sermon as a tool for instructing the ignorant and exciting the indifferent.

Before long, others joined Zunz to work in the Science of Judaism. Studying the Bible and Talmud in this new way brought forth a flood of information about earlier times. Jewish books and magazines of all kinds were published and widely read. Zunz, who lived to be ninety-two, saw German-Jewish society totally changed by the results of his work, as generations grew up with a new feeling of pride in their religious heritage and a rich knowledge of the Jewish past.

Samson Raphael Hirsch and Neo-Orthodoxy

From the work of Zunz and his followers, the Reformers learned that Jewish practice had changed in the past. To the

Reformers this meant that Judaism should always change to meet the times. That was one way to understand the Science of Judaism—but it was not the only way. A very different view was taken by a man who tried to combine European culture with Orthodox tradition: Samson Raphael Hirsch.

Hirsch, like Geiger, had a traditional upbringing. Like Geiger, he went to the University of Bonn—in fact, the two were good friends there. (They studied Talmud together, and practiced delivering sermons to each other.) And, again like Geiger, he saw that changes in Jewish life were necessary. When he was a rabbi in a very traditional community, he seemed to be a reformer, bringing order and beauty back to the service, improving Jewish education, and encouraging studies in non-Jewish fields. Hirsch shared with the Reformers the belief that a good Jew must be deeply involved in improving the world.

But on the basic issue of Reform—the question of whether change should be permitted—Hirsch stood firm. For him, Jew-

---

Did Reform Go Too Far?

The early Reform leaders all believed that Jewish laws could change. But they did not always agree on which laws should be changed, or how many traditions should be abandoned.

One of the most radical Reformers was Samuel Holdheim, who in 1847 became the first Reform rabbi in Berlin. Holdheim held Sabbath services on Sunday instead of Saturday mornings, and he taught that Jewish boys need not be circumcised. In fact, Holdheim was ready to discard just about all the teachings of the Talmud. "In the Talmudic age," he said, "the Talmud was right. In my age, I am right."

Few Reformers spoke so bluntly, but many of them shared Holdheim's disregard of tradition. Meeting in Pittsburgh in 1885, the leaders of the American Reform movement pledged to uphold the "moral laws" of Judaism, while rejecting all "ceremonies" that were "not adapted to the views and habits of modern civilization." They denied that the Jews were a nation, and held out no hope for a return to Zion.

In time, the Reformers came to see that they had lost as well as gained in their break with tradition. More than fifty years after the Pittsburgh meeting, American Reform leaders gathered in Columbus, Ohio, to reexamine their beliefs. They showed a new openness to traditional "customs, symbols, and ceremonies," and they looked forward to the day when a Jewish homeland in Palestine would be both "a haven of refuge for the oppressed" and "a center of Jewish culture and spiritual life."

A Jewish woman from Hamburg, dressed in the height of nineteenth century fashion.

to the level of the Torah. The lesson of Jewish history, Hirsch said, is that the Jews must always stand apart.

Hirsch dedicated his life as a rabbi, writer, and educator to teaching these ideas. Through his teaching, he created a more modern type of Orthodoxy, often called NEO-ORTHODOXY (or New Orthodoxy). Neo-Orthodox Jews act as full members of the modern world but still keep their age-old Jewish practices. Much of modern Orthodox life has been the result of Hirsch's work.

Zacharias Frankel: a middle way

Something of a middle road was established by Rabbi Zacharias Frankel. His study of Jewish history convinced him that the Jewish tradition had always permitted and required change. But he felt that the Reformers had often gone too far. His final split with Geiger and Reform came over the question of Hebrew. A conference of Reform rabbis voted that Hebrew was no longer absolutely essential for Jewish worship, although "for the present" it should still be used. For Frankel, Hebrew was a basic part of Judaism. The idea that there might be a time when Jews could do away with the use of Hebrew was something Frankel could not accept.

But Frankel faced the same problem the Neo-Orthodox and Reformers faced. How can we know what can be changed in Judaism to make it more modern; and how can we know what may never be changed? This is the question of authority: Who shall decide what is wrong and what is right in Jewish law? Orthodoxy insisted that the laws in the Torah and Talmud were true and unchangeable forever. Re-

ish law could be found where it had always been: in the Torah. We have been chosen by God to live for what is true and perfect, he said. To do this, we must observe the Law which the Lord has given us.

Both Hirsch and the Reformers wanted to make it possible for Jews to live in the world of the nineteenth century. But, as Hirsch saw it, the Reformers were trying to do this by bringing the Torah *down* to the level of the world. It would be better, he taught, to bring the world *up*

form said each Jew had to decide on his or her own beliefs and practices. Frankel's answer was that only the Jewish people as a whole could change traditions. The will of all Jews would decide the practice of our religion.

Frankel's theory was not totally clear. How can we be sure of the will of all Jews? In practice, he believed that changes should be made at a slow but steady pace. This idea appealed to many, and later became one of the basic building blocks for the American movement known as CONSERVATIVE JUDAISM.

Toward a new era

Thus, the work done by Geiger, Hirsch, and Frankel in the 1830's and 1840's established the three main forms of modern Judaism.

Of course, it did not happen as simply as we have made it appear. For a time, the governments in Germany allowed most cities to have only one Jewish congregation, which meant that each city's rabbi had to serve Jews of all shades of belief. As a rabbi, Geiger was called upon to make decisions on questions of Talmudic law for Orthodox Jews which he taught were no longer binding for Reform Jews!

Moreover, after the failure of the revolutions of 1848, all liberal movements were put down. The desire to update Jewish practice was slowed, and the branches of German Jewry made peace with each other. All congregations, regardless of what they called themselves, followed a ritual which was very much the same.

Nevertheless, the German Jews had successfully fought the great battles of modern Jewish religious thinking. Reform would find a new home in America. Orthodoxy was reborn. And European Jewry was about to enter its greatest era.

SUMMARY *The great split in Jewish religious thought took place in the 1830's and 1840's over the question of Jewish law. The Reformers, led by Abraham Geiger, insisted that, although the spiritual message of Judaism was eternal, each person had to decide what forms of Jewish practice were still meaningful. (They supported their argument by pointing to the work of Leopold Zunz and other scholars who developed the Science of Judaism.) Samson Raphael Hirsch taught a Neo-Orthodox approach, allowing certain changes but insisting that Jews must keep their traditional practices. Zacharias Frankel took a position favoring moderate change. The major forms of modern Judaism developed from these three viewpoints.*

7

Heroes of Emancipation

The rapid changeover was almost impossible to believe. In 1790 not a single European Jew was a citizen of the land in which he lived. By 1880 total equality had come to almost the entire Jewish population of Central and Western Europe.

Jews used this new freedom to earn fame in a wide variety of fields. In Great Britain, the first Jew to win national renown was, of all things, a boxer! His name was Daniel Mendoza, and from 1792 to 1795 he was the boxing champion of England. He raised boxing to a new level by approaching it "scientifically." Until his time, the sport was nothing more than two strong men trying to punch each other until one fell, unconscious. But Mendoza, though smaller than most boxers, used his speed, agility, and strong left jab to defeat larger and more powerful opponents.

At the time of Mendoza's career, Jews had only been permitted to live in England for a little over a century. Just as the success of Negro baseball players in the 1940's and 1950's helped win new respect for blacks in America, so the achievements of Mendoza and other Jewish boxers helped our people gain respect in eighteenth century England.

The Rothschilds

The Jew who really dazzled the British was anything but an athlete. He was a short, plump German who settled in London in 1805. He never learned to speak English properly, and when he talked he was honest to the point of rudeness. But in the world of banking, he had few equals. His family became the leaders of European finance, and its name still stands for wealth and splendor. He was Nathan Mayer Rothschild.

Rothschild and his four brothers were

born in the Frankfurt ghetto. Their father gained some wealth and influence by handling business affairs for a German prince. Each son settled in a different major city of Europe, but they worked together to create the world's first international bank. Nathan was known as the leader of the five, and his career combined brilliance and courage.

One of his most spectacular feats came while England was fighting Napoleon in Spain. England needed to send money to the continent to pay its soldiers, but the French forces were patrolling the Spanish coast. The British government could not find a way to get the money safely to its troops in Spain.

Nathan Rothschild could. He hit upon the seemingly strange idea of sending funds to fight the French directly through France! For anyone else, the idea of sending a key shipment across enemy territory would have been insane. For the Rothschilds, it was only incredibly bold. With the help of the family's branch in Paris, the money was smuggled across the French countryside, then over the Pyrenees mountains to the English army in Spain. The plan was carried out with flawless timing, and the funds arrived on schedule.

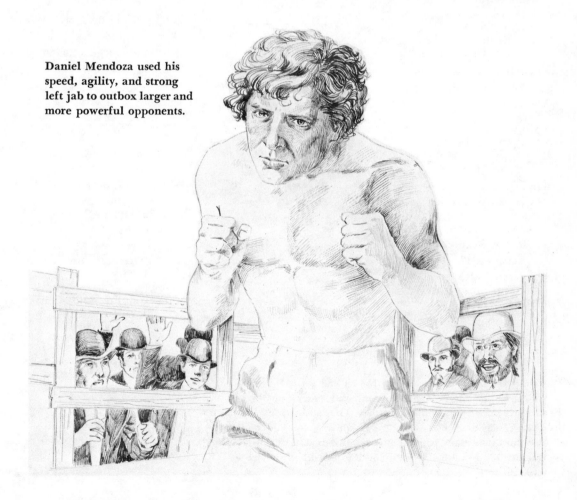

Daniel Mendoza used his speed, agility, and strong left jab to outbox larger and more powerful opponents.

THE ROTHSCHILDS:
A FAMILY TREE

FRANKFURT

Mayer Amschel Rothschild
1743–1812
- banker in Frankfurt
- father of five sons

LONDON

Nathan Mayer Rothschild
1777–1836
- key financial figure during Napoleonic Wars
- sister-in-law (Judith Cohen) married Moses Montefiore

Lionel Nathan de Rothschild
1808–1879
- first Jewish member of Parliament
- helped finance Suez Canal

Nathaniel Mayer, 1st Baron Rothschild
1840–1915
- first Jewish member of House of Lords

Lionel Walter, 2nd Baron Rothschild
1868–1937
- received Balfour Declaration in 1917

Amschel Mayer von Rothschild
1773–1855
- supported Neo-Orthodox movement

VIENNA

Salomon Mayer von Rothschild
1774–1855
- financed construction of first Austrian railroad

NAPLES

Karl Mayer von Rothschild
1788–1855
- made large loans to Sicily, Papal States, and other regions of Italy

PARIS

James Jacob Mayer de Rothschild
1792–1868
- most powerful banker in France
- leader of French Jewry
- gave large sums to charity

Baron Edmond James de Rothschild
1845–1934
- major supporter of early Jewish settlements in Palestine

This chart shows the importance to Jewish and world history of Mayer Amschel Rothschild, his five sons, and several members of the family's Paris and London branches. The family tree itself has been very much simplified—a complete family history of the Rothschilds would take many pages. For more on Edmond de Rothschild, see Chapter 13; on Lionel Walter, 2nd Baron Rothschild, see Chapter 16.

Leaders of European Jewry

Throughout the nineteenth century, the Rothschilds held center stage among the leaders of European Jewry. Facing page, the Rothschild family's coat of arms in England; bottom left, the Rothschild house in Frankfurt, Germany; bottom right, Salomon Mayer von Rothschild, head of the family's Vienna branch. Other Jewish leaders during this era included Sir Moses Montefiore (top left), who was related by marriage to the Rothschilds; and Adolphe Crémieux (below), who worked together with Montefiore to protect Jewish rights and interests.

Services in the Great Synagogue at Duke's Place, London.

Moses Montefiore

Perhaps even more remarkable than Nathan Rothschild was his handsome, six-foot three-inch brother-in-law, Moses Montefiore. As a young man, Montefiore received the support of his uncles. At the time only twelve spaces on the stock exchange were allowed for Jews. Montefiore's uncles bought him one of these twelve spaces, and Montefiore began to buy and sell stocks. He did extremely well, partly by working with the Rothschilds, partly through his own courageous investments. He was especially successful with two inventions which scientists warned him were very risky. One was gas-lighting, which would soon brighten cities all over the globe. The second was a vehicle that would soon change the face of the world—the railroad.

By the time he was forty, Montefiore had much more money than he could possibly need. He and his wife, Judith, realized that they were now free to leave the business world and spend the rest of their lives working on what mattered to them most. They were deeply Orthodox Jews. They never traveled without a Torah scroll and they refused to eat non-kosher food, even at banquets given by the Queen! And because of their beliefs they agreed to spend their lives helping others—and especially helping the Jewish people.

Because of their deep love of the land of Israel, the two set out in 1827 to see for themselves the way the Jews of Palestine were forced to live. In those days, the journey from London to Jerusalem took months, and was filled with such dangers as pirates, bandits, and disease. Nevertheless, the Montefiores made the trip five times.* They were disturbed to find the land in pitiful condition. The few thousand Jews who lived there were suffering under

* After his wife's death, Sir Moses—he was the first Jew in modern times to be knighted—returned twice more to Eretz Yisrael, the last time at the age of ninety.

harsh Turkish rule and badly in need of outside help.

The Montefiores gave money to the Jews of the Holy Land—but, beyond that, they gave a new vision. Their goal was to make the Jewish settlement financially independent. The English couple helped set up farm colonies at Jaffa, Safed, and Tiberias. They opened an industrial school and a girls' school, began building a hospital, and ordered the construction of a windmill (which still stands) so the Jews could grind their own grain. These were the first steps toward making Eretz Yisrael once again a land "flowing with milk and honey."

Adolphe Crémieux

Though Sir Moses and Lady Judith Montefiore were particularly devoted to the Jews of Palestine, they were ready to help Jews anywhere. In their most famous effort to protect our people, they were joined by the leading Jew of France, Adolphe Crémieux.

Crémieux was a lawyer who spent much of his life defending human rights. He successfully fought for better treatment of criminals, freedom of the press, and citizenship for the minorities living in the French colonies of North Africa. He served for a while as the French minister of justice—the first practicing Jew to hold such a high-ranking post in a modern government.

And while he was busy in politics, Crémieux remained active in Jewish causes. Until his time, any Jew testifying in a French court had to take a complicated "Jewish Oath" which called down horrible curses if the Jew spoke falsely. The government believed that a Jew could not be trusted to take the simple oath required of a Christian. Crémieux insisted that the same standards of honesty should be expected of all French citizens, and fought until the insulting "Jewish Oath" was abolished.

Hard as this task was, it was minor compared with the problem posed by an awful event in Syria.

The Damascus Affair

Syria, like Eretz Yisrael, was part of the decaying Ottoman Empire. Though Syria was mostly Muslim, people of many faiths lived there.

Early in 1840, a Catholic priest mysteriously disappeared from the streets of Damascus, the Syrian capital. Normally this would have attracted little notice. In this case, however, it was suggested to the local police by an important French official that the priest had been murdered by Jews who wanted to use his blood in making Passover matzah. False charges of this type, called BLOOD LIBELS, were not uncommon during the Middle Ages. Now this slander was revived by a "civilized" modern Frenchman.

The Syrian police took up the case with cruel enthusiasm. They arrested many Jews—some of them children—and tortured them horribly. Two Jews died. Others "confessed," only to deny their guilt as soon as they were freed from the torture chamber. This so-called "Damascus Affair" brought international protests; but, in a pattern that has become all too familiar in modern history, the nations of the West were afraid to take action for fear of angering the rulers of the Middle East.

Thus, the Jewish community found itself fighting alone. Jewish leaders around the world took up this challenge by uniting—for the first time—to act in defense of our people. Moses Montefiore, Adolphe Crémieux, and their wives were chosen to travel to the Middle East to demand justice for Syrian Jewry.

Muslim officials were not blind to the criticism being heaped on them in the European press, and offered to compromise. A pardon could be given to the Jewish prisoners. Or, the government said, those who had died under torture could be declared guilty, while those still alive would be freed. Montefiore and Crémieux refused to accept any statement which would mean that even a single Jew was guilty of murdering another human being in order to eat his blood. At last, as world pressure mounted, the agents of the Sultan gave in. All those accused were cleared, and the Jews still in prison were released. Furthermore, Montefiore was able to persuade the Sultan to forbid the use of torture in the prisons under his control.

The Jewish delegation returned to Europe to be greeted as heroes by both Jews and Gentiles. At a dinner in his honor, Crémieux told why he had undertaken the dangerous task:

> I am a lawyer, and I saw that there were unfortunates to be saved; I am a Jew, and I saw religious persecution to be fought; I am a man, and I saw the barbarity of torture to be abolished; how could I have hesitated without myself committing a crime? . . . I felt within myself the strength of right, and strength of spirit; would not my silence have been shameful cowardice?

The Alliance Israelite Universelle

It soon became clear that the fight for Jewish rights was more than a few individuals could handle. In 1858, officers of the Pope kidnapped a seven-year-old Jewish boy from his home in Bologna, Italy. They kept him in hiding, and raised him as a Roman Catholic. (They said this was legal because his nurse had secretly baptized him.) Despite international protests and the personal efforts of Moses Montefiore, the Church refused to return the child.

This kidnapping led to the creation of an agency that would work full-time to protect Jewish rights and defend Jews from attack. Thus was the Alliance Israelite Universelle (Universal Jewish Alliance) founded in 1860, with the tireless Crémieux as its first president. In addition to being a defense organization, the Alliance took an active role in providing education and job training for backward Jewish communities. Today it runs a network of all-day Jewish schools in fourteen countries, having helped more than 700,000 Jewish children with both Jewish and general education.

Jewish rights in Europe

Crémieux and Montefiore remained active world leaders throughout their remarkably long lives: Crémieux lived to be 85, Montefiore to be nearly 101! Over the years, other figures joined them in their struggle for Jewish rights. Again, the name of Rothschild was prominent.

Lionel de Rothschild was the son of Nathan Mayer Rothschild. A shy man,

Lionel disliked appearing in public. But he was also a devoted Jew, and so he entered politics to right a wrong: the law which made it impossible for Jews to serve in the Parliament of England.

Strangely, it was not illegal for Jews to *run* for Parliament, and Rothschild was duly elected. When he came to take his oath as a member of the House of Commons, the law required him to swear "on the true faith of a Christian." He naturally refused, and was forced to leave. He was elected a second time—and again was not allowed to sit in the Commons. All in all, he was elected seven times over an eleven-year period before the oath was finally changed so that he could take it. In 1858,

with his head covered and his hand on a Hebrew Bible, Lionel de Rothschild was sworn in as the first Jewish member of Parliament. Twenty-seven years later his son, Baron Nathaniel Rothschild, completed the task of gaining political rights for British Jewry by becoming the first Jew to sit in the House of Lords.

In Central Europe, Jews were also involved in the struggle for freedom. Ferdinand Lassalle was one who believed, like Washington and Jefferson, that the duty of a government is to make every citizen free and secure. But he also believed that the only way to set workers free was to allow them to own the factories, railroads, and other means of production. He orga-

Outrages like this kidnapping of a seven-year-old Jewish boy by papal officers inspired the formation of a new agency to protect Jewish rights—the Alliance Israelite Universelle.

nized the German laborers around this idea, and created the largest socialist party on the continent.

Another outstanding figure in the struggle for equal rights was Gabriel Riesser. When he was a young man he found that there were German laws to keep a Jew from becoming a lawyer. Many other Jews of his time, faced with the same problem, converted to Christianity in order to practice law. Riesser decided to fight. He founded a magazine called *Der Jude* ("The Jew") in which he demanded equality for the Jewish people. Many read his articles and, during the revolution of 1848, he was elected vice-president of the liberal parliament. Soon the old nobility returned to power, but Riesser kept working for change. In 1859 he became the first Jewish judge in Germany.

Decades of progress

Throughout Western Europe, our people felt that a new age of freedom had arrived. In 1830, the Jews of Belgium received full rights. Jews became citizens of Denmark in 1849, of Austria in 1867. In 1869, just six years after Gabriel Riesser's death, a new constitution in Germany granted political equality to all. The following year, after decades of struggle, the Italians freed their land from foreign control and gave the Jews full citizenship. Strangely, Switzerland and Sweden, which

A dressmaking workshop organized by the Alliance Israelite Universelle for the young Jewish women of Paris.

sheltered many Jews during World War II, were among the last to give freedom to our people. They finally did so in the 1870's; Norway followed suit in 1891.

There were, to be sure, a few troubling signs. A French writer named Renan suggested that there were basic differences between Semitic peoples (such as Jews) and Aryan peoples (such as Christian Europeans). Another Frenchman, the Count Gobineau, argued that people of the white race (especially those with blond hair and blue eyes) were superior to all others. But these racist arguments seemed unimportant at a time when the Jewish people was being accepted by the modern world. When the sun is shining brightly, we are not bothered by a few clouds. And, for the Jews of Western and Central Europe, the sun was shining as it never had before.

SUMMARY   *The period from 1840 to 1880 was one in which the Jews of Western and Central Europe enjoyed startling success. Anti-Jewish laws in England and France were repealed, allowing men like Moses Montefiore, Adolphe Crémieux, and the Rothschilds to represent the best both of Judaism and of the spirit of their nations. Elsewhere, Jews were gaining rights and influence, though more slowly. By 1880 the Jewish people had full rights of citizenship in most countries of Europe, and were looking toward a future of unending progress.*

8

America Before 1880

Of the many Jewish families who lived in the United States during its early years, none was more outstanding than that of Michael Gratz. He and his brother built a profitable trading and shipping business. They also took an active part in the struggle for American independence. Michael Gratz's sons were patriots. Two of them mined most of the saltpeter needed for America's gunpowder during the War of 1812, taking it from the cave owned by the family in Kentucky—now a tourist attraction known as Mammoth Cave.

Members of the Gratz family were founders and leading supporters of the first synagogue in Philadelphia, Mikveh Israel. One son helped establish Gratz College, the first college in the United States to train teachers for Jewish schools.

But the most outstanding member of the family was not one of Michael's seven sons, but one of his five daughters—Rebecca Gratz.

Rebecca Gratz

Rebecca Gratz was charming, intelligent, and radiantly beautiful, a woman who from early days found her greatest satisfaction in helping others. Before she reached the age of twenty, she helped run a private welfare agency with a poetic name: The Female Association for the Relief of Women and Children in Reduced Circumstances. She was a founding member of the Philadelphia Orphan Asylum. What she learned working for these agencies helped her create special agencies to meet the needs of the Jewish community in the New World.

In Europe, the synagogue was the center of a community's Jewish life—including all forms of tzedakah. In America, Jewish society was more divided. Poor immigrants from one region might create a synagogue of their own rather than become members of a wealthier synagogue established by

Jews from another region. This made it impossible for major charities to work through synagogues.

So Rebecca Gratz helped found the Female Hebrew Benevolent Society. This independent agency was the parent of today's huge network of Jewish charitable organizations.

Similarly, Jewish education had worked well in Europe, where the lives of children were centered on schooling, and where there were many scholars able to teach basic Judaism from traditional Hebrew texts. Scholars were few in the United States, so American Jewish children were getting almost no religious education. Rebecca Gratz spoke about this problem to Rabbi Isaac Leeser, another great leader and organizer. (He was the first to give sermons in English in an American synagogue.) Together they founded the first

Hebrew Sunday school in the United States. Miss Gratz directed it for twenty-seven years, until she was eighty-four.

In addition to the fame she won through her own work, Rebecca Gratz was known far and wide for another reason. In her early twenties she fell in love with a Christian, but out of loyalty to Judaism she refused to marry him, and remained single throughout her long life. This story was told to a British writer, Sir Walter Scott, who used her as a model for the noble Jewish heroine of his famous novel *Ivanhoe*— and he called his heroine Rebecca.

Judah Touro

Another American Jew to win fame was Judah Touro. He was the son of the rabbi of Newport, Rhode Island. Orphaned be-

The beautiful Rebecca Gratz (1781–1869).

Her father, Michael Gratz (1740–1811).

fore his Bar Mitzvah, young Judah was raised by an uncle in Boston. He then moved to New Orleans, where he was probably the first Jewish settler. Judah enlisted and fought in the War of 1812. Wounded and left for dead on the battlefield, he was rescued by a young Virginian, and the two men became friends and partners.

Touro was an excellent businessman, and in a surprisingly short time their firm was able to earn a large fortune. But he was a strange, lonely man, with a limited social life. From the privacy of his own rooms, he sent money wherever he felt it was needed. He was one of the two largest contributors to the monument in Boston which commemorates the Battle of Bunker

A Scene from "Ivanhoe"

Sir Walter Scott first heard about Rebecca Gratz from a mutual friend—the American writer Washington Irving. Scott was so struck by her story that he gave her name to the heroine of his novel Ivanhoe, *which is set in twelfth century England. In the novel (published in 1820), Rebecca is the daughter of a moneylender named Isaac. Captured by an evil Christian knight and threatened with death, she bravely answers his slanders against the Jewish people.*

"Thou hast spoken [about] the Jew," said Rebecca, "as the persecution of such as thou art has made him. Heaven in ire has driven him from his country, but industry has opened to him the only road to power and to influence which oppression has left unbarred. Read the ancient history of the people of God, and tell me if those, by whom Jehovah wrought such marvels among the nations, were then a people of misers and usurers!—And know, proud knight, we number names amongst us to which your boasted northern nobility is as the gourd compared with the cedar. . . ."

Rebecca's color rose now as she boasted the ancient glories of her race, but faded as she added, with a sigh, "Such *were* the princes of Judah, now such no more!— They are trampled down like the shorn grass, and mixed with the mire of the ways. Yet there are those among them who shame not such high descent, and of such shall be the daughter of Isaac. . . . Farewell! I envy not thy blood-won honors—I envy not thy barbarous descent from northern heathens—I envy thee not thy faith, which is ever in thy mouth, but never in thy heart nor in thy practice."

Hill. He organized, and to a great extent paid the bills for, the Jewish community of New Orleans.

His most spectacular gifts, however, were made in his will. He left money to practically every Jewish congregation in America, large donations to most of the nation's charities, and $50,000 to be spent for the benefit of the Jews of Palestine. (This large sum was sent to Moses Montefiore, whom Touro had never met! It made possible the building of the first dwellings in what was to become the new city of Jerusalem.) In addition, Judah Touro and his brother gave the money for a fund to preserve the beautiful synagogue of Newport, which is today the oldest synagogue building in America and a national shrine.

Rabbis in America

The number of Jewish congregations in America increased tenfold during Judah Touro's lifetime—from five in 1775 to about fifty in 1854. But these synagogues lacked leaders. The "rabbi" was often just one of the group who was given the title, even though he knew little Hebrew, little Judaism, and, for that matter, little English.

No remedy for this was in sight. The average salary for a "rabbi" was $250 a year, and though money was worth more in those days than it is now, this amount was still very small. Furthermore, there was no school in the United States where one could study to become a true rabbi. The state of Jewish learning is shown by the experience of a young immigrant who walked into one of the oldest Orthodox congregations in New York and asked for a copy of the Mishnah. The synagogue

Dedicated in December 1763, the Judah Touro Synagogue of Newport, R.I., is the oldest synagogue building in North America.

members only laughed at him. How could someone be so foolish as to think he could find a classic Hebrew book in the New World?

But this particular immigrant was already determined to change Jewish life in America. His name was Isaac Mayer Wise.

Isaac Mayer Wise

Wise came to the United States to live in a free land and to teach Geiger's principles of modern Judaism. He soon found that American Jewry was hardly yearning for his message of Reform. Wise took the job as rabbi of a synagogue in Albany, New York. But some members of his con-

Isaac Mayer Wise (1819–1900), pioneer in the U.S. Reform movement and founder of its leading religious organizations.

ite, as well as a German-Jewish newspaper to be read by the majority of American Jews who still spoke German. To spread his ideas about modern religious life, he wrote a new prayer book, articles of all kinds, and even plays.

One of his most popular ideas was a new way to observe the Sabbath. Traditionally, the Torah was read on Monday and Thursday mornings during the week, as well as the Sabbath morning. The Shabbat evening service was a short ceremony at sundown attended almost entirely by men. Wise created a major service with a sermon for Friday evenings after supper, a time when entire families could attend—even those whose schedules were controlled by the business week of the Gentile world. This late Friday service is still popular throughout America.

His great goal, however, was to create

gregation were upset at the changes which Wise introduced. In fact, the president of the synagogue stood up in the midst of a Rosh Hashanah service and slapped the rabbi in the face! A fight broke out which had to be stopped by the police.

While still in Albany, Wise was able to organize those who approved of his work into a new Reform congregation. But it was in Cincinnati, Ohio, that he found his true spiritual home. Cincinnati in the 1850's had the second-largest Jewish population of any city in America (after New York), and there Wise was able to develop a wide range of important projects. He started a Jewish newspaper, *The Israel-*

AMERICAN JEWISH RELIGIOUS ORGANIZATIONS
(with date each was founded)

	REFORM
CONGREGA-TIONS	Union of American Hebrew Congregations (1873)
RABBINICAL BODIES	Central Conference of American Rabbis (1889)
MAJOR RABBINICAL SCHOOLS	Hebrew Union College–Jewish Institute of Religion (1875)

organizations which would unify Jewish life in the United States. He asked all synagogues to take part in conferences, and in 1873 succeeded in creating the Union of American Hebrew Congregations. Two years later he opened the first successful rabbinical school in the Western Hemisphere, the Hebrew Union College (HUC). This school first met in the basement of his Cincinnati Temple and had a library of just fourteen books; today, after merging with the younger Jewish Institute of Religion, it has branches not only in Cincinnati but also in New York, Los Angeles, and Jerusalem. Finally, in 1889, Wise organized the HUC graduates and other Jewish leaders into the Central Conference of American Rabbis.

The word "Reform" does not appear in the names of these groups. Wise hoped that *all* American Jews would unite. He was a moderate in the Reform movement, and thought that soon every Jew (and, indeed, every Christian!) would come to see modernized Judaism as the only true religion. But the Orthodox refused to have anything to do with his groups. The institutions he created came to serve only Reform Judaism. Nevertheless, they worked so well that when the Orthodox and Conservative movements later developed formal organizations, they patterned their groups after those which Wise had founded.

Immigrants from Germany

Jewish groups grew and succeeded because the American Jewish population grew and succeeded. During the first decades of the nineteenth century, the

NSERVATIVE	ORTHODOX	RECONSTRUCTIONIST
ited Synagogue of erica (1913)	Union of Orthodox Jewish Congregations of America (1898)	Reconstructionist Federation of Congregations and Fellowships (1954), under the Jewish Reconstructionist Foundation (1940)
bbinical Assembly 00)	Rabbinical Council of America (1923)	Reconstructionist Rabbinical Association (1975)
vish Theological ninary (1886)	Rabbi Isaac Elchanan Theological Seminary of Yeshiva University (1896)	Reconstructionist Rabbinical College (1968)

Temple Emanu-El, in New York City, was built in 1868 by the American Jewish architect Leopold Eidlitz.

number of Jews in America was small. If there were 2500 Jews in the Colonies in 1776, there were only 15,000 by 1840. But by 1880, the Jewish population soared to 250,000. The rapid growth came from a wave of immigration from Germany, which reached its peak from 1840 to 1860.

This wave of immigrants included Germans of many faiths who crossed the ocean in search of freedom. Particularly after 1848, it was clear to all Germans that the best place to find political liberty was in the New World. The Jews who lived in the south German province of Bavaria, however, had a special reason to look for new homes. The Bavarian king not only placed heavy taxes on Jews, but also set strict limits on the number of Jewish marriages which could take place in any year. Most of the young people who wanted to marry were forced to leave the country.

Of these, the majority chose to go to the United States.

From packs to riches

The German Jewish immigrants arrived in America with little education—and less money. Many a Jew found the best way to survive was as a peddler. With a small investment, he could fill a pack with one or two hundred pounds of goods. Then, hoisting his wares on his back, he would trudge on foot between the scattered towns of the Midwest and South, selling to those who lived far from a general store.

The German Jews had arrived at an ideal time, when America was first realizing its size and wealth. Those who left Europe in 1848, for example, arrived just before the California Gold Rush of 1849.

Some of the hardworking German
Jewish immigrants achieved remarkable
business success. At right, Julius Rosenwald, who helped build Sears, Roebuck
into the world's largest retail company;
below left, Levi Strauss as he looked
when he came to California during the
Gold Rush. Below right is an 1880's
ad for Levi's "spring bottom" pants—
notice the price, $13.50 a dozen!

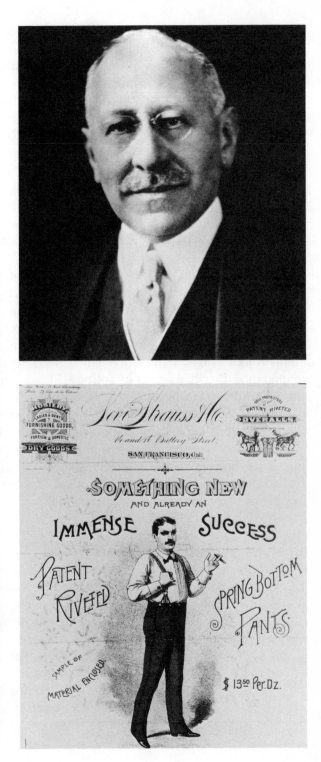

In this time of growth, the peddler was soon able to make enough money selling on foot to invest in a cart and horse. Through hard work and careful saving, he might even earn enough to open a small shop. These shops often grew until, in many American towns, they became local department stores.

A few of the peddlers (or more often their children) were able to rise to astounding levels of success. Adam Gimbel, who began as a peddler in the Mississippi Valley, ended his career by founding the huge chain of Gimbel's stores. Nathan Straus, the son of an immigrant, built Macy's into the largest department store in America. The profits from Meyer Guggenheim's knapsack, invested in mining, made him one of the richest men in the country. Julius Rosenwald left the store which his immigrant father had set up in Springfield, Illinois, and rose to become the president of Sears, Roebuck, and Company—now the largest retailing firm in the world.

Many of these fortunes were built by improving service to the public. Gimbel, for example, pioneered the service of giving refunds to unhappy customers. (Before, any sale was thought of as final.) Furthermore, many of the Jewish millionaires worked actively for charities. Nathan Straus saved thousands of children from disease and death by working for the pasteurization of milk in America. Julius Rosenwald contributed to charity the staggering sum of $70 million, much of it for Negro education.

This did not all happen by 1880, but by that year German-American Jewry was well established. Immigration had slowed down, and those who arrived two or three decades earlier had worked themselves out of poverty into the middle (and, in a few cases, the upper) class. The German Jewish community was well organized, and religious Reform, which seemed so radical in the 1840's, was now accepted as the country's leading form of Judaism. American Jews, like their brothers and sisters in Western Europe, looked forward to a brighter future.

They were not disappointed in their hopes of a good life in the United States. But they would soon face a new and unexpectedly serious challenge.

SUMMARY *During the early years of the United States the Jewish community was quite small, but people like Rebecca Gratz and Judah Touro made important contributions to both American and Jewish life. The organization of American Judaism was pioneered by Isaac Mayer Wise. A major change in the size of the American Jewish population took place between 1840 and 1860, when a wave of German immigrants arrived. The newcomers were mostly poor, but within a generation many had become prosperous (and sometimes wealthy) businessmen. By 1880 the Jewish future in America, as in Europe, looked endlessly bright.*

PART THREE

Eastern Europe Before 1880

A Century Under the Czars

All of us today are in some way the heirs of Eastern European Jewry. First and most obviously, many of us in fact have Jewish parents, grandparents, or great grandparents who fled Eastern Europe at the turn of the century. These Jews took with them their language, their culture, their religious heritage, and their unquenchable hopes for a better life.

Second, the Yiddish culture that developed in Eastern Europe during the eighteenth and nineteenth centuries became so powerful and pervasive that today, for many people, it seems the very essence of Jewishness. Out of this great reservoir flowed many of the movements, trends, and habits of mind (along with certain foods and a distinctive kind of humor) that the world has come to identify as uniquely Jewish, and that all our people share to some extent.

Feasting and dancing, laughter and joy . . . ever since
Talmudic times, the Jewish wedding has been a great
community celebration. Of course, the marriage ceremony
itself was a serious matter, as you can see from this scene
painted in 1861 by the German artist **M. D. Oppenheim**.
But waiting in the background, at the top of the stairs,
was the badḥan, or wedding jester. When the solemn
ceremony was over, he would make music, crack jokes,
poke fun at some of the important guests, and
sing songs in praise of the bride.

Third, Zionism — the national movement of the Jewish people — is
unthinkable apart from the contributions of Eastern European Jewry.
Nearly all the pioneers of the 1880's came to Eretz Yisrael from
Russia and Rumania. When some Western Jewish leaders wavered, it
was the Russian Jews who insisted that a homeland in Zion (and not
Uganda, or some other land) was the only true goal for a Zionist
movement. Messianic passion, a pure religious longing for
redemption, and deep Jewish national feeling were currents that ran
strongly throughout Eastern Europe. These qualities sustained the
Zionist movement, and they continue to inspire many Israelis today.

ABBA EBAN

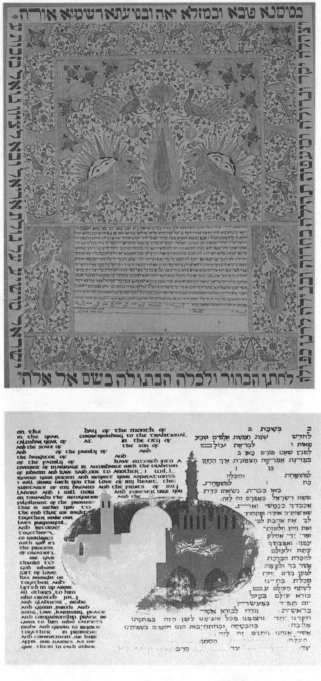

Right, a nineteenth century Persian marriage contract; bottom right, a modern ketubah in Hebrew and English; bottom left, the traditional Moroccan bridal costume, from an exhibit at the Israel Museum in Jerusalem.

Right: a new treatment of the traditional wedding headdress, offered by an American jeweler, features antique ivory, bone, and sterling silver. Below: an elegant ketubah drawn up in the Iranian city of Meshed in 1901.

Two rural couples: a
kibbutz wedding
(above), and a painting
of Ruth and Boaz in
the fields (right)
by the Israeli artist
Shalom of Safed.

84

9

INTRODUCTION TO PART THREE:

Eastern Europe Before 1880

This book is about modern Jewish history. Up to now we have concentrated on the places where the modern era began—Western and Central Europe and America. But these lands held only a small minority of world Jewry throughout the nineteenth century. For the entire modern period (until the time of Hitler), and for at least 100 years before, 50 percent or more of the total Jewish population lived in the countries of Eastern Europe.

Early settlements

Jewish history in Eastern Europe goes back very far. In fact, Jews were living in what is now Russia many centuries before there was such a thing as the "Russian" people. Our ancestors settled near the north shore of the Black Sea about the first century B.C.E., when the Temple was still standing in Jerusalem. They brought with them nearly 2000 years of history, and the Law of Moses. The native peoples, on the other hand, were primitive idol-worshippers living in small, independent tribes. They all spoke Slavic languages (that is, languages related to modern Polish and Russian), but had little else in common.

During the early seventh century C.E., a Turkish group known as the Khazars built a huge empire on the plain that lies between the Caspian and the Black Seas. They became friendly with the Jewish communities there, and our people taught the newcomers how to read and write. The Khazars were so impressed by Jewish culture that their king and 4000 of his nobles converted to Judaism. Their land was the largest Jewish state of all time.

From "Russes" to Russians

Things began to change about the year 850. A group of Scandinavian adventurers known as "Russes"—close relatives of the

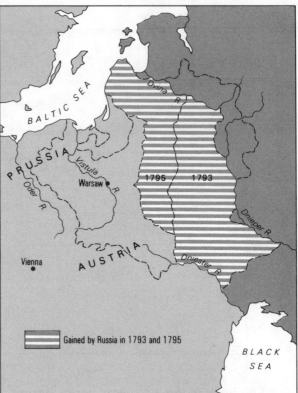

RUSSIA'S WESTWARD MARCH

It took less than fifty years for Russia to swallow up all of Poland—and with it, the world's largest Jewish community. The first Partition of Poland, in 1772, resulted from a treaty designed to stave off war between Russia, Austria, Prussia, and Ottoman Turkey. This treaty left standing a government called the Polish Commonwealth, but political rivalries and two large-scale revolts by Polish patriots during the 1790's led to the complete eradication of the Polish state. By 1795, Russia controlled the regions known as Lithuania, White Russia, and the Western Ukraine, along with such cities as Vilna (see Chapter 3) and Berdichev (see Chapter 10). The defeat of Napoleon in 1815 pushed Russia's frontier still further westward to include Warsaw and Lublin, but not Galicia.

Boundary of Poland before 1772

Russia in 1772

Gained by Russia in 1772

Gained by Russia in 1793 and 1795

— — — Western boundary of Russia in 1815, after the defeat of Napoleon

○ Towns with large Jewish populations

0   300 miles

0   300 kilometers

Harold Faye

Vikings who were invading and looting the West during the same period—attacked Eastern Europe. They were accepted as leaders by the native Slavic peoples, and around them the first "Russian" state was born. It grew stronger and stronger until, during the 960's, it was strong enough to invade the land of the Khazars and break the power of the Jewish kingdom.

The Russian city of Kiev then became the center of Eastern European life—the hub of a state so huge that, except for the Holy Roman Empire, it was the largest nation in Europe. Kiev itself grew to a population of 80,000, equal to that of Paris, the largest city in the West.*

The Russian Slavs gave up idol worship and became members of the Eastern Orthodox Church. (This is a branch of Christianity somewhat like Roman Catholicism, except that Orthodox Christians do not accept the Roman Pope.) Happily, they were willing to take in Jewish settlers.

* Even so, all Christian cities were small and primitive compared to those of Muslim Spain, which at this period was in its Golden Age. Cordova, for example, was home to half a million people. For more on this, and on the Khazars, see Volume One, Chapter 12.

Litvaks and Galitzianers

In Yiddish, a Lithuanian Jew was called a "Litvak," and a Galician Jew was known as a "Galitzianer." After the Partitions of Poland, the Galitzianers were governed by Austria, while the Litvaks were ruled by Russia.

In time, folk traditions grew up around the two groups. Litvaks thought of Galitzianers as bookish but naïve; Galitzianers thought of Litvaks as clever but shallow.

One thing the Litvaks, Galitzianers, and other Eastern European Jews could agree on was their dislike for what was happening in France and Germany. They viewed Berlin as a city of a lost souls—in fact, the Yiddish word "Berliner" was used to mean a person who had completely abandoned Judaism!

A shtetl in Galicia.

The triumph of Genghis Khan and his Mongol warriors in the 1220's put an end to democracy and toleration in Russia.

Although these Jews were sometimes mistreated, in general the Jewish community of Kiev became secure and prosperous. International trade was beginning to revive and expand after the Dark Ages in Western Europe, and Jews were deeply involved in setting up trading centers in Germany and Russia. The importance of our people in trade can be seen in coins of the period, which were minted by Jewish coinsmiths and use Hebrew letters.

The Mongol empire

The good times came to a sudden end in the thirteenth century. Out of north-

eastern Asia burst Mongol warriors, led by the fierce general Genghis Khan. They conquered China, swept across Central Asia and Persia, destroyed the remnants of the Khazar kingdom, and overran Russia. When their advance finally stopped, the Mongols were rulers of a giant empire which reached from Poland to the Pacific, and which they were able to control for more than two centuries.

Under the stern eye of the Khans (as the Mongol kings were called), the Asian mainland was fairly peaceful. One could travel safely across the entire continent; so, for the first time, Western Europeans visited China. The most famous of the men to make this trip was an Italian named

Marco Polo, who for many years served the great Mongol emperor of China, Kublai Khan.

Russia reborn

Though Mongol rule may have helped a few adventurous travelers, it was a disaster for Russian society. The Mongols did away with what freedom and democracy there had been in Kiev. When Russia was reborn the new Russian kings imitated the Mongols in their ferocious cruelty.

The first of these new dictators was Ivan III ("Ivan the Great"). When he came to the throne of Moscow in 1462, the land he ruled was small; but the Mongol power was gradually fading. The young monarch soon began to conquer new lands for himself. By the end of his forty-three-year reign, he had created a modest-sized empire, somewhat larger than the modern state of Greece.

His grandson, Ivan IV, continued this war of conquest, more than doubling the size of the empire he inherited. However, he is best remembered not for his battles

Peter I ("Peter the Great," 1672–1725) was one of the few czars who showed kindness to the Jews. He heard Jewish requests while sitting in his favorite tavern.

but for his insane cruelty. This is the man who is known to history as "Ivan the Terrible." Even before his time, Russian rulers were driving the Jews out of their lands, but Ivan the Terrible added new vigor to the anti-Jewish policies. He spoke of our people as "importers of poisonous medicines and misleaders from the Christian faith," and once he had 300 Jews drowned for refusing to convert to Christianity.

In Poland and Lithuania

West of Russia, Jewish life was far better—at least for a time. Poland asked for Germans to help rebuild the country after the Mongol invasions, and German Jews were among the many who came. Over the centuries the Polish Jewish community grew stronger and richer—until 1648. In that year and for ten years more, bands of raiding Cossacks invaded Poland from Russia and began a series of massacres in which at least 100,000 Jews were murdered.

Despite this disaster, Polish Jewry held to its traditions of study and prayer. Lithuania, a neighboring country which also had a large Jewish population and which had merged with Poland during the Middle Ages, became an outstanding center of traditional Jewish scholarship.*

Then came the Partitions of Poland (see Chapter 3), and Polish-Lithuanian Jewry found itself split into three sections. About 150,000 Jews came under the control of Prussia (though most were expelled to Russian-held territory). Another 250,000, those who lived in an area called Galicia, became subjects of Austria. But by far the greatest number, more than 500,000 Jews, were swallowed up by the empire of Russia.

We will see in the next chapters what happened when one of the world's most anti-Jewish governments came to rule the world's largest Jewish community.

* The history of the Jews in Poland and Lithuania is discussed in detail in Volume One, Chapters 21 and 22.

SUMMARY *The Jews have a long history in what is now Russia. The modern part of that history begins with the decline of the Mongol empire, when the rulers of Moscow started to acquire the lands which make up today's Russian state. These tyrants excluded Jews from their territory until, through the Partitions of Poland, Russia suddenly found itself with a Jewish population of more than 500,000.*

10

In Shtetl and Ghetto

The pattern of Jewish life in Eastern Europe was set long before Poland was divided in the late 1700's, and in many ways that pattern remained unchanged well into the 1930's. But today that Jewish world is only a memory.

It is only a memory because it was totally destroyed. A Jewish civilization over 600 years old was swept away in only six years.

It is only a memory because in most cases only memories have survived. Homes, synagogues, community records, and millions of Jewish people—all are gone.

For that reason, much of what we know comes from the words of those who escaped before it was too late. And, not surprisingly, different people have very different feelings about what life was really like.

Life in the "old country": pro and con

Everyone agrees that Jewish life in Eastern Europe was hard, and often dangerous. But many believe this difficulty helped create a wonderful Jewish spirit. When scholars interviewed a large number of immigrants from Eastern Europe, for example, they found a great love for the beauty of Sabbath observance in the "old country." Here is what they were told:

> Father in a silken caftan and velvet skullcap, mother in black silk and pearls; the glow of candles, the waves of peace and joy, the glad sense that it is good to be a Jew, the distant pity for those who have been denied this foretaste of heaven.

This is the warm feeling we get in the stories of the greatest of the European Jewish writers, Sholem Aleichem. His tales

Sholem Aleichem gave a glowing picture of shtetl life. For a story by this Yiddish author, see pages 130–131.

were turned into a musical called *Fiddler on the Roof*, which during the 1960's became the longest-running show in the history of Broadway theater.

But there is another, more bitter story to tell. Golda Meir, the fourth prime minister of Israel, said of her early childhood in Russia:

> I have very few happy or even pleasant memories of this time. . . . [The popular idea of a community] on whose roofs fiddlers eternally play sentimental music has almost nothing to do with anything I remember, with the poverty-stricken, wretched little communities in which Jews eked out a living, comforting themselves with the hope that things would somehow be better one day and with their belief that there was a point to their misery.

Can both of these memories be correct? Yes—for each person sees and reacts in a different way. Here we can only look at "facts" about Jewish life in Russia, but we must remember that these "facts" meant different things to the people who lived them.

The shtetl—a world apart

Most of the Jews of Eastern Europe lived in small villages. The word for village in Yiddish is SHTETL, שטעטל (*plural:* SHTETLACH, שטעטלעך), but shtetl came to mean especially "the Jewish community *within* a village." Jews and Christians lived side by side in these little towns, but the two worlds were very far apart.

They were separated by prejudice. Christians tolerated the Jews, but did not really accept them, and at any moment might attack the shtetl.

They were separated by Jewish law. Jews kept a weekly day of complete rest on the Sabbath—the Gentiles did not. Jews ate only kosher food—the Gentiles raised and ate pigs. The Jews studied the Torah and Talmud—most Gentile peasants could not even read.

And they were separated by language. Jews spoke Yiddish, and knew little of the Polish or Russian spoken by their Gentile neighbors. Yiddish grew out of the medieval German which the Jews spoke when they first arrived in Eastern Europe. Mixed with the German is Hebrew, as well as words and forms picked up in Poland and Russia.* Yiddish is written with Hebrew characters, which means that the Jews did not even use the same alphabet as their Christian neighbors.

* SHTETL, for example, comes from the German word *Stadt* (city). The L at the end is an Eastern European way of saying "little."

Family life

Life in the shtetl was terribly hard, and nearly every Jew was poor. Even when each member of a family worked at a trade—or at more than one trade—there was still barely enough money to make ends meet. Many Jews were small-scale merchants or innkeepers; others worked at skills such as tailoring or shoe repair. But a large number were merely unskilled laborers, who often had no regular work at all.

Houses were shabby, with bare earth for

Abba Eban Remembers:
Golda Meir

Golda Meir (1898–1978).

Golda Meir's chief attribute was her ability to dominate any gathering in which she found herself. It was, of course, perfectly possible for ministers in her cabinet to oppose her or to vote against her, and we often did this. But in general, she was so emphatic in her convictions that most of her colleagues hesitated before coming into conflict with her.

When she spoke she used to simplify problems and avoid their complexities. This was not always a virtue, since some problems really are complex, so that if you simplify them you are not really describing them accurately. But what gave her strength was her sense of total rectitude. She was convinced that the Israeli position was 100 percent correct on every point, and that only wickedness or folly prevented others from seeing things that way. Her favorite posture was to be in lonely defiance of a hostile world, rather as a grandmother likes to protect grandchildren against being bullied by neighborhood toughs.

She was sometimes excitable at the wrong moments, but was always very calm in times of crisis. I shall never forget coming back one night from difficult talks in Washington to see Golda in her small house in Jerusalem. Instead of discussing matters of state, she insisted on going into the kitchen and making coffee and cookies for me and for her. I shall always remember the sense of security that she created in a situation that was really hair-raising in its explosive possibilities.

Another of her qualities that not all Israeli leaders share was an ability to see the Jewish destiny in its total universal framework. The Jewish people for her consisted of Israel *and* the Jewish Diaspora, and the willingness on her part to take Diaspora Jews into her confidence was rewarded by them with an attitude of the utmost affection and respect.

Even for the poorest families, Shabbat in the shtetl was a special occasion.

the floor. After a hard day's work, the dinner was usually just potatoes and herring. Some Jews were so poor that they would live all week on bread and potatoes, in the hope of saving enough to buy "something special" for the Sabbath. Simple and scanty though the food was, there was likely to be someone eating at any time of the day. There were no set mealtimes, except on the Sabbath, and neighbors felt free to drop in at any time for a chat and a cup of tea. All this made the Jewish community like one large bustling household.

Families were large. Children were thought of as a great blessing, and were pampered as babies. But from an early age children began doing household duties, and working at the most important activity in the life of a Jew—study.

Education

Boys began to go to school by the time they were five, and sometimes as early as three. Their elementary school was called a HEDER (חֶדֶר)—which means "room"—because the classes were almost always held in a room of the teacher's house. Classes were held from 8 A.M. to 6 P.M., five days a week, plus half a day on Friday. The ḥeder was crowded. Fifteen or twenty children would study together in the same room, each chanting a different lesson. Young and old, they studied together.

The absolute master of the ḥeder was the elementary school teacher, the MELAMED (מְלַמֵּד). He might be a person of limited intelligence—but no one expected him to be clever, or to make lessons interesting. His only job was to watch over the children as they learned the letters of the Hebrew alphabet, and to give a beating to those who did not do their work. In time, the students did learn enough to graduate to the study of Torah with the commentaries of Rashi. (For the life and work of Rashi, see Volume One, Chapter 13.) By the time he was eleven or twelve, each boy would again be promoted, this time to the most valued part of a Jewish education: the study of Talmud.

Girls had far shorter school days than boys, and fewer years, too. Not many girls could understand the Hebrew they learned to read mechanically. Most learned only enough Hebrew to write a simple letter. They were deeply involved in another kind of Jewish study, however. Each girl had to work with her mother, learning to maintain a home so that every detail of family living would be totally kosher.*

This kind of schooling would not make us happy today, but it worked rather well. It produced generation after generation of men and women who were familiar with Jewish law, and totally devoted to it. Indeed, one of the reasons Jewish education worked so well was that the students knew their parents had deep respect for Jewish learning, and observed Jewish laws. No one felt that religious education was "just for children."

A boy's formal education might end at Bar Mitzvah, for lack of money. A family would scrimp on everything to raise tuition to send their son to ḥeder, but many could not afford more. Still, an excellent

---

* This system of schooling gave women one curious advantage. While boys were limited to the study of classic Hebrew texts, girls had time to read Yiddish books. Similarly, when secular schools were opened to Jews, girls were more likely to attend than boys because a woman was not expected to have a "serious" (that is, Jewish) education. So women often gained more general knowledge than did many of the scholarly males.

male student had almost limitless chances to pursue his studies. After Bar Mitzvah, the young scholar would leave home to study with a respected teacher. If his parents could not pay for his food and lodging, he was supported by the town in which he stayed. A community would take pride in the number of students its rabbi could attract, even though this meant that the citizens had to feed, clothe, and house the poor scholars. The young men seldom remained poor, however. A fine scholar was almost certain to marry into a well-to-do family, and his father-in-law would often agree to support the newlyweds for a year or two after that, so the boy could learn still more.

Marriage and love

The brightest boys usually were paired with the most desirable girls when a marriage was arranged—and "arranged" it was! Parents decided when a teenager was old enough to marry, and selected the "right" marriage partner. Young people usually had no choice of whom they would wed, and sometimes did not even meet their bride or groom until the day of the wedding. The law was that no one was forced into a marriage—a girl did have the right to reject a man she did not want. But the truth was that children usually did what they were told.

The parents worked very hard to give their children a "good match." Social position was carefully considered. It was far better to marry into a family of learned rabbis than into a family of laborers. The bride's family was expected to provide a dowry—cash and wedding gifts for the couple, and often for the family of the bridegroom. (Brides from wealthy families were much in demand, for the richer the family, the larger the dowry.) And, as we have seen, a scholarly bridegroom was valued highly.

Love did not usually enter into the arrangement of a marriage, but this did not mean that marriages were loveless. Love was thought to *follow* marriage, growing as a man and woman shared the joys and sorrows of life together. Perhaps the idea is worth thinking about, for while divorce is fairly easy to obtain under Jewish law,

---

A Shtetl Marriage Contract

Arranging a marriage was not a simple matter. In his lively autobiography (published in 1793), the philosopher Solomon Maimon described one of his father's many unsuccessful attempts to find him a bride.

A ketubah
from Germany.

Mr. L. of Schmilowitz, a learned and rich man who had an only daughter, was so enchanted with my fame as a scholar that he chose me for his son-in-law without having seen me.

My father made the journey to Schmilowitz, saw his future daughter-in-law, and had the marriage contract drawn up. Two hundred gulden were paid to him on the spot. He was not satisfied with this, however, and insisted that he would not agree to the marriage unless he received 400 gulden in all. Therefore, the bride's family had to pay him 200 gulden more, and to hand over to him the so-called "little presents" for me, namely a black velvet cap trimmed with gold lace, a Bible bound in green velvet with silver clasps, and so on. With these things he came home full of joy, gave me the presents, and told me that I was to prepare to give a lecture on my wedding day, which would be in two months' time.

Already my mother had begun to bake the cakes she was expected to take with her to the wedding, and to prepare all sorts of preserves. I began to think about the lecture I was to give, when suddenly the sad news arrived that my bride-to-be had died of smallpox. My father could easily accept this loss, because he thought that he had made 400 gulden by his son in an honorable way, and could marry me off again to make 400 gulden more. I, too, who had never seen my bride, could not really mourn her loss.

My mother alone was heartbroken. Cakes and preserves will not keep long. All my mother's work was made fruitless by this fatal accident; and to this must be added that she could find no place to protect the delicious cakes from my secret attacks!

it was rare among East European Jews. In our modern world, where we pride ourselves on the freedom each person has to "marry for love," divorce is much more common.

Unity and division

Not all brides came from wealthy families; most families were poor, but the shtetl was well prepared to aid those in need. There were societies to raise money for dowries for poor brides, to visit the sick, to bring food and help to the needy, to care for orphans, and to bury the dead. Every person belonged to at least one society; and the societies took the place of taxes to keep the community going.

It seems there was a great unity in Jewish life. This is largely true. Yet differences in wealth, learning, and social position often divided the Jews, and there was tension and even hatred between different groups. Moreover, the Talmud itself could be a source of division: though not every Jew was a scholar, everyone understood the Talmudic idea that every opinion must be considered. Thus, each Jew felt that his or her own ideas were of value, and should be heard before a decision was reached. This was a kind of democracy, but one which sometimes kept the shtetl from operating effectively or as one unit.

Even love for Judaism sometimes gave rise to bitter divisions. In Chapter 1 we saw that there was a major split between the traditionalists (the Mitnagdim) and the followers of the Baal Shem Tov (the Ḥasidim). Within these movements, there were even further divisions and subdivisions.

Some Mitnagdim believed that knowledge of mathematics, science, and foreign languages could help a person better understand Judaism. Other traditionalists felt that only the study of the ancient Hebrew sources was worthwhile. They loved a form of study called PILPUL (פִּלְפּוּל): finding difficulties in the Talmud and then finding clever ways to solve them. Pilpul offered mental exercise, but little real knowledge.

Israel Salanter and Musar

Then there were those who felt that too little attention was being given to the ethical ideals of Judaism—the basic principles of right and wrong. A Lithuanian rabbi named Israel Salanter organized groups for studying the traditional writings on ethics—writings known as MUSAR (מוּסָר). The Musar groups met to discuss moral questions, and to help improve the conduct of their daily lives.

Salanter himself was a man of great saintliness and courage. Once in 1848, cholera spread through the city of Vilna at the time of the High Holy Days. The rabbi was told that Jews who fasted would be more likely to catch the dread disease, so he ordered his congregation to eat on Yom Kippur. Knowing that it was the holiest day of the Jewish year, and that the Jews would feel bad about not fasting, he himself set the example. It is said that on this Yom Kippur, Israel Salanter stood before the entire congregation and ate! This was entirely in keeping with Talmudic law, which says that a commandment may be broken when life is in danger; but few rabbis would have dared to act out this idea so boldly.

Ḥasidic sects and traditions

Although the Ḥasidim were united against the traditionalists, they too were

**"I, Levi Yitzḥok, son of Sarah of Berdichev,
Have come for a judgment against You . . ."**

divided into differing, and sometimes warring, sects. Among the Ḥasidic leaders—called ZADDIKIM (צַדִּיקִים) or REBBES (רביים)—were those who claimed the power to perform miracles, and the ability to serve as a direct link between God and man. The Ḥasidim treated their rebbes almost as gods, actually fighting for crumbs that might drop from their leaders' table. Some of these rebbes were little more than crooks, setting up splendid "courts" where they became wealthy at the expense of their followers.

Yet some Zaddikim were truly great men. One of the greatest was Levi Yitzḥok of Berdichev, a rabbi whose kindness became legendary. It is said that one Yom Kippur he failed to arrive for services. Why? He had heard a baby crying. Its mother had left for the synagogue, so the

rabbi stayed in the house to comfort the unhappy child.

Yet Levi Yitzḥok was also a man of strength and courage—a man who was even prepared to challenge the power of heaven. When he could no longer bear the suffering of the Jewish people, he stood before the Holy Ark and cried to God:

*I, Levi Yitzḥok, son of Sarah of
    Berdichev,
Have come for a judgment against You,
On behalf of Your people Israel.
What do You want of Your people
    Israel?
Why do you afflict Your people
    Israel? . . .
There must be an end of this,
The exile must end!*

A very different way of life was taught by the branch of Ḥasidism known as ḤABAD (חב״ד).* This name is formed from the initials of three Hebrew words: חָכְמָה (wisdom), בִּינָה (understanding), and דַּעַת (knowledge). As these words suggest, life in Ḥabad is based on reason, learning, and study. In modern times, the movement has also been trying in imaginative ways to reach out to non-observant Jews and persuade them to return to traditional practices.

Legacies of the shtetl

Thus, the world of Eastern European Jewry was complex, filled with variety, passion, and searching. Yet it was also surprisingly simple. Almost all Jews agreed that Jewish law was the only basis for a good life, and that God—in His own time

* The founder of Ḥabad was Shneur Zalman, whom we met earlier. The movement is also called LUBAVITCHER ḤASIDISM because Shneur Zalman's son and successor settled in a Lithuanian town named Lubavitch.

—would bring the Jewish people back to Eretz Yisrael.

These beliefs are shared by all Orthodox Jews. But in Western Europe they were developed creatively. Western Jews tried to combine Jewish knowledge with a modern life. But a majority of Eastern European Jews guarded their traditions largely by ignoring everything else. They used Judaism to build a wall, a ghetto of the mind designed to keep out whatever the Gentiles might bring against them.

In this they were very successful. The traditional civilization of Eastern European Jewry survived everything except the guns and gas chambers of World War II, and even these did not prevent the establishment of groups in Israel and the United States which today preserve the attitudes and ideals of the shtetl.

Eastern Europe also survives in another way. Many Jews continue to remember with love a world where the highest respect was paid to Jewish knowledge, and where nothing was more important than living a fully Jewish life.

SUMMARY *Most Jews of Eastern Europe lived in shtetl communities, usually small, and always poor. The Jews devoted themselves to education, and successfully raised many generations who were rich in Jewish learning. Society was unified in the shtetl, but it also had many divisions. The major religious split was between the Mitnagdim and the Ḥasidim, each with its own sects and branches. All but a small minority, however, agreed that Jewish law was sacred, and that God alone would save Jews from their suffering.*

11

In the Grip of the Czars

We think of the world as a place of change: the horse and buggy give way to the automobile, fashions come and go, singers and artists are famous one day and forgotten the next. Changes of this kind have come to Russia, of course. Yet the surprising thing about Russian history is that two basic things have remained the same, whether the country has been ruled by czars or by Communist dictators.

First is the desire of the Russians to expand their territories—to conquer and rule as much land as possible.

Second is their determination to eliminate Judaism from the lands under Russian control.

The Pale of Settlement

For years, these policies did not come into conflict. Ivan the Terrible and other early Russian rulers simply expelled native Jews and tried to prevent other Jews from entering the country. In time, however, Russia swallowed up the part of Poland where most of world Jewry lived. Empress Catherine II of Russia ("Catherine the Great"), the woman who directed the Partitions of Poland, had promised religious liberty to all who came under her rule, so new ways of dealing with the Jews had to be found. Catherine began by treating our people fairly.

This worried a number of Christians. Many Polish Jews were poor merchants who were willing to offer their goods at low prices. Soon the Russian merchants were complaining to the Empress about Jewish competition. What would happen if the Polish Jews were to move everywhere in the Russian lands, forcing prices down throughout the empire?

One possible answer was that lower prices would help the poor Russian peasants—but this was not something that interested Catherine. Instead, she decided to protect the Russian merchants by forbidding Jews from settling in any lands which had historically been part of Russia.

Jewish citizens were forced to stay in the districts where they had been living at the time of the Partitions—an area which became known as the PALE OF SETTLE-MENT (in Hebrew, תְּחוּם־מוֹשָׁב). In short, Jews were to be ruled *by* Russia, but were not really to be part *of* it.

This became the cornerstone of the Russian government's policy toward Jews, a policy which has continued in spite of the Communist revolution and two world wars. Rights usually given to all other Russian citizens were denied to Jews, or were handed out as special privileges to only a few. Even today, our people are given "Jewish" (not Russian) passports, and face special difficulties and persecution.

Of course, staying in the Pale of Settlement—the area where they had lived for years—might not have been a hardship for the Jews if only the Russian government had left them in peace. But the czars had no intention of doing so.

Czar Alexander I

Under Czar Alexander I, taxes on Jews were raised to double those of the Gentile population. Then the czar's government set out to change and destroy the shtetlach. Some Jews were sent to farm colonies—supposedly to help them learn new skills, actually to break their contacts with traditional Judaism. Many more Jews were driven from their homes and forced to look for jobs in large towns and cities.

But there were no jobs to be had. The cities had no use for the sudden flood of homeless wanderers. On the other hand, the Jews *were* needed in the villages where they and their families had lived for centuries. They had served their townsmen,

both Jewish and Gentile, in important jobs—as merchants, innkeepers, tailors, cobblers, tinsmiths, and carpenters. One of the few government documents to speak honestly reported:

It is not true that the village Jew enriches himself at the expense of the peasant. On the contrary, he is generally poor and ekes out a scant existence from the sale of liquor and by supplying the peasants with the goods they need.

In time, the attempt to resettle the Jews was given up—but by then, thousands had been driven from their homes and left penniless in towns and cities.

Despite all this, the Jews tried to be loyal to their Russian rulers. Actually, the Jews did not have much choice—they had nowhere else to go. And, in a strange way, the Russian government was protecting the traditional Jewish way of life by keeping out the new ideas of freedom and equality which were coming from the West. Most of the leaders of East European Jewry agreed that what was happening in France and Germany was not healthy for Jewish religious life.

Thus, many Jews were willing to give their support to the Russian government. The Russians showed no gratitude. Instead, the czar who came to the throne in 1825, Nicholas I, was the most vicious ruler our people had known in centuries.

Czar Nicholas I

Nicholas used every power of the state in an attempt to destroy the Jewish religion. During his thirty years on the throne, some 600 anti-Jewish laws were passed. Jewish self-government was abolished. All Jewish books were censored.

The Pale of Settlement was made smaller. Even traditional Jewish clothing was forbidden.

Most terrifying of all was the practice of drafting (or sometimes kidnapping) Jewish boys between the ages of eight and twelve. Torn from school and home, the young boys were sent into the Russian army for thirty years or more. These CANTONISTS, as they were called, were stationed far from home, where they became helpless victims of whatever brutal treatment their officers found amusing. Many children died from cruel treatment. Some converted to Christianity in order to avoid further suffering; others were forced to be baptized. It is truly amazing that some of these children remained Jewish and survived the endless years of torture, returning as middle-aged men to their homes and their people.

Czar Nicholas sometimes hid his cruelty behind a mask of kindness. Once, he opened government schools for Jews, claiming that he wanted to improve Jewish education. He even invited a gifted German rabbi, Max Lilienthal, to come to Russia and develop a modern Jewish school system. Lilienthal, who was only twenty-four at the time, thought this was a marvelous opportunity to serve his people, and readily accepted. He worked hard on the project for four years, until he realized he had been tricked; in truth, the czar wanted to use the new schools to guide young Jews toward Christianity. Lilienthal immediately abandoned the project, and fled in horror to the United States.*

* Lilienthal became one of the founders of the American Reform movement. He conducted the first confirmation in the United States, and was one of the first teachers at the Hebrew Union College.

Far from home, the Cantonists were tormented by Russian army officers and often forced to convert to Christianity.

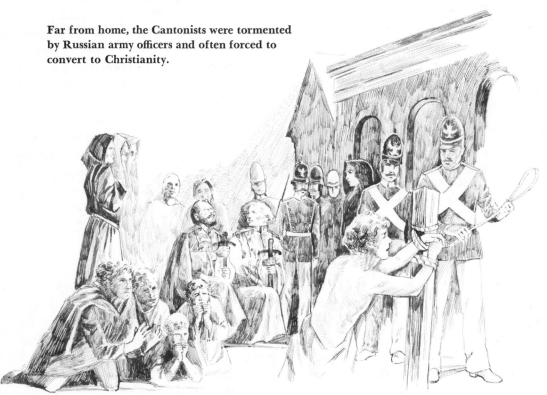

The Cantonists

The conditions under which Jewish children were taken across Russia to become soldiers was vividly described by a Russian author, Alexander Herzen. He was talking with an officer who was transporting a group of them, and who complained that half of them would die before reaching their destination:

"Epidemics?" I inquired, stirred to the very core.

"No, not exactly epidemics; but they just fall like flies. Well, you know, these Jewish boys are so puny and delicate. They can't stand mixing dirt for ten hours, with dry biscuits to live on. . . . Everywhere strange folks, no father, no mother, no caresses. Well, then, you just hear a cough and the youngster is dead. . . ."

The little ones were assembled and arrayed in military line. It was one of the most terrible spectacles I have ever witnessed. Poor, poor children! The boys of twelve or thirteen managed somehow to stand up, but the little ones of eight and ten . . . no brush, however black, could convey the terror of this scene on the canvas.

Pale, worn out, with scared looks, this is the way they stood in their uncomfortable, rough soldier uniforms, with their starched, turned-up collars, fixing an inexpressibly helpless and pitiful gaze upon the garrisoned soldiers, who were handling them rudely. White lips, blue lines under the eyes betokened either fever or cold. And these poor children, without care, without a caress, exposed to the wind which blows unhindered from the Arctic Ocean, were marching to their death.

Alexander II

In 1855, Nicholas I died. People hugged in the streets as they told each other the wonderful news. The Jews rejoiced at the death of the Haman of Eastern Europe.

The new czar, Alexander II, soon gave the Jews more reasons for rejoicing. He freed many political prisoners and made the military duties of Jews the same as those of Gentiles; best of all, he ended the drafting of Jewish children. During his reign, Jews with higher education were allowed to live outside the Pale, to hold government office, and to practice some professions that had earlier been closed to them.

Welcome as these changes were, they stopped far short of making the Jewish people citizens of Russia. Though the worst horrors of military life were ended, those Jews who did serve in the army were rarely promoted. Few Jews rose even to the rank of sergeant. Basically, Alexander was willing to give privileges to that tiny minority of Jews who were well-to-do, but he did little for the poor Jewish masses. Worse still, he tried to close Jewish schools.

In short, Alexander, like Nicholas, divided Jews into two groups: those who were useful to him, and those who were not. But while Nicholas punished those who were not to his liking, Alexander rewarded those whom he liked. Life under Nicholas had been so bad that Alexander's tactics seemed to many Jews to be a major opening in the wall of traditional Russian hatred against them. Men and women began to speak of a wonderful new era. Acceptance and equality, the goals that had given hope to the Jews of Western Europe since the French Revolution, appeared at last to be coming to Russia.

Beginnings of Haskalah

This hope had a powerful effect on the Jewish upper classes. Those who had moved out of the shtetlach and gained some success in the Gentile world saw limitless opportunities ahead of them. Especially hopeful were those who had been trying to bring to Russia the Western idea that Jews should take part in the general culture. These people were known as the MASKILIM, מַשְׂכִּילִים (*sing.*: MASKIL, מַשְׂכִּיל), and their movement was called HASKALAH, הַשְׂכָּלָה ("Enlightenment").

The maskilim thought of the shtetl world as old-fashioned, backward, and filled with superstition. A leading early maskil, Isaac Ber Levinsohn, suggested broad changes to modernize Russian Jewish life. Jews should learn languages other than Hebrew and Yiddish—above all, the language of the country in which they live. Modern schools, open to both sexes, should be set up. Bible study should continue, but our people should cut through the layers of commentary upon commentary, and return to the simple meaning of the text. All this, said Levinsohn, would help prepare Jews for the new jobs now open to them in fields such as farming and handicrafts.

To us, Levinsohn's program sounds like

The "Jews' walk" at Odessa, a Ukrainian port on the Black Sea. Between 1880 and 1920, Odessa and Warsaw were the two leading centers of urban Jewish life under czarist rule.

common sense, but in Eastern Europe in the middle of the nineteenth century it sounded like a call to revolution. Though there were a few who praised Levinsohn, the vast majority of Jews condemned him for his untraditional ideas. He spent his life as an outcast, and died in poverty. Only after his death was he widely praised by Jewish intellectuals, who called him "the Russian Mendelssohn."

Achievements of the maskilim

In the 1860's the maskilim began to publish books and newspapers. Whenever possible, they wrote either in Russian or Hebrew. The Russian works were written for Gentiles as well as Jews. In them, the maskilim argued for the political rights of Russian Jewry and defended the merits of Judaism as a religion. The Hebrew writings were meant for educated Jews, who were urged by the maskilim to modernize and take part in Russian life. Using Hebrew, the maskilim helped revive the ancient language as a medium of modern thought and literature. For the first time, Jewish spiritual ideas began appearing in such secular forms as plays and novels.

The maskilim tried not to write in Yiddish. Most of them sneered at the language of the common people because it was neither real German nor real Hebrew.* Nevertheless, the young writers did want to reach the large Yiddish-speaking majority of Russian Jewry. In time, this forced them to use the language they hated in order to speak with those who knew no

* The young intellectuals were often indifferent, or even hostile, to the needs of the Jewish poor. At times, the maskilim urged the Russian government to meddle in the lives of poor Jews—for example, by censoring Hasidic books.

Mendele Mocher Sforim, sometimes called the "grandfather of Yiddish literature."

other tongue. Soon there were magazines and newspapers in Yiddish.

This new Yiddish press had an unexpected effect. The new journals, which were meant to bring political ideas to the Jewish masses, also searched for top-quality Yiddish writers. One of the best was Shalom Jacob Abramovich, who used the pen name MENDELE MOCHER SFORIM ("Mendele the Bookseller"). He began to write about the ordinary Jews of Russia in their own language. Mendele's work became very popular. Even today, it is read wherever Yiddish is spoken. And his work was the beginning of modern Yiddish literature, which reached its Golden Age in the next generation.

The maskilim were always few in number, and their attitude toward most Russian Jews was sometimes intolerant and unkind. Nevertheless, they accomplished a great deal. Their ideas awakened even in many traditional Jews a desire to study modern culture and science. Unlike the German Enlightenment, which led to widespread conversions and the abandonment of Hebrew even by many who remained loyal to

Judaism, Haskalah led few Jews toward Christianity and breathed new life into two Jewish languages: Hebrew and Yiddish.

Weaknesses of Haskalah

But the Haskalah movement was trapped by the problems of Jewish life in the modern world. The conflict between traditional ways and the new ideals is shown most clearly in the life of the leading Jewish poet of the time, Judah Loeb Gordon. His poems spoke out against the privileged classes among the Jews, and showed concern for the poor—especially for Jewish women. He criticized the power that traditional Orthodoxy held over the life of Russian Jewry.

Yet when the time came for a new plan of action, his ideas were far less clear. Gordon told Jews to be modern, to adopt Russian dress and culture in public, while keeping their Jewishness private. "Be a Jew in your house and a man in the street," he urged.

What did this mean? Never before had it occurred to our people that being a Jew was something less than, or other than, being human. Indeed, to past generations of Jews, to be Jewish was to take part in the very noblest of human experiments, to live for all that was meant by the word "humanity." Now, for many of the maskilim, as for Jews throughout Western Europe, all that was gone. In its place stood little more than a desire to be accepted—to be a Russian, a German, or a Frenchman "like everyone else." Jewish religion seemed little more than a "Jewish persuasion" which was no longer set apart by its goals, ideals, or practices.

Such was the common attitude among leading Jewish writers in the Russia of 1880. But events were about to force them into a sudden and complete change of thought.

SUMMARY *The Russian government has always been anti-Jewish. Empress Catherine II confined our people to the Pale of Settlement. Czar Alexander I tried to break up the shtetl communities by forcing Jews into farm colonies and cities. Czar Nicholas I approved more than 600 anti-Jewish laws, including ones forcing Jewish children into almost endless years of military service. By comparison with the other czars, Alexander II was generous. During his reign, the liberal movement of Jewish intellectuals—Haskalah—reached its peak. The followers of this movement, the maskilim, helped revive Hebrew and Yiddish literature. However, their dream of being completely accepted in Russian society proved to be a false one.*

PART FOUR

Europe at Its Height

Migration – and the Birth of Zionism

We sometimes think of the early Zionists as people who made great material sacrifices by going to Palestine. Were they not leaving behind the comforts of life in Europe or America to settle in a swampy, disease-ridden, undeveloped land? This is only partly true.

The Milwaukee which Golda Meir left behind was not, for her, a scene of great wealth, and David Ben-Gurion's home in Poland was far from well-to-do. It is true that both of them faced greater hardships in their new land. Yet they hoped to create not only a rich cultural life in the land of Israel, but also a dynamic society and economy. In any case, the early Zionists were for the most part indifferent to the niceties of material well-being. Freedom and self-expression meant much more to them than personal comfort.

If you stood on Dizengoff Street, in the heart of Tel Aviv,
what would you see? Trees, cars, fashionable stores,
strollers and shoppers, busy sidewalk cafes—a thoroughly
modern scene. But if you had stood on the same spot
early in 1909, you would have seen nothing but sand dunes.
It took money and machinery to work this miracle, to
build a new city and to rebuild an ancient nation.
But most of all it took people—people with a vision of
what they wanted their nation to become, and with the
knowledge and determination to turn that vision
into reality.

The early Zionists came to Eretz Yisrael not so much because they
were driven there by the hardships of their previous homes, but
because they were drawn by the promise of a new life. They wanted
the special joy and challenge of building one's home from the very
foundations, instead of merely inhabiting a society whose
foundations and main structure had already been built. Above all,
they wanted a future in which the Jewish people could simply be
itself and live within its own origins, its own landscapes, its own
language and faith and background. They sought and found a deep
harmony between their human and their Jewish identities.

ABBA EBAN

An old photograph (left) showing what Tel Aviv looked like around 1920 contrasts sharply with an artist's version (below) of the present city skyline and the Mediterranean Sea. The facing page portrays some of the young people on whom Israel's future depends: scholars in a yeshiva (top) and students in a computer class at the Haifa Technion (center).

An Indian Jew
farms in the Negev.

City life would be impossible in Israel, as
elsewhere, without farmers to supply the city
dwellers with the food and agricultural products
they need. Above, workers crate eggs on a
moshav near Ramla (for more about life on
a moshav, see page 146). At the top, the
kibbutzniks of Gan Shmuel take time out
for dancing.

12

INTRODUCTION TO PART FOUR:

Europe at Its Height

From 1880 to 1914, Western Europe enjoyed the world's highest standard of living and ruled most of the peoples of the earth. Proud and confident, Western Europeans looked forward to a future of constant progress in which they would forever be the lords of humanity.

The scramble for colonies

The model of this security and power was Queen Victoria, who came to the English throne in 1837 as a girl of eighteen and reigned for sixty-four years. During this time, Britain added nearly all of East Africa and Southern Asia to her colonies, creating the empire "over which the sun never set." In 1876, at the suggestion of Prime Minister Benjamin Disraeli (a Jew who had been baptized by his father at the age of thirteen after an argument with the London synagogue), Victoria became empress of India.

Other European nations did not lag far behind. Belgium took a large section of central Africa and called it the Belgian Congo (now Zaire), setting off a scramble for African lands. By 1900 the nations of Europe had carved up almost all of Africa. In the same way they divided the decaying Chinese empire into "areas of influence," where they could set laws and taxes for their own convenience and profit.

At times, the Asian and African peoples revolted against European rule, but their weapons were no match for those of the industrial nations. In 1898, for example, 50,000 Muslim tribesmen marched against the British in the land known as the Sudan, south of Egypt. They were wiped out by British machine guns. In 1899, a Chinese society called the Order of Literary Patriotic Harmonious Fists (nicknamed the "Boxers" by Westerners) staged a rebellion, but this uprising was crushed within two years by an army of soldiers from the Western nations.

Benjamin Disraeli (1804–1881), a Jewish-born statesman who was prime minister of Great Britain in Queen Victoria's time.

The rise of Japan

One of the few nations able to resist the power of Europe was Japan. From an early date, the Japanese had thought of outsiders as a threat, and for nearly two centuries (from 1660 to 1854) Japan had sealed itself off from the rest of the world. No Europeans, other than a few Dutch traders, were allowed to live in the country, and no Japanese were allowed to leave. It was a crime for any Japanese to build a boat large enough to sail the high seas.

Within its island home, the nation grew wealthy. While a military dictatorship kept order, Tokyo (then called Yedo) grew larger than London or Paris, and twenty times as large as any city in the United States. But Japan lacked modern military equipment. And so, when the American Commodore Matthew Perry sailed his steam-driven warships into Yedo Bay in 1853, the Japanese could only agree to his demand that they open up trade with the West.

Learning the power of modern science, the Japanese decided to use it for their own ends. They proved, as they would a second time after World War II, how quickly they could make use of the ways of outsiders when their national survival was at stake. Japan's military dictator was replaced with a parliament. The warrior nobility—the Samurai—became army officers. A national school system was established. The economy was modernized. Almost overnight, Japan became one of the world's foremost trading nations.

Perhaps not surprisingly, the Japanese also adopted the Western passion for taking foreign lands. In 1904 they invaded China, attacking an area which was held by the Russians. The Russo-Japanese War which followed was the first full-scale war in modern times between a major nonwhite power and a European army.

To the amazement of the West, the Russians were soundly defeated. Japan had shown that the Europeans were not all-powerful. Now, all across Asia (and later in Africa) there were growing demands for independence and self-rule. But the effects in Russia and in Western Europe were even more immediate and more devastating.

The two maps on the opposite page show Europe and the Near East at the close of the Napoleonic Wars (above) and after World War I (below). Notice how many more unified, independent nations there were in 1920 than in 1815. (Two countries shown on the 1920 map, Latvia and Lithuania, were later taken over by the Soviet Union.) Although Transjordan is shown on the 1920 map, it was not officially established until 1922, when the British divided Palestine and placed most of it under Arab rule.

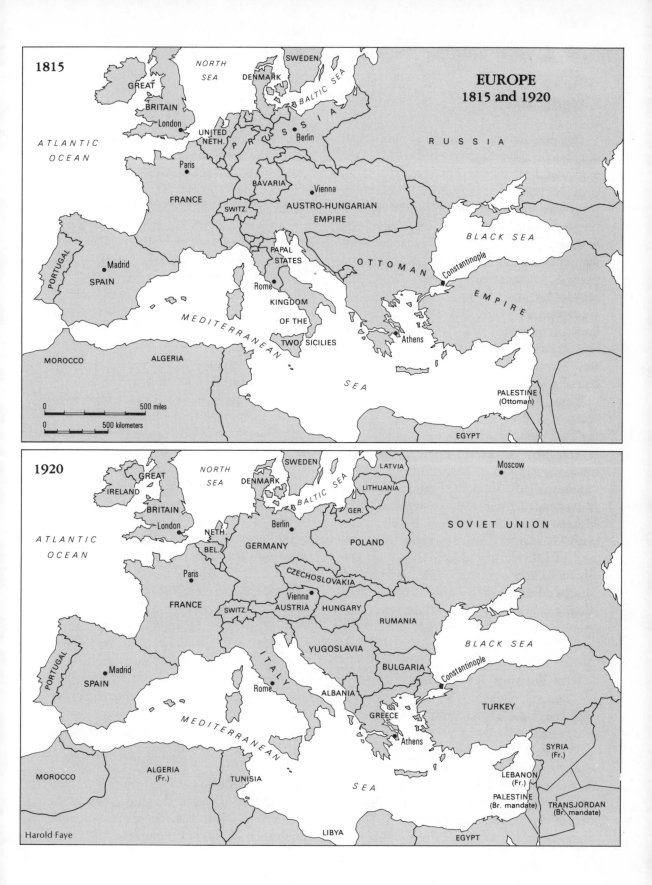

1815

NORTH
SEA

SWEDEN

DENMARK

BALTIC SEA

GREAT
BRITAIN

London

UNITED
NETH.

P R U S S I A

Berlin

R U S S I A

EUROPE
1815 and 1920

ATLANTIC
OCEAN

Paris

FRANCE

BAVARIA

SWITZ.

Vienna

AUSTRO-HUNGARIAN
EMPIRE

BLACK SEA

PORTUGAL

Madrid

SPAIN

PAPAL
STATES

Rome

KINGDOM

OF THE

TWO SICILIES

O T T O M A N

Constantinople

E M P I R E

M E D I T E R R A N E A N

Athens

MOROCCO

ALGERIA

S E A

PALESTINE
(Ottoman)

500 miles

500 kilometers

EGYPT

1920

NORTH
SEA

SWEDEN

DENMARK

LATVIA

Moscow

BALTIC SEA

GREAT
BRITAIN

IRELAND

London

NETH.

BEL.

Berlin

GERMANY

LITHUANIA

GER.

POLAND

S O V I E T   U N I O N

ATLANTIC
OCEAN

Paris

FRANCE

SWITZ.

CZECHOSLOVAKIA

Vienna

AUSTRIA

HUNGARY

RUMANIA

BLACK SEA

PORTUGAL

Madrid

SPAIN

I T A L Y

Rome

YUGOSLAVIA

BULGARIA

Constantinople

ALBANIA

M E D I T E R R A N E A N

GREECE

Athens

TURKEY

SYRIA
(Fr.)

MOROCCO

ALGERIA
(Fr.)

TUNISIA

S E A

LEBANON
(Fr.)

PALESTINE
(Br. mandate)

TRANSJORDAN
(Br. mandate)

LIBYA

EGYPT

Harold Faye

World War I

The Russians were unhappy with their oppressive government even before the war was lost to the Japanese. By 1914, Czar Nicholas II was frantically searching for a way to turn the attention of his people from their problems. Certain Slavs who lived in Austria-Hungary were demanding more rights, and Nicholas decided to pose as a champion of their cause. He moved his army against Austria and—in a moment of tragic rashness—also to the German border. The Germans insisted that the Russian forces be withdrawn; when this demand was ignored, Germany declared war on Russia.

There had not been a major conflict in Europe in more than forty years, but during that time the great powers had formed several firm alliances. France was committed to support Russia, and England was committed to support France—so both those countries joined the struggle. Austria-Hungary and the Ottoman Empire sided with Germany. Thus, the most backward part of Europe was able to drag the most advanced nations into a war of destruction. World War I lasted from 1914 to 1918, leaving nearly 10 million soldiers dead and another 20 million wounded.

The Russian Revolution

In the midst of the fighting, the Russian czar was overthrown.

World War I caused serious food shortages throughout Russia. The hunger, added to the many years of cruel government policies, caused the people to rise up against the government, and in 1917 the czar was forced to resign. For the first time since the Mongol invasion, nearly 700 years earlier, there was freedom in Russia.

Most of the nation rejoiced at the success of the revolution, but one group saw it as a chance to set up their own form of dictatorship.

This group, which came to be known as the COMMUNISTS (in Russia they were called BOLSHEVIKS), drew their ideas from the writings of Karl Marx. Marx was a German born of Jewish parents, but he had been baptized as a young child. Later he developed a philosophy which was very non-Jewish, and at times even anti-Semitic.

Marx saw the world as a great economic machine. History, he argued, has been a constant struggle between those who have wealth and power and those who do not. Each time those in power are overthrown, the victors in this war oppress a new class of poor people, leading to a new revolution. Marx believed that this struggle would go on for many years—but not forever. Finally a "classless" society would be created, one in which no group would oppress another, and all wealth would be shared in a fair and reasonable way.

Marx's ideas were based on the belief that people in power in Europe would hold on to every bit of their wealth until the poor had no choice but to revolt. Marx died in 1883, too soon to see that in Western Europe this did not happen. Laborers created unions and political parties which brought them great power—sometimes through violent struggle, but without the need to overthrow society.

Only in Russia was the state so opposed to change that it made revolution necessary. Oddly enough, the fact that Marx was wrong about Europe never bothered the leader of the Communists, who had taken the name Lenin. He boldly seized control of the Russian government, dissolved parliament (which had been elected by a four-to-one *non*-Communist majority), and set up the harsh dictatorship which remains in power to this day.

A new world order

Lenin withdrew the Russian army from World War I, but by that time the United States had entered the fighting on the side of England and France. This brought the added power needed to defeat Germany, and on November 11, 1918, the bloodshed was brought to an end.

The world was again at peace, but it did not look like the world Queen Victoria had known. The three great nations of Eastern Europe—the Russian, Austro-Hungarian, and Ottoman empires—had all collapsed. From their territories many new European states would be formed or recreated: Poland, Lithuania, Rumania, Czechoslovakia, Austria, Yugoslavia, Hungary. The Ottoman lands in the Middle East were divided into separate states—Turkey, Syria, Lebanon, Iraq, and Palestine—each of which would in time become independent. England and the other nations on the winning side still held their empires, but Europe was no longer the supreme ruler of the world. Japan had been its own master since defeating Russia, and the United States had proved itself one of the leading international powers.

Jews, as loyal citizens of many of the nations caught up in these great events, took part in world affairs at every level. But even more important to them as Jews were certain things that happened within their own countries. These things led many Jews to wonder if they could ever be safe in Europe. While many European Jews looked for homes in the New World, others decided that the Jews would never be safe until they had a homeland of their own.

The period when Europe's power was at its height was for our people the era of Migration—and the Birth of Zionism.

SUMMARY   *Between 1880 and 1914, Europe reached the peak of its power. The Western nations had carved out great empires and were first challenged in 1904–1905 by the victory of Japan in the Russo-Japanese War. Then came World War I, which brought the collapse of the great empires and the rise of Communists in Russia. All these things affected the Jews. But, even more, Jews were concerned with certain key events within their own countries.*

13

Death of an Old Dream, Birth of a New

On March 13, 1881, the hopes of Russian Jewry were crushed as Czar Alexander II was murdered by revolutionaries. The dream of freedom which he had inspired was turned into a ghastly nightmare by his son, Alexander III.

Pogroms

The younger Alexander wanted revenge for his father's death. He also needed something to turn aside the attention of the Russian masses from their anger against the government. And he was a Jew-hater. He was able to combine all three elements by blaming "the Jews" for his father's murder.

In fact, very few Jews took part in the revolutionary groups which were springing up throughout Russia. The only Jewish member in the group which killed Alexander II was a young woman who kept a secret hideout for the terrorists. But facts were never allowed to get in the way of prejudice and politics when the czar dealt with the Jewish people. So Alexander III organized riots, called POGROMS, in which Christians brutally attacked the Jewish communities.

The rioters were not stopped by the police as long as they pretended that attacking the Jews was their own idea and not the idea of the government. They could loot, destroy, rape, and murder. Most rioters were Russian peasants. But sometimes they came from the "better" parts of society. University students sometimes joined in the violence. Respectable newspapers printed articles praising the riots. The leading Russian writers remained silent. The police stood watching as bloodshed raged, or took weapons away from Jews who tried to defend themselves. (In the few cases where arrests were made, Jews who fought back were punished as

When Russian peasants savagely attacked the Jews
of Kishinev, army officers did nothing to stop them.

severely as the Gentiles who attacked them.) The Gentile revolutionaries, who usually opposed all government actions, joined the government in approving the torture and murder of their Jewish neighbors.

The czar was arranging to have Jews murdered. And the czar's Christian subjects approved.

May Laws

While Russian Jews were struggling to understand this horrible truth, Czar Alexander signed his cruelist edict: the so-called MAY LAWS. These laws imposed strict quotas on the number of Jews who could attend schools and universities. Christians were given the right to drive out "vicious Jews" from their communities— a "right" which Christians were only too happy to use. Innocent Jews suddenly found themselves thrown out of their homes and forced to squeeze into those towns where our people were still permitted to live. Huge numbers were forced to move—20,000 from Moscow alone. The surviving Jewish communities became incredibly crowded. Fully 40 percent of the

Jewish population needed charity in order to survive.

The suffering caused by the May Laws was no accident. When a more kindly high official sent a report asking the czar to end the oppression, Alexander III wrote in the margin this comment: "But we must not forget that it was the Jews who crucified our Lord and spilled his priceless blood." A leading official bragged about what was planned for the Jews: "One-third will emigrate, one-third will be baptized, and one-third will starve."

Under Nicholas II

Alexander III reigned only thirteen years, but his cruelty continued with his son—the last of the czars, Nicholas II. Nicholas was not very bright, and often followed bad advice. And there was much bad advice about our people.

Of all the czars, Nicholas had the best reason to think well of the Jews, for many of them served him loyally in the Russo-Japanese War. (Jewish soldiers were usually sent to Siberia, the furthest section of Russia, which was near the battle lines.) The Jews fought bravely to defend Russian land, though they were fighting in an area where they were not allowed to live. But even though the Jews fought for him, Nicholas said: "As long as I am czar, the Jews of Russia shall not receive equal rights."

To his credit, Nicholas II rejected a book called THE PROTOCOLS OF THE ELDERS OF ZION, which said that Jews were organizing to destroy Christendom and take over the world. The work was a fake sent to him by the Paris office of the Russian police, and even the czar could see it was nonsense. The "Protocols" seem to have been forgotten for a time, but after the Russian Revolution, copies were sent all throughout Western Europe. The book has been translated into many languages, and has been used by both Nazis and Arabs for propaganda.

Another crude plot against the Jews was the trial of Menaḥem Mendel Beilis. Beilis was accused of murdering a Gentile boy in order to use his blood for Jewish rituals. The Russian police investigated this ridiculous charge for two years, but the evidence against Beilis was so flimsy that not even a Russian court would find him guilty. In the end he was freed, and left the country for Palestine.

The Kishinev pogrom

Though false charges against the Jews might fail, the government knew that violence would always succeed. In 1903, state agents organized a major pogrom in Kishinev. For two days, Russian peasants savagely attacked the Jews of the city. All the while, army officers, claiming they were "awaiting orders," did nothing to stop the massacre, and educated Russians turned the other way or even encouraged the peasants to do greater violence.

Forty-seven Jews were killed. Today it may not seem like many. We have become so used to hearing of nations murdering their citizens by the hundreds, thousands, or millions that this number really seems rather small. At the beginning of this century, however, one writer could call the events of the Kishinev massacre "bestialities such as find few parallels even in the history of the most barbarous ages."

The pogrom shocked the Jewish people not only because of the murders, but also because the victims had been totally unable to defend themselves. A thirty-year-old writer, Ḥaim Naḥman Bialik—who would become the greatest Hebrew poet of modern times—poured out his fury at this helplessness, imagining that God Himself was angered by the weakness of the Jewish people:

> *They pray of Me forgiveness for their*
> *sin.*
> *Their sin? the sin of shadows on the*
> *wall,*
> *The sin of broken pots, of bruised*
> *worms!*
> *What will they? Why stretch out their*
> *hands to me?*
> *Has none a fist?* *

The Kishinev pogrom—and the challenge of Bialik's widely read poem—led to the creation of Jewish self-defense units. This marked a turning point for Russian Jewry, as some Russian Jews tried to take control of their own lives. A more common reaction to the pogroms, however, was escape. Millions realized that Russia was no longer their home in any meaningful way. As we shall see in Chapter 15, most of these people came to America.

But for a third group, it seemed pointless to continue to search for safety in the Diaspora. What Russia was today, America could become tomorrow. To these people, the only solution was a permanent home for Jews in the land of Israel. Jewish nationalism—Zionism—was born again.

---

* Bialik's literary career led him from Russia to Eretz Yisrael, where he settled in 1924. There he was, among other things, the creator of the Sabbath celebration known as ONEG SHABBAT (עֹנֶג שַׁבָּת).

The rebirth of Zionism

Jews had always dreamed of returning to Eretz Yisrael. But, in the past, Jews had only prayed for a Messiah to bring our people back to the Holy Land. Through the movement called ZIONISM (צִיּוֹנוּת) Jews sought to create a Jewish homeland out of their own dedication and hard work.

The first to turn to Zionism were those who before 1881 had been furthest from it: the maskilim. At first these men thought that anti-Semitism was just a holdover from the Middle Ages. The maskilim believed, as Mendelssohn had taught, that when Jews became more and more part of the modern world they would be more and more accepted by Gentile society.

The pogroms destroyed this belief. It was clear that modern Jew-hatred was widespread in the government and in every social class. This was well understood by a maskil named Moses Leib Lilienblum. Until 1881 he had lived in a state of great confusion. Because he wanted more than the traditional Jewish education he received, he was scorned by the Orthodox. He fell in love, but could not marry the one he loved because he had been wed at the age of sixteen in a marriage arranged by his father. He turned from his family and taught that Jews should wear Russian clothing and learn secular culture, but when he did these things he still felt that something was wrong.

Then came the pogroms, and Lilienblum finally realized what had been missing in his life:

> When I became convinced that it was not a lack of high culture that was the cause of our tragedy—for foreigners we are and foreigners we shall remain even if we be-

The Making of
Modern Hebrew

Eliezer Ben-Yehudah
worked tirelessly to make
Hebrew the language of
the Holy Land.

Although Hebrew remained a "holy language" through
all the years of Jewish wandering, it was not revived
as a spoken language until the late 1800's, when large
numbers of Jews began arriving in Eretz Yisrael from Europe,
North Africa, and the Middle East.

These immigrants came from many lands and spoke
many different languages—Yiddish, Ladino, Arabic, German,
and French, among others. Using Hebrew made them feel
that they were now one people meeting on common ground.
Speaking a new language, even though it was an ancient
one, also helped to separate the immigrants from their old
homelands. Moreover, Hebrew was the language
of the Bible, and it was through the Bible that Israel had
been remembered as the Promised Land. The choice of
Hebrew reflected the immigrants' hope that they were
pioneering a new "golden age" in Eretz Yisrael.

It was not easy to adapt the language of the Bible to the
realities of everyday life in the modern world. As
Ben-Yehudah said, "Whoever wishes to write something of
wisdom and science, and especially someone like myself, who
speaks Hebrew at home with the children, about everything
in life, feels every moment a lack of words without
which living speech cannot take place." Ben-Yehudah sadly
observed that Hebrew had no word for "tickling,"
a simple everyday action. New words had to be formed.

They were formed in three ways. The first method
was to give new meanings to older Hebrew root-words.
When the Israelis needed a word for calling someone by
telephone, they used the old word for ringing, מְצַלְצֵל ,
to mean "ringing up" or "calling." The second method was
to borrow a word from another language. Scientific terms were
taken from Greek, Latin, and German; technical
terms were very often borrowed from English (especially
during the days of the British mandate, when many English
speakers lived in Palestine). Thus, the constellation which the
Greeks called Andromeda became אַנְדְרוֹמֶדָה in Hebrew.
A radio, undreamt of in Biblical or medieval Hebrew, is
simply called רַדְיוֹ . The third way to make new words
depended on the wit and imagination of the people.
For example, it was a popular pastime in Tel Aviv to take
weekend walks around Dizengoff Square; and so, a word
for "taking a stroll around Dizengoff Square" (לְהִזְדַּנְגֵּף)
suddenly appeared in the Hebrew vocabulary.

Taking a walk around Tel Aviv's Dizengoff Square became
so popular that a new word was invented for the pastime.

Many new words in Hebrew have fascinating histories.
Electricity, for example, was unknown in Biblical times, so a
new Hebrew word for it was needed. There was a Hebrew
name in the Bible for an alloy of gold and silver
which is called, in Latin and English, *electrum*. And so the
Hebrew name for electrum (חַשְׁמַל) became the new
name for "electricity."

Bulldozers were important in rebuilding the Jewish State,
but what would they be called in Hebrew? To solve the
problem two words were combined: דָּחַף , which means "push,"
was joined to חָפַר , which means "dig," to make the word
for bulldozer, דַּחְפּוֹר .

Something else important to modern society is the
babysitter. But here again there was no word in Hebrew.
So, by taking a word meaning "baby" (טַף) and joining it to a
word meaning "guarding" or "watching" (שָׁמַר), the word
for babysitter (שְׁמַרְטַף) was created.

Another way of using old words to build new ones is by
making an acronym. An acronym consists of the most
important (usually the first) letters of several words.
For example, take the first letter of the word for knife (סַכִּין);
add the first letter of the word for spoon (כַּף); then the
Hebrew letter for "and" (וֹ); and finally the first letter of the
word for fork (מַזְלֵג). What you get is the Hebrew word
for "silverware" (סַכּוּ"ם).

The Haifa Technion today.
As early as 1913, students
and teachers demanded
that Hebrew be used in
the school.

With little or no farm experience, the BILU pioneers found it hard to make their living from the soil.

come full to the brim with culture—all the old ideals left me in a flash.

He spent the rest of his life working to create a Jewish state.

Eliezer Ben-Yehudah and the revival of Hebrew

Throughout Eastern Europe, Jews were caught up by the spirit of the Zionist movement. Meanwhile, a Lithuanian Jew had settled in Jerusalem in order to take an important practical step in building a homeland for the Jews. Eliezer Ben-Yehudah was determined to make Hebrew the language of the Holy Land.

Today it seems obvious that Hebrew should be spoken in Eretz Yisrael, but in 1881 it was not. Most Jews spoke Yiddish; and, more and more, the new books Jews were reading were written in Yiddish. Hebrew was used only in prayer and study. The religious community of Jews living in Palestine since ancient times thought of Hebrew as the "holy" tongue. They refused to use it for everyday speaking. Even those highly educated Jews who used Hebrew as a spoken language found that there were no words in the ancient language for the many modern inventions.

But Ben-Yehudah realized that Hebrew was the only language which could unite Jews no matter what country they came from. And so he set about his task, writing many works in Hebrew—including a dictionary in which he coined new words to meet modern needs.

His work was painstaking, and sometimes caused difficult personal problems.

Because he would speak only Hebrew, he and his family were separated from many members of the Jewish community. But his triumph was complete. Through his work Hebrew was truly reborn. In 1913, a German Jewish group founded the Haifa Technion (Technological School) and announced that German would be the school's official language. Both students and teachers went on strike with the slogan "No Hebrew, No Technion." The striking scholars refused to give up their ancient but now modern speech. Hebrew became the language of the Technion.

Foundations of the yishuv

Of course, just having a language for Eretz Yisrael would mean nothing if no Jews were willing and able to settle there. At that moment many of the Jews of Russia were ready. The wave of pogroms was hardly over when Jewish students in Russia began to organize as Zionist pioneers. The first of these groups was called BILU (בִּיל״וּ), from the initials of the Hebrew words of Isaiah 2:5:

$$\text{בֵּית יַעֲקֹב לְכוּ וְנֵלְכָה}$$

House of Jacob, come let us go up.

Fifteen young men and women reached Palestine in the summer of 1882, and others followed. They settled and began work as farmers.

Sadly, these brave settlers had learned little about farming in Russia, and nothing about farming in Eretz Yisrael. Centuries of neglect had turned once fertile land into deserts and swamps. Some of the young people died; others were ready to give up

and return to Russia or go to America. But for every settler that died and for every one that left, several new pioneers would make the hard trip from Russia to Palestine. The story was often the same: the newcomers came with enthusiasm, but were soon sick, unhappy, or discouraged. Then, at this critical moment, huge sums of money arrived from Europe to save the small colonies from bankruptcy and starvation. At first, the donor was unknown. Before long, however, the settlers learned that it was the leading Jew of France, Baron Edmond de Rothschild, who had rescued them.

Rothschild's interest in Palestine came out of one of the strangest meetings imaginable. The rich man had met with a Russian rabbi, Samuel Mohilever. The rabbi did not know French, and spoke with such a bad stammer that he could only com-

Baron Edmond de Rothschild (center) visiting Eretz Yisrael in 1914.

municate with Rothschild by chanting in Hebrew and having his song translated! Yet somehow, despite his handicaps, the rabbi shared his deep feeling for the land of Israel and the needs of its people.

Rothschild was caught up by the rabbi's message. During the next fifty years he gave more money to Palestine than did all the rest of the Jews in the world put together! He bought 125,000 acres of land for our people. His money and the experts he sent drained swamps, developed irrigation projects, and started industries producing products such as perfume and wine. He also gave of himself, visiting the country five times. He held a tight rein on all his projects, which sometimes led to disagreements with those actually living in Palestine; but through his help, newcomers to Eretz Yisrael found work, and the land began to revive.

By 1897, sixteen years after the first pogrom, and only fifteen years after the arrival of the first modern Zionist pioneers, the YISHUV (יִשׁוּב)—the Jewish settlement in the Holy Land—was a living reality. Farm colonies rose like lush green islands from the swamps and dunes of Northern Palestine, islands created in a spirit of joy and sacrifice. The first step toward restoring the Promised Land to the Jewish people had been taken.

SUMMARY   *The pogroms which began in 1881 marked a turning point in Jewish thought, for Russian Jewry came to see that neither the czarist government nor the Gentile community would protect Jews from mob violence. Some Jews did their best to endure or resist the cruel May Laws, the Kishinev massacre, and other types of oppression. Millions of Jews fled, mostly to America. Others developed Zionism, the movement to build a Jewish homeland in Palestine. By 1897, thanks in part to the generosity of Baron Edmond de Rothschild, the Jewish settlement in Palestine (the yishuv) was a reality.*

14

The Herzl Miracle

ALIYAH (עֲלִיָּה) is a Hebrew word which means "going up." It was the word for the pilgrimage up to the Temple in ancient Jerusalem. It is the term for "going up" from the congregation to take part in the reading of Torah during a synagogue service.

And it is the word for "going up" from the Diaspora to the Holy Land—immigration to the land of Israel.

First pioneers

After the destruction of the Second Temple, there were few Jews willing to join groups returning to Israel. Some came toward the end of the eighteenth century, and between 1850 and 1880 more than 20,000 Jews settled in Eretz Yisrael. They came mainly to live in the Holy Land, hoping to earn merit for themselves and the Jewish people. They spent most of their time in study and worship, and to support themselves and their families they took charity from Jews in other lands.

The BILU pioneers who arrived in 1882, and those who followed them, were different. They wanted to work the land, supporting themselves on farm colonies. They wanted to settle and rebuild our homeland, and at the same time to create a new spirit of Jewish independence and self-reliance.

The First Aliyah—the wave of Jewish immigration from 1882 to 1903—was a good beginning. These 25,000 immigrants founded many new farm communities. This was the yishuv—the Jewish settlement in Palestine. But it was still not a nation. For one thing, the yishuv did not have a legal right to exist! The Turkish government, which ruled Palestine, had not stopped the immigrants from settling, but it had not given them permission to do so.

Zionism began as the pioneering of a few idealists. Later it became the mass movement which would create a Jewish state. This great change was brought about by the will of one man: Theodor Herzl.

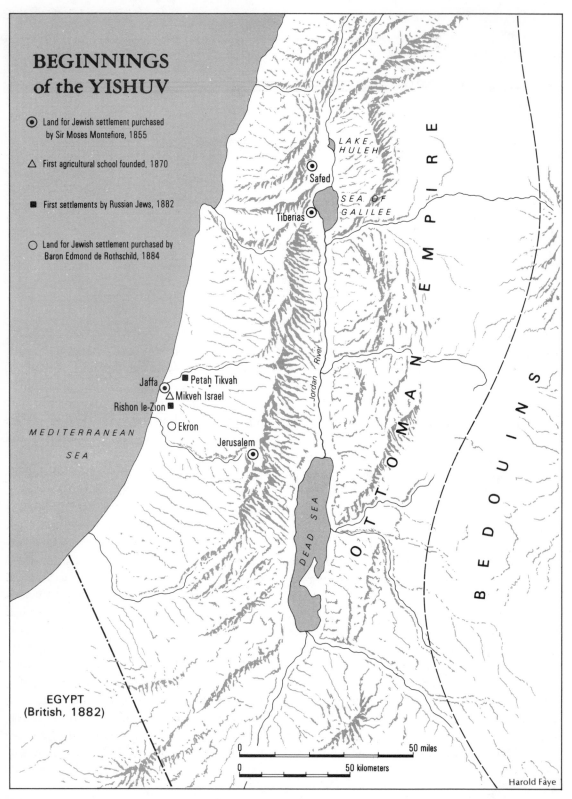

BEGINNINGS
of the YISHUV

⊙ Land for Jewish settlement purchased
by Sir Moses Montefiore, 1855

△ First agricultural school founded, 1870

■ First settlements by Russian Jews, 1882

○ Land for Jewish settlement purchased by
Baron Edmond de Rothschild, 1884

LAKE HULEH

⊙ Safed

SEA OF GALILEE

⊙ Tiberias

Jordan River

Jaffa ⊙ ■ Petaḥ Tikvah
△ Mikveh Israel
Rishon le-Zion ■

○ Ekron

MEDITERRANEAN SEA

Jerusalem ⊙

DEAD SEA

O T T O M A N E M P I R E

B E D O U I N S

EGYPT
(British, 1882)

0 _____ 50 miles

0 _____ 50 kilometers

Harold Faye

Herzl's early career

Herzl was born in Budapest on May 2, 1860, an only son to adoring parents. His Jewish education ended with his Bar Mitzvah—indeed, he never learned much of either Hebrew or Judaism. He became a lawyer in Vienna, but then followed his childhood dream of becoming a writer. He found it hard to win fame, however, and at twenty-two he wrote in despair:

> I haven't even the tiniest success to show, not the slightest achievement of which to be proud.

Nine years later he found an important job as a reporter for a leading newspaper, the *New Free Press* of Vienna. His new job brought him to Paris, where he felt anti-Semitism on the rise around him.

Herzl was soon haunted by the question of anti-Jewish prejudice. He almost convinced himself that the solution lay in the complete disappearance of the Jews through conversion and intermarriage. Then, realizing how much he really loved his heritage, he wrote a play called *The New Ghetto* in which he strongly reaffirmed his Jewishness. Nevertheless, the major change in his life came when he was sent by his newspaper to report on the Dreyfus case.

Although nearly all the pioneers of the 1880's came from Eastern Europe, the yishuv could not have succeeded without the help of Jewish leaders in the West. Land for settlement in Eretz Yisrael was purchased in 1855 by a British Jew, Sir Moses Montefiore, using funds provided by an American Jew, Judah Touro. The Mikveh Israel agricultural school was founded in 1870 by the Alliance Israelite Universelle, whose president was a French Jew, Adolphe Crémieux. And the money to support the Russian and Rumanian pioneers came from another Frenchman, Edmond de Rothschild.

Theodor Herzl with his three children.

The Dreyfus case

Alfred Dreyfus was a French army officer who was accused of selling secret information to the Germans. The evidence against him was slim—an unsigned letter which a cleaning woman had found in a wastebasket at the German embassy. The handwriting on the letter was similar (but not identical) to that of Dreyfus. He had no reason to betray his country, and over and over said that he had not done so.

Dreyfus was rich, cold, snobbish, and boastful. But it was clear from the trial, and all that happened after, that Dreyfus' worst sin was that he was a Jew. This fact Dreyfus could hardly understand. He did not think of himself as a Jew, but as a loyal Frenchman. Would the court—with no real evidence and no real witnesses—punish him just for being a Jew? The court found him guilty of treason and sentenced him to life imprisonment on Devil's Island, off the coast of South America.

A small group, led by Dreyfus' brother, pressed for a further inquiry. Government officials discovered that the real traitor was Major Ferdinand Esterhazy, a free-spend-

Dreyfus in Kasrilevka   *In his short story "Dreyfus in Kasrilevka," Sholem Aleichem recalls that the Dreyfus affair was as meaningful to Jews in the shtetls and ghettos of Eastern Europe as it was to Jews in the West. Sholem Aleichem was living in Kiev while the scandal was raging in Paris; he based his fictional town of Kasrilevka on the Ukrainian shtetl where he grew up.*

Zeidel, Reb Shaye's son, was the only person in Kasrilevka who subscribed to a newspaper. The townspeople learned all the news of the world from him, or rather through him. He read and they interpreted. He spoke and they supplied the commentary. He told them what he read in the paper, but they turned it around to suit themselves, because they understood it better than he did.

One day Zeidel came to the synagogue and hold how in Paris a certain Jewish captain named Dreyfus had been imprisoned for turning over government papers to the enemy.

This went in one ear and out the other. Someone remarked in passing, "What won't a Jew do to make a living?"

And another added spitefully, "A Jew has no business climbing so high, interfering with kings and their affairs."

Later, when Zeidel came to them and told them a fresh tale, that the whole thing was a plot, that the Jewish Captain Dreyfus was innocent and that it was an intrigue of certain officers who were themselves involved, then the whole town became interested in the case. At once, Dreyfus became a Kasrilevkite. Whenever two people came together, he was the third.

"Have you heard?"

"I've heard."

"Sent away for good."

"A life sentence."

"For nothing at all."

"A false accusation."

[News that Dreyfus would be given a new trial filled Kasrilevka with excitement. Everyone waited anxiously to hear the verdict.]

When the last day of the trial came, the Kasrilevkites shook as with a fever.

At the first sign of dawn they rushed to the post office. The outer gates were closed, and the street was filled with people. Men walked up and down, yawning, stretching, pulling their earlocks and praying under their breath.

When, at last, Zeidel came to the post office, opened his paper, and read the news aloud, there arose such an outcry, such a clamor, such a roar that the heavens could have split open. The outcry was not against the judges who gave the wrong verdict, not at the generals who swore falsely, not at the French who showed themselves up so badly. The outcry was against Zeidel.

"It cannot be!" the people of Kasrilevka shouted with one voice. "Such a verdict is impossible! Heaven and earth swore that the truth must prevail. What kind of lies are you telling us?"

"Fools!" shouted Zeidel, and thrust the paper into their faces. "Look! See what the paper says!"

"Paper! Paper!" shouted Kasrilevka. "And if you stood with one foot in heaven and the other on earth, would we believe you? Such a thing must not be. It must never be! Never! Never!"

And—who was right?

ing officer who was heavily in debt; but they also decided that it would be bad for the army to admit that it had made an error. To cover up, new "evidence" against Dreyfus was forged, so when Esterhazy was tried by court-martial he was declared completely innocent.

The whole affair then became even more heated. Beginning with the bold words *J'accuse* ("I accuse"), the Gentile novelist Emile Zola attacked Esterhazy's acquittal as a "crime against humanity." There was an instant reaction. Much of the public, including the military and the Catholic clergy, feared that admitting the truth of Zola's charges would hurt the army. The novelist was accused of libel, and had to flee France to escape imprisonment. In France, huge crowds plundered Jewish stores, beat up Jews, and publicly burned Zola's article. A mob paraded along the streets of Paris shouting "Death to Zola! Death to the Jews!" Petitions demanded the expulsion of all Jews from France. The nationalist press urged that all Jewish workers be fired from their jobs, and some university professors who supported Dreyfus were either suspended or forced to resign.

Nevertheless, the Dreyfusards—those who believed that Dreyfus was innocent—continued to demand justice, and in 1899 Dreyfus was returned to France for a new trial. His four and a half years in prison had left him a broken man—at thirty-nine he was bent and thin. Despite the clear evidence in his favor, he was again found guilty, though his sentence was reduced to ten years because of "extenuating circumstances." Later the president of the Republic granted him a pardon; but it was not until 1906, twelve years after the affair began, that Dreyfus was declared innocent of all crimes.

"The Jewish State"

Theodor Herzl was present at the first Dreyfus trial in his role as a newspaper reporter. What he saw was deeply shocking. He believed from the outset that Dreyfus was innocent, but this was not what bothered him most. As he wrote in his diaries:

The Dreyfus case contains more than a miscarriage of justice; it contains the wish of the vast majority in France to damn one Jew and through him all Jews. "Death to the Jews!" the crowd yelled when they ripped the Captain's stripes from his uniform. And since that time, "Down with the Jews" has become a battle cry. Where? In France. In republican, modern, civilized France, one hundred years after the Declaration of the Rights of Man. . . .

Up to that time, most of us had believed that the solution of the Jewish question was to be expected from the gradual progress of mankind toward tolerance. But if an otherwise progressive, surely highly civilized people could come to such a pass, what was there to be expected from other people?

Thus, Herzl began his search for a way to make our people safe from anti-Semites. At last he came up with an idea that was both very simple and totally revolutionary: the Jews had to have a country and a government of their own. In 1896 he published his call for an independent nation in a small book which he named *The Jewish State*. In it he wrote:

I believe that a wondrous generation of Jews will spring into existence. The Maccabeans will rise again.

Let me repeat once more my opening words. The Jews who wish it will have their State.

We shall live at last as free men on our own soil, and die peacefully in our own homes.

The world will be freed by our liberty, enriched by our wealth, magnified by our greatness.

Herzl's book broke upon the world like a bolt of lightning. Everywhere people spoke of it. The German press, both Jewish and non-Jewish, said Herzl's ideas were those of an insane dreamer. Russian Zionists, though they shared his dream, were afraid to trust Herzl. They had never heard of him, and wondered why he did not mention either the Hebrew language or any of those who had earlier called for Jewish national independence.

In fact, Herzl had never heard of the Zionists in Russia. He later said that he would not have written his book if he had known anything about them! He had been driven to pour out his ideas in the belief that they were original—and it was this freshness of imagination that inspired others. From everywhere came calls for Herzl to lead the Zionist cause.

The First Zionist Congress

Now Herzl turned all his energy to the task of creating a Jewish state. First he looked for support to the wealthy, both Gentile and Jewish. He failed to convince even Baron Edmond de Rothschild of the need for statehood, though the Frenchman had been the mainstay of the yishuv. This made Herzl decide that he could get nothing from the well-to-do. "Let us organize our masses immediately," he said. And so political Zionism was born.

Herzl's first major project was to organize a Jewish congress. Using his own funds he created a weekly publication to publicize and define the idea. On August 29, 1897, the First Zionist Congress met in Basel, Switzerland. This was the first official, worldwide gathering of Jews in history—and it was the work of one man.

Almost 200 Jewish leaders attended the meeting. They came from Eastern and Western Europe, from England, America, and Algeria—young and old, Orthodox and Reform, capitalist and socialist. The Congress set up a World Zionist Organization in order to create "for the Jewish people a home in Palestine secured by public law." A Jewish flag and national anthem were adopted, both of which served as models for the flag and national anthem of the State of Israel. Prophetically, Herzl wrote in his diary:

At Basel I created the Jewish State. In five years, perhaps, and certainly in fifty, everyone will see it.

Opponents of Zionism

Knowing, as we do, that independence for the State of Israel was approved by the United Nations just fifty years after these words were written, it is hard for us now to understand why so many Jews *opposed* the Zionist movement; but they had a great deal of logic on their side. The ultra-Orthodox believed that a Jewish state should only be established by the Messiah. There were millions more who thought it would be impossible to recreate a nation which had been destroyed some 1800 years earlier. Furthermore, Palestine was hardly a pleasant site for a homeland: it was a poor, backward, and unfriendly corner of the Ottoman Empire.

Many (including Edmond de Rothschild) feared that having a Jewish state in

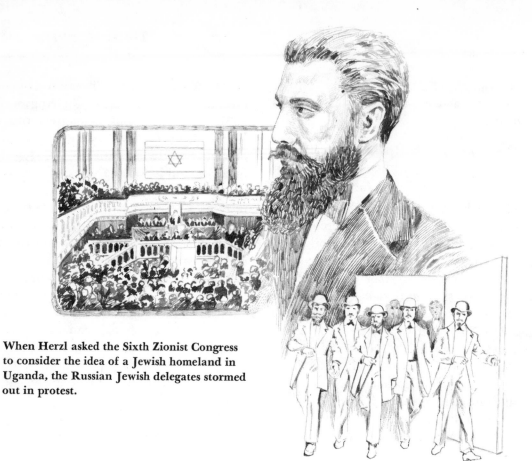

When Herzl asked the Sixth Zionist Congress to consider the idea of a Jewish homeland in Uganda, the Russian Jewish delegates stormed out in protest.

Palestine would be bad for the Jews of the Diaspora. People might begin to think that those Jews living in Europe and America were more loyal to the land of Israel than to the countries in which they lived—exactly what anti-Semites had been saying.

Aḥad Ha-Am

The most powerful argument against Herzl came from a Russian Jew who was himself a loyal Zionist. His name was Asher Ginzberg, but we know him by his pen name, AḤAD HA-AM ("One of the People").

Aḥad Ha-Am did not believe, as Herzl did, that Jews would be left in peace as soon as a Jewish state was established. He saw that the geographical position of Pales-

tine, as well as its religious importance, would always put the Holy Land at the storm center of world politics.

His disagreement with Herzl, however, was even more basic. What business, asked Aḥad Ha-Am, do the Jewish people have creating an "ordinary" state? He believed deeply that the task of Judaism was to teach the world the highest values. For him, Zionism meant creating a worldwide Jewish community that would pursue that task. Palestine, in his view, should be a home for a small group of men and women who would dedicate themselves to the finest in the Jewish spirit, and who by the quality of their lives would inspire the world. The Jewish masses could find homes in other lands.

The Zionist movement followed Herzl and did not accept Aḥad Ha-Am's views of "cultural Zionism." But Aḥad Ha-Am worked for Jewish rights in the Holy Land and settled there in 1922. He became the "secular spiritual leader" of a growing Jewish community in Eretz Yisrael, and was so widely admired that his street in Tel Aviv was closed to traffic during his afternoon rest hours. When he died in 1927, the whole city turned out for his funeral.

A homeland outside Palestine?

Herzl had no time for Aḥad Ha-Am's skepticism and doubt. As the first president of the World Zionist Organization, he needed all his energies for the Zionist program. He traveled constantly to gain support for Zionism. He visited Palestine, where the lack of such basics as clean water and modern sanitation only made him more eager to create "a glorious new Jerusalem."

Year after year there were Zionist congresses, bringing ever greater numbers of Zionists together. Real achievements were made at these meetings. At the Fifth Congress in 1901, for example, the Jewish National Fund was created to purchase, develop, and rebuild land in Palestine on behalf of the Jewish people. Still, the political results of Herzl's work were small. The Ottoman sultan met with the Jewish leader after huge bribes had been paid to Turkish officials, but he would not give the Zionists official permission to settle in the Holy Land.

By 1903, the year of the Kishinev massacre, the plight of Russian Jewry was becoming more and more desperate. Just at this point, the English government offered the Zionists land in Africa, in the British-held territory of Uganda, to use as a home for oppressed Jews. Herzl saw this as a temporary solution to the mounting refugee problem, a "shelter for the night" un-

---

The Jewish National Fund

The Jewish National Fund (קֶרֶן קַיֶּמֶת לְיִשְׂרָאֵל) began buying land in Palestine in 1905, though it was not able to begin large-scale activities until 1921. By 1978, the JNF had achieved amazing results. It had:

- planted 135,000,000 trees.
- built more than 2300 miles of roads.
- acquired more than 660,000 acres of land.
- developed 849 rural settlements.

Much of the money needed for this work was raised through the "Blue Box." Jews all over the world have used these boxes to collect coins for purchasing territory in the Holy Land. In Russia, where commitment to a Jewish homeland has been illegal since czarist times, Jews have secretly moved these little tin containers from place to place, until they could be smuggled across the border and into the West.

Today, some 1,160,000 Israelis live on land owned or developed by the JNF.

A little "Blue Box."

til large-scale Jewish immigration to Palestine became possible. He proposed to the Sixth Zionist Congress that a commission be set up to explore the idea of a Jewish homeland in Uganda, and the Congress agreed.

Then a remarkable thing happened—a classic conflict between faith and reason. Representatives of the Russian Jews, who had the most to gain from the Uganda plan, stormed out of the Congress! They insisted that the task of Zionism was to build a home in Eretz Yisrael, not to worry about the temporary suffering of the Jewish masses. They wanted a Jewish state in Eretz Yisrael—and nowhere else. Herzl was astounded. "These people have a rope around their necks," he said, "and still they refuse."

As the Congress ended, it seemed the Zionist movement was about to collapse. But Herzl had always believed in unity, and he called a special conference to heal the wounds he had unintentionally created. All parties agreed to abandon the Uganda plan. No Jewish state would be founded outside of Eretz Yisrael. In the battle between faith and reason, faith had won.

Herzl's achievements

Bringing about this Zionist unity was Herzl's last great deed. He had been very ill before the Sixth Zionist Congress. When it was over, he tried to regain his health with a six-week rest cure; but even then he could not stop working. Finally, on July 3, 1904, he was overcome by pneumonia and died. News of his passing shattered the Jewish world: the fallen hero was only forty-four years old.

Only nine years and seven months had passed since Alfred Dreyfus was first sent to Devil's Island. Yet in that short time Herzl had worked a miracle. He had given the Jews the will to shape their own lives, to take the future into their own hands.

They, in turn, would fulfill his last wish. With perfect faith in the Zionist cause, Herzl had requested in his will that his final resting place be the Jewish state. And so, in 1949, the grateful citizens of Israel brought his coffin from Vienna and buried it on a hill overlooking Jerusalem. Just forty-five years after his death, the Jewish state was no longer a dream—it was a reality.

SUMMARY *Zionism as a political movement was created by Theodor Herzl. Shocked by the anti-Semitism he witnessed in France during the Dreyfus case, he decided that Jews could only be safe if they had a land of their own. Though faced with strong opposition, with questions from the brilliant thinker Aḥad Ha-am, and with divisions within the Zionist movement, Herzl almost single-handedly created the World Zionist Organization and began the chain of events which led to the creation of the State of Israel.*

15

The Golden Land

Millions of Jews could not wait for Herzl's dream of a national homeland to come true. Crushed by poverty and government oppression, they looked to the New World for refuge.

South American settlements

Some were able to find homes in South America, thanks to the charity of a German Jew, the Baron de Hirsch. Hirsch built his huge fortune by investing in European railroads, and gave more than $100 million to charities—particularly to the rescue of Eastern European Jewry. First he offered to set up craft and agricultural schools in Russia to improve the lives of the Jews there; but czarist officials refused to allow Hirsch to do this. So Hirsch decided that the only solution was for every Jew to leave.

With $10 million of his own money, Hirsch established the Jewish Colonization Association, hoping to resettle many Russian Jews on farms in Argentina. But only a handful of Russian Jews were willing to leave their cities to try their luck on South American farmland. Baron de Hirsch was disappointed. His high hopes vanished, but several Jewish farm colonies were successfully begun. A new wave of immigrants came after World War I and Argentina grew to have, today, the fifth largest Jewish community in the world (after the United States, Israel, the Soviet Union, and France).

The flood of immigrants

The goal of the vast majority of East European Jews, however, was to reach the "Golden Land"—the United States.

The Jews were not unique in this respect. The late nineteenth century was a period when Europeans of many religions flooded into America. America wanted workers, and there were few limits on immigration. The newcomers only had to register at receiving centers, where they were tested for disease; but 99 percent passed the examinations and were allowed into the country. Irish and Scandinavians, Italians and Greeks joined the Eastern Europeans (both Jewish and Gentile) in the increasingly crowded slums of the eastern port cities. Large as the Jewish group was (between 1880 and 1924 some 2,378,-000 of our people came to America) it made up only 8 percent of the total immigration to the United States during that period.

Yet if the Jewish migration was not unique in size, it was special in two ways. First, fully 20 percent of world Jewry came to America—one out of every five Jews. Thus, the beginning of our century saw a major movement of our people from Eastern Europe to the United States.

Second, most Jews were forced to leave their European homes forever. Members of some other groups came to America to earn money and return to the Old World. For the Jewish immigrants this was impossible. Once they came to America, there was no turning back.

From Eastern Europe to the Lower East Side

The first task for the new immigrants was to create a community in which they could feel at home. The Lower East Side of Manhattan (where nearly three-quarters of the Jewish immigrants settled) and, to a lesser extent, downtown sections of other American cities took on the noisy, hectic air of the shtetl.

The center of Jewish life in America was, as it had been in Europe, the synagogue. The immigrants organized small Orthodox SHULS, each of which served refugees from a particular town or region. The shuls were usually small, crowded, and unattractive, but they gave the worshippers a chance to pray together with old friends, and to gossip about the old country and old times. By 1916, New York alone had more than 500 of these little synagogues.

The immigrants spoke Yiddish, so there was an explosion of Yiddish culture. Five Yiddish daily newspapers were founded, together reaching more than half a million people a day. The largest and most important was the *Forward*, a socialist paper

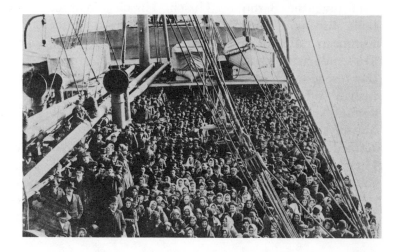

More than 2 million European Jewish immigrants steamed across the Atlantic into New York Harbor on crowded ocean liners like this one.

The Lower East Side of Manhattan was like a city within a city, where a rich Yiddish culture helped the new-comers cope with the grim world of slums and sweatshops.

which at its peak had eleven local and regional editions reaching as far west as Chicago.

There was also a rich diet of Yiddish literature, scholarly Yiddish lectures, and, somewhat later, Yiddish films and radio programs. In 1931 the *Forward* created in New York the world's first and only full-time Yiddish radio station.

The Yiddish theater

Perhaps the immigrant's greatest love was the Yiddish theater.

The first modern Yiddish theatrical troupe was created by Abraham Gold-faden in his native Rumania in 1876. For seven years his company toured Europe with much success. Then, after the czar-ist government banned performances in Yiddish, Goldfaden came to America.

As the "Father of the Yiddish Theater," Goldfaden was actor, producer, and play-wright. His company presented dramas which mixed scenes of immigrant life in America with flashbacks to the "old coun-try." In addition, Goldfaden put on operas and light operettas. Since he was not a trained musician, he wrote by borrowing melodies from the synagogue ritual or taking tunes from well-known European operas! This was hardly great art, but it was very popular—and the simple, sentimental tales were just what the audience wanted.

When the number of Yiddish theaters increased, quality also improved. Fine writers like Sholem Aleichem (who spent his last years in America) wrote for the Yiddish stage. In 1918 an actor named Maurice Schwartz founded the Yiddish Art Theater. He went on to produce more than 150 plays, including not only Yiddish works but also international classics like the works of Shakespeare in Yiddish translation.

Slums and sweatshops

The joys of Yiddish were a welcome escape from the hardships of daily life.

The Germans who arrived during the 1840's found small towns growing rapidly in the South and Midwest, and moved into these communities with ease. For the Eastern European immigrants of the 1880's, however, the only work was in large city industries. The jobs paid poorly, and the workers were forced to live in dreadful slums. To make matters worse, the Russian immigrants had to do more than support themselves: they had to save enough money to bring all their loved ones to America, for those Jews who remained in Russia faced the constant threat of pogroms.

Many thousands of Jews found jobs in the "needle trades," making ready-to-wear clothing. The working conditions were truly hideous. Factory buildings were overcrowded and unsafe. One factory fire alone brought a horrible death to 146 workers. More often, a clothing firm was not in a factory at all, but was a small business operating in a slum—perhaps not even a separate shop, but just a corner of a Jewish home. As many as a dozen people might be jammed into a tiny, dirty room. Because such places felt like ovens in the heat of a New York summer, they became known as "sweatshops"—though they were freezing cold in winter. When business was at its height, men, women, and children worked sixteen hours a day, five or six days a week.

The struggle for workers' rights began almost immediately. Labor unions were organized to demand decent treatment, and to organize strikes when demands were not met. One of the leaders of this movement was Samuel Gompers, a Jewish cigar maker from England who founded the American Federation of Labor (AFL). Today, joined with the Congress of Industrial Organizations in the AFL-CIO, it represents some 17 million workers—by far the largest group of its kind in America.

Uptowners and downtowners

The established Jewish community was startled by the flood of penniless Jewish immigrants. Well-to-do Jews soon deserted the Lower East Side, leaving it to the new arrivals. The wealthier Jews moved to better homes uptown. Thus there developed in New York (and in other Jewish communities) two separate groups. The "uptowners" were prosperous, Americanized, and of German (or sometimes Sephardic) origin. Most were Reform Jews. The "downtowners," on the other hand, were poor and Eastern European. Many of the downtowners were either old-fashioned in outlook and rigidly Orthodox in religious practice, or eager to establish a socialist government and frankly non-religious.

The uptowners had little understanding or affection for their poor relations downtown—but they felt responsible for their fellow Jews. The established Jewish community organized to provide the help which the immigrants desperately needed.

As early as 1882, the Young Men's Hebrew Association in New York set up a downtown branch with classes in Americanization, English for foreigners, and related subjects. Fathers and sons could sit side by side, learning their ABC's together. Hebrew Relief Societies were set up in dozens of cities, giving aid to families in need. New organizations such as the Council Education Alliance in Cleveland, the Jewish People's Institute in Chicago, and the Abraham Lincoln School in Milwaukee offered the newcomers classes in Western art, music, health education, and even sports.

One of the most lasting and important of these institutions was the Education Alliance in New York. Among those who studied there were David Sarnoff, a pioneer in radio and television broadcasting; Eddie Cantor, a comedian who also worked tirelessly offstage for the poor, the sick (he helped found the March of Dimes), and the State of Israel; George Gershwin, a composer whose musical masterpieces include *Rhapsody in Blue* and *Porgy and Bess;* and well-known artists like Sir Jacob Epstein and Ben Shahn.

Emma Lazarus

The religious devotion and deep Jewish commitment shown by so many of the

Emma Lazarus, whose poem "The New Colossus" is inscribed at the base of the Statue of Liberty, at the entrance to New York Harbor.

newcomers also had an effect on the uptowners. One of them was a remarkable woman: the poet Emma Lazarus.

For the first thirty years of her life, Emma Lazarus showed little concern for her Jewish heritage, either in her life or in her poetry. But as she read of the Russian persecutions and saw the refugees arriving in New York, her thinking began to change. She gave of her time to teach the immigrants, and began writing original works on Jewish themes.

She studied Hebrew so that she could translate the poems of Solomon ibn Gabirol and Judah ha-Levi into English. Her most famous poem, "The New Colossus," which speaks of the Statue of Liberty as the symbol of hope for the oppressed, was inspired by the Eastern Europeans she saw arriving at Ellis Island, the receiving station in New York harbor.

Moreover, she became a Zionist even before there was an organized Zionist movement. She died tragically at the early age of thirty-eight in 1887, seven years before the Dreyfus affair, but she had already become the first American to appeal for funds to create Jewish colonies in Palestine. One of her poems sounds today like a prophetic call to arms for Theodor Herzl:

O for Jerusalem's trumpet now,
　To blow a blast of shattering power,
To wake the sleepers high and low,
　And rouse them to the urgent hour! . . .

Let but an Ezra arise anew,
To lift the Banner of the Jew!

A rage, a mock at first—erelong,
　When men have bled and women wept,
To guard its precious folds from wrong,
　Even they who shrunk, even they who slept,
Shall leap to bless it, and to save.
Strike! for the brave revere the brave!

Conservative Judaism

The Zionism for which Emma Lazarus longed would later become a powerful force in America. For the newcomers, however, the problem was not how to create a Jewish state. It was how to adjust to life in the United States! The difficulties were great, especially for children who wanted to adopt a modern American lifestyle but whose parents still held to the ways of the shtetl. These tensions tore some families apart. Young people turned their backs on the ways of the "old country," sometimes rejecting the most basic values of Judaism.

Yet among these young people—and sometimes even more strongly among their children—there often remained a deep desire for Jewish life. They did not believe in the ways of Orthodoxy, and many could not accept the ways of Reform.* Fortunately, these Jews found a new movement which allowed religious change but which was basically traditional in practice. This movement was Conservative Judaism.

Conservative Judaism could trace its origins to Zacharias Frankel's work in the 1840's (see Chapter 6); its American roots reached back to 1886, when the Jewish Theological Seminary was founded as a school for traditional rabbis. But the movement really began in 1901—the year Solomon Schechter agreed to become president of the Seminary.

Schechter was the scholar who discovered the Cairo GENIZAH (גְּנִיזָה), the hiding place for old manuscripts in the Cairo synagogue. (See Volume One, Chapter 11.) He could have spent the rest of his life sorting, translating, and studying these manuscripts—there were more than 200,000 pages, some of them 1000 years old. Yet when Schechter was asked to come and teach in America, he seized on this chance

　. . . to establish a training school for Rabbis which, adopting what is best in modern thought but at the same time teaching traditional Judaism in such a manner as to awaken fresh interest in our glorious past, should create a Conservative School removed alike from both extremes of Radical Reform and Hyper-Orthodoxy.

---

* During this period, some Reform congregations were moving to extremes, even holding Shabbat services on Sunday mornings. Reform returned to more traditional practices after World War I.

Famous in England for his work on the documents of the Cairo genizah, Solomon Schechter became known in America as a founder of Conservative Judaism.

Under Schechter, Conservative Judaism developed as a separate branch of our religion. The United Synagogue of America, the union of Conservative congregations which he founded in 1913, became the fastest-growing Jewish organization in America. In the 1970's, it included more than 850 congregations with a combined membership of over 1,500,000.

The rapid growth of Conservative Judaism showed how quickly the immigrants adjusted to American life. Within a single generation, they stopped living in the world of the Middle Ages and began living in the twentieth century. They worked and studied their way out of the slums, becoming members of the middle class.

Much was lost in the midst of this rapid change: the great loss of Yiddish culture is only now being widely felt. But something new and remarkable had been built. New York City became the largest Jewish community in history. And the Jewish population in America, though still small, was large enough to have an important effect on the life of the United States.

SUMMARY *Although some Jews settled in South America, most of those who left Eastern Europe came to the United States. Here they developed a thriving Yiddish culture. Life was hard in the slums and sweatshops of America's port cities, but the newcomers were helped by—and had an important effect on—the Jewish community already in the United States, which now included many well-to-do "uptowners." There were great pressures to Americanize, and many Jews broke away from traditional Judaism. Solomon Schecter's Conservative movement helped hundreds of thousands of them return to their heritage.*

16

New Leaders, New Opportunities

Even as millions of Jews were coming to America, Jewish immigration to Palestine was also increasing. From 1904 to 1914—a decade known as the Second Aliyah—more than 35,000 Jews went from Eastern Europe to the Holy Land.

Like their friends and relatives heading to the United States, these Jews wanted to escape pogroms and persecution. And they felt they had a special reason for choosing the hard life of Eretz Yisrael over the dream of wealth in the New World: a desire to preserve Zionism even after the death of Herzl.

Building a new life

Many also wanted to create a new way of life for our people. In Russia, most Jews had lived by serving strangers (often as innkeepers), or by selling the products of strangers (as merchants). The young immigrants to Palestine wanted to prove that they could support themselves, care for each other, and grow their own food. To do this they created a new type of settlement, the KEVUTZAH (קְבוּצָה), based on the socialist idea that each person should work as much as he or she can, and receive from the group as much as he or she needs. From the success of the kevutzah sprang the KIBBUTZ (קִבּוּץ), a collective farming village guided by the same spirit of total equality.

Early in the Second Aliyah, in September 1906, a short, bushy-haired twenty-year-old arrived in Palestine. He immediately went to Petah Tikvah, a settlement seven miles east of the sand dunes where Tel Aviv would be founded in 1909, and began a lifelong dedication to farm labor. He also continued the active political life which he had begun in Russian Poland. There he had been called David Gruen, but in the Holy Land he adopted a Hebrew name, one which became famous long before he was chosen to be the first prime minister of the State of Israel. That new name was David Ben-Gurion.

Jacob Schiff

Two months after Ben-Gurion arrived in Palestine, the leading Jews of America met in the New York mansion of Jacob Schiff.

Schiff came to America from Germany in 1865, when he was only eighteen, and within twenty years had become one of the leading figures on Wall Street. Through brilliant investments, particularly in railroads, he made his banking firm one of the two largest in the country. In the first five years of this century, its sales had a value of more than $175 *billion*!

Even while building his financial empire, Schiff remained deeply involved in Jewish life. He established the Judaica collections at the Library of Congress in Washington and at the New York Public Library. He was a major supporter of the Jewish Publication Society, which was and continues to be an important publisher of Jewish books in English. And, though Schiff was a Reform Jew and a supporter of the Hebrew Union College, it was he who helped reorganize the Jewish Theological Seminary and invited Solomon Schechter to be its president—key events in the growth of Conservative Judaism.

Schiff also supported the printing of the English–language *Jewish Encyclopedia*, not only the first major scholarly work on Judaism produced in America, but also the largest and finest work of its kind to appear in any language up to that time. The encylopedia, edited by a German immigrant named Isidore Singer, was so outstanding that even today it remains an excellent source of information.

Schiff was also concerned with Jewish politics. During the Russian pogroms, he helped collect vast sums to aid victims of the massacres. During the Russo-Japanese War, his company raised $200 million for Japan to fight the anti-Semitic government of czarist Russia.

American Jewish Committee

It was for political reasons that the German-Jewish leaders met at Schiff's New York home. There they agreed to

Does the young man in the center look familiar to you? He's David Ben-Gurion, in a photograph taken about forty years before he became Israel's first prime minister.

Kevutzah, Kibbutz, Moshav

Young kibbutzim.

A kevutzah is a small collective farm. A kibbutz is a collective village which may include industry along with farming; as a rule, kibbutzim are larger than kevutzot. Both are based on the same ideals of shared wealth and political freedom that have been preached, but never practiced, in Communist countries.

A third kind of settlement, the moshav (מוֹשָׁב), has been popular with immigrants coming to Israel since 1948. Like the kevutzot, most moshavim are devoted to farming. Members cooperate in buying and using heavy equipment and in selling their crops. The major difference is that while members of a kevutzah own and operate one large piece of property, families belonging to a moshav live and work separately on their own small plots of land.

form an organization to protect the rights of Jews in the United States and throughout the world. They called this organization the AMERICAN JEWISH COMMITTEE (AJC).

Within five years the AJC had scored its first great triumph: convincing the United States to revoke a seventy-year-old treaty.

When American Jews visited Russia, they received the same humiliating treatment the czars gave their own Jewish subjects. But this violated a trade agreement between Russia and the United States which had been signed in 1832 and which required that all visiting Americans be treated equally. President William Howard Taft knew that the Russians were acting unfairly, but he was afraid to take any action which might endanger the millions of dollars of business between the two countries.

The American Jewish Committee publicly insisted that the rights of Americans were more important than money. Every person carrying a United States passport deserved equal protection from the Ameri-can government, said the AJC. No foreign state should be allowed to say that some American citizens were acceptable and some were not.

The U.S. Congress fully supported this position by an amazing vote of 300 to 1 in the House of Representatives and 72 to 0 in the Senate. As a result, President Taft ended America's treaty with Russia. This set a precedent which has been used by the United States government on other occasions to protect both Jews and other minority groups.

Joint relief efforts

The American Jewish Committee also gave charity to the needy. It helped rebuild Jewish institutions destroyed by earthquakes in San Francisco and in Italy, aided the victims of Russian pogroms, and fed starving Jews in Persia.

But World War I created a need for relief funds far greater than any single organization could provide. Because Eastern Europe was a major battleground, many

Jews who still lived there were left homeless and desperate. Moreover, the war cut off the Jews in the Holy Land from their supporters in Europe; thus, almost as soon as fighting broke out, the Jews of Eretz Yisrael were faced with the threat of mass starvation.

To meet these needs, the AJC combined its relief efforts with those of Orthodox and labor groups to form the AMERICAN JEWISH JOINT DISTRIBUTION COMMITTEE —popularly called "Joint." Through Joint, American Jewry for the first time took a commanding role in world Jewish affairs. By 1918, Joint was distributing $16 million a year, the largest privately financed program of rescue and reconstruction up to that time. (The work Joint did during and after World War II was even greater, and Joint continues today to serve our people through funds raised by the United Jewish Appeal.)

Jews in World War I

Four percent of America's soldiers in World War I were Jewish, though Jews were only 3 percent of the total population. In all, there were some 200,000 Jewish soldiers—more than the entire Jewish population of the United States at the time of the Civil War! Jews also helped in the American war effort by serving on the War Industries Board.

Although the United States issued a bold declaration of war, the nation was far from ready for combat: the armed forces did not have enough equipment for a major campaign. To meet this emergency, the government set up a commission to tell American industry how to produce the needed weapons and supplies. Of the seven

men named to this commission, three were Jews: Samuel Gompers, president of the American Federation of Labor; Julius Rosenwald, president of Sears, Roebuck, and Company; and Bernard Baruch, a self-made millionaire from New York.

Baruch had expert knowledge of raw materials and was brilliant at organization. Soon he became chairman of the War Industries Board. In this post, he held vast power over the American economy.

Under the leadership of Baruch and the other members of the Board, civilian industries were converted to wartime use. Piano factories turned out airplane wings, and 75,000 tons of tin were saved by not making toy wagons for children. Because of this kind of creative thinking and clever planning, American industry broke all production records, and American power reached Europe in time to bring victory to the Allies.

There were also Jews fighting against the Allies. Since there was no specifically Jewish issue in World War I (as there would be in World War II), the Jews of Germany and Austria quite naturally supported their own countries. Just as Bernard Baruch directed American industry, a Jew named Walter Rathenau organized the production of German war materials, preventing his nation from being defeated early in the conflict.

Rathenau was a chemist and industrialist. In peacetime, he had been a man of deep human feelings. He wrote on philosophy and politics, calling for a society of justice and equality. Following the war, he served as foreign minister of the new German republic, and did much to restore the honor of his country—until he was shot and killed in 1922 by German anti-Semites.

Chaim Weizmann

Of all the Jews who took part in World War I, surely the most important from the viewpoint of Jewish history was Chaim Weizmann. To tell his story, however, we must turn back the clock to 1906, when David Ben-Gurion was beginning a new life in Palestine and the American Jewish Committee was forming in New York.

Weizmann was only in his early thirties, but he was already a famous chemist and had been invited to teach in England at Manchester University. By 1906 he had been in Britain less than two years, and his English was far from perfect. Still, because he was a leader in the Zionist movement, the English statesman Arthur James Balfour asked Weizmann to explain why the Zionists had refused to accept Britain's offer of Uganda as a temporary homeland for the Jews.

Balfour hoped to convince Weizmann that the Zionists were wrong. Instead, Weizmann convinced Balfour that Palestine was the only possible homeland for the Jews! From that day on, Balfour became a committed Zionist.

Weizmann became well-known in Britain through his skills as a chemist. World War I had hardly begun when England was faced with a shortage of a basic ingredient of ammunition: acetone. Weizmann solved this problem by finding a way to make the chemical from corn and chestnuts. By this method he was able to use materials that were common in Britain to keep naval guns armed and active.

Partly because of his fame as a chemist, Weizmann was able to win leading British Gentiles, as well as certain prominent Jews, to the Zionist banner. Herbert Samuel, the first professing Jew to be a member of the British cabinet, supported Zionism. So did Lord Walter Rothschild, the unofficial leader of British Jewry.

But there were those against Zionism among the Jewish people. Even many who supported Jewish *settlements* in Palestine saw the idea of a Jewish *state* as a threat. Anti-Semites had been arguing for years that Jews were disloyal outsiders just waiting for a chance to desert their Diaspora homes and run off to the Holy Land. A Jewish nation might be taken as proof of such disloyalty. It might serve as an excuse for governments to take away the rights which the Jews in Western Europe had won so recently.

The Balfour Declaration

It was a strange moment in history. Through the work of Weizmann and other Zionists, Britain's Gentile government was ready to recognize Jewish rights in the land of Israel. But it could not do so because of a small but influential group of Jews! The deadlock was not broken until the president of the United States, Woodrow Wilson, cabled the British government with America's support of the Zionist goal. Finally, on November 2, 1917, Lord Balfour issued a letter which declared:

> His Majesty's Government view with favour the establishment in Palestine of a national home for the Jewish people. . . .

This BALFOUR DECLARATION signaled the start of a British military campaign in Palestine led by Lord Edmund Allenby. Among his troops were members of the "Jewish Legion," a group of volunteers from England, the United States, Canada, and Palestine. On the first day of Hanukkah in 1917, Lord Allenby's forces entered

Abba Eban Remembers:
Chaim Weizmann

Chaim Weizmann
(1874–1952).

There is no doubt at all that it was Chaim Weizmann, more than any other man, who changed the course of Jewish history by obtaining recognition of the principle of Jewish statehood long before we had any real strength to show for our work in Eretz Yisrael. There were only a few thousand Jews there. We had little physical or economic strength. We couldn't seriously threaten anybody or penalize any government that sought to oppose us. It can be said of Chaim Weizmann that no other statesman ever achieved such great ends with such limited means at his disposal. Whereas Ben-Gurion secured recognition of Israel's achievements, Weizmann had the more difficult task of getting the world to accept Jewish statehood on the basis of a hope and a dream.

As a very young worker in the Zionist Political Office, I had close contact with Weizmann, then at the height of his power and prestige. It was not easy to work with him because he only had two moods: one was unlimited ecstasy and the other was unlimited depression. He passed from one to the other without any visible transition, and when we who worked for him used to set out for the office in the morning, we would never know precisely in what mood we would find him.

It is fitting that Chaim Weizmann became the first president of our state. It is very difficult for later generations to have any idea of the special air of majesty that he diffused around himself. One of his devices for promoting a Jewish state was to behave as though it already existed. For many decades preceding Israel's statehood, he went around London and other major capitals as though he was already a head of state engaged in a permanent summit mission. His dignity, his tall, commanding appearance, his social grace, and the deep passion of his advocacy all lent credibility to the idea. The fact is that Israel had a president before it even had a state.

Jerusalem. Only one month after the Balfour Declaration, Judea was liberated.

But while this military triumph was important, the Balfour Declaration itself was the great Jewish victory of the period—indeed, it was the key diplomatic victory for the Jewish people in modern times. To claim, as Weizmann and Balfour did, that the Jewish people had the right to build a national home in Palestine was to challenge all the facts and traditions of international law. Nobody knew what a "national

After World War II, the Joint Distribution Committee helped thousands of refugees like these fulfill their dream of emigrating to Israel.

home" really was. The "Jewish people" was not a group that was legally recognized anywhere. There was not even such a country as "Palestine"; there was only the southern district of Syria, which, at the time of the Balfour Declaration, was under the rule of the Ottoman Turks.

Weizmann's power came from his ability to see, and to show others, that the needs of Jewish history must overcome the obstacles of "reasonable" thinking. Moreover, he was able to imagine what the national home might be—a land of the Jewish spirit as well as of the Jewish people. As he wrote in his autobiography:

Whether prophets will once more arise among the Jews in the near future is difficult to say. But if they choose the way of honest and hard and clean living, on the land in settlements built on the old principles, and in cities cleansed of the dross which has been sometimes mistaken for civilization; if they center their activities on genuine values, whether in industry, agriculture, science, literature, or art; then God will look down benignly on His children who after a long wandering have come home to serve Him with a psalm on their lips and a spade in their hands, reviving their old country and making it a center of human civilization.

SUMMARY   *The early years of the twentieth century saw a wave of immigration to the land of Israel (which included a future prime minister, David Ben-Gurion), and efforts in America to defend Jewish rights, especially through the formation of the American Jewish Committee. Jews in the United States, in Germany, and in Palestine played important roles in World War I. Most important was Chaim Weizmann, whose efforts, both political and professional, persuaded the British government to issue the Balfour Declaration, calling for the establishment of a Jewish homeland in Palestine.*

PART FIVE

Depression and World Conflict

Holocaust and Rebirth

There are, of course, hundreds of thousands of Israelis who experienced the Holocaust personally: people who fled from concentration camps and who still have tattooed numbers on their arms, and people who escaped from Nazi-occupied Europe as children but who still carry the horrifying memories of the slaughter and plunder to which European Jews were subjected. For many Israelis, however, the Holocaust has been lived not as a personal experience but as a national memory.

Those of us who were already in Israel between 1941 and 1945 were, strangely enough, living in one of the more serene and secure areas of the world. Palestine itself was not very close to the front. The general comforts and amenities were greater than in many of the more advanced countries of Europe and the Mediterranean. The perils we endured were not personal but national.

I shall never forget how the first news of the Holocaust began to seep into Jerusalem in 1941 and 1942. The stories were so hair-raising that at first there was a tendency to think they were

The Polish artist Maurycy Gottlieb was still a young man
when he painted his masterpiece, "Day of Atonement in the
Synagogue." And yet he had only a few months left to live.
By 1879, when Gottlieb died at the age of twenty-three,
Jews had been living in Poland for more than six centuries.
But for Polish Jewry also, time was running out.

---

exaggerated. Eventually, however, and certainly by the beginning of
1943, there was no room for doubt that the Nazis planned to
exterminate the Jewish communities of Europe. There was, for us, a
curious sense of contrast between the sunshine and freedom of Tel
Aviv, Jerusalem, and Haifa, and the knowledge that our brethren in
Europe were being subjected to the worst hatred and violence that
had ever been visited on any family of the human race.

In April 1945, when news of the Allied victory in Europe reached us
in Jerusalem, there was a brief night of dancing in the streets. And
yet our celebration was overshadowed by gathering clouds. We had
the feeling that as soon as the sound of victory died away, we would
face two traumatic experiences. First the curtain would go up,
showing us the full horror of what had happened to our people in
Europe. Next, with the common enemy of Hitlerism absent, the
Jewish population of Palestine and the British government would
pass from uneasy truce into open conflict. The danger of German
conquest had been pushed out of our minds, but the perils of a clash
with the British and the Arabs had come closer.

ABBA EBAN

The two insets offer charming glimpses of Jewish life
in Poland before the Holocaust. Above, a band of
musicians from Galicia; below, a heder for girls in 1910.
The scene at left, based on a familiar photograph,
shows Eastern European Jews seeming ill at ease and out
of place in the forward-looking Vienna of 1915.

Warsaw was never known as a great center of Jewish culture.
During the Holocaust, however, the Warsaw Ghetto became a symbol
of the Jewish resistance against the Nazis (see Chapter 20).
In today's Poland, all that remains of the heroic Warsaw Ghetto
uprising are memories, some documents, and this monument,
completed by a sculptor named Rapaport in 1948. The ghetto area
has been turned into an apartment house complex by the Polish
government, which, during several waves of official anti-Semitism,
managed to shut down the few Jewish cultural institutions that
sprang up in Warsaw when World War II ended.

17

INTRODUCTION TO PART FIVE:

Depression and World Conflict

The strange little Austrian looked around his prison cell. Clearly the man was a misfit. He had dropped out of school at the age of sixteen, and never held a job for any length of time. Yet he was filled with supreme confidence in his own genius. He wrote a book, which he called *Mein Kampf* ("My Struggle"), to teach the world his ideas:

> Mankind has grown great in eternal struggle, and only in eternal peace does it perish.

> The stronger must dominate and not blend with the weaker, thus sacrificing his own greatness. Only the born weakling can view this as cruel.

> Those who want to live, let them fight; those who do not want to fight, in this world of eternal struggle, do not deserve to live.

He wanted to lead Germany in this "eternal struggle." He promised to do away with democracy, which he hated.

Next he would conquer France, "the mortal enemy of the German people." Then he would expand eastward, largely at the expense of Russia. The pure German people—"the Aryan race"—would dominate Europe. Inferiors such as Jews and Slavs would not be allowed to mix or breed with the master race.

Although *Mein Kampf* became a bestseller and made its author a millionaire, it was ignored or laughed at in the Western democracies. This proved disastrous, for the book was a blueprint for the bloodiest decades in human history.

The author of *Mein Kampf* was Adolf Hitler.

Legacies of World War I

Hitler was able to come to power and begin World War II partly because of the treaties which ended World War I. The victorious Allies in 1918 required Germany to pay huge amounts in war damages. The Belgians, for example, asked for a sum larger than the entire wealth of Belgium! Germany was made to accept guilt not only for starting World War I but also for all the damage caused by both sides. This idea was so grossly unfair that no reasonable German leader could be found to sign the documents based on it.

The treaties also posed other problems. The map of Europe was redrawn to give each people its own state. Old empires were swept away, leaving new (or re-created) states such as Czechoslovakia, Yugoslavia, Poland, and Lithuania. Yet these new countries were not truly based on national cultures—for example, a large number of German-speaking people suddenly found themselves in the new Czechoslovakia.

Finally, the American President Woodrow Wilson called for complete world disarmament, and for a world council—the League of Nations—to take charge of the newly peaceful planet. Instead of following his noble ideals, the Western democracies forced Germany to give up its weapons, while keeping their own armed forces. Worst of all, the League of Nations was weak and ineffective. Germany was not allowed to join until 1926, Russia until 1934. And the United States never joined.

The fact that the United States refused to belong to an organization proposed by an American president showed how much the country wanted to stay out of the affairs of Europe. One war had been enough. There was a deep feeling in the United States—as well as in Britain and France—that if each nation minded its own business, the world would take care of itself.

Indeed, during the first years after the war, the Allies found little to worry about. Business was good, and new developments like the automobile, commercial air service, and motion pictures brought pleasure and excitement to millions. America passed through the giddy age known as the "Roaring Twenties."

In Germany, things were quite different. Inflation was so great that paper money became all but worthless. By the end of 1923, it took more than four *trillion* German marks to equal a dollar, and people had to carry suitcases full of cash in order to pay for their groceries. It was during this period of chaos that Hitler tried to overthrow the German republic, was sent to prison, and wrote *Mein Kampf*.

Unemployed Germans line up for free soup in Berlin in 1930. Hitler exploited the economic hardships of the Great Depression to catapult himself into power.

British Prime Minister Neville Chamberlain hoped to avoid war by letting Hitler take what he wanted.

Depression—and the rise of Hitler

When he was released in 1925, life in Germany had begun to improve, and Hitler's political party—the NAZI party *—received little support.

Then came 1929, and the world economy collapsed in the Great Depression. The value of shares on American stock exchanges dropped so rapidly that fortunes were wiped out almost overnight. Similar disasters struck Europe. Business activity nearly ground to a halt, and millions of people lost their jobs. Everywhere there was a cry for quick, simple solutions to the crisis.

In Germany, Hitler and his followers suddenly enjoyed widespread popularity. Hitler's ideas were simple enough for everyone to understand, and his promise of

---

* A contraction of the party's full name: National Socialist (in German, NAtionalsoZIalistiche) German Workers' Party.

greatness for Germany and the Germans gave hope to those who had lost it. In the next national election the Nazis became the second largest political party in the country. In January 1933, Hitler—who a year before had not even been a German citizen—was named chancellor (prime minister) of Germany.

Working with a ruthless disregard for law and ethics, he moved to increase his power. He arranged to have the German parliament building set on fire, blamed the Communists for this crime, and used the fire as an excuse to unleash a campaign of terror against all non-Nazi parties.

By the autumn of 1934, Adolf Hitler was the absolute dictator of Germany.

World War II

Still following the plan he had outlined in *Mein Kampf*, Hitler rearmed Germany and took control of Austria. Then he pretended that he wanted to "free" the Germans living under Czech rule—and conquered the whole of Czechoslovakia.

France and Britain did nothing to stop Hitler. They were terrified of another war. (France alone had lost nearly 1,400,000 men in World War I.) Hitler played on their fears in a masterful way. Time after time he threatened to fight if his demands were not met. Time after time Britain and France gave him what he wanted, hoping each time that he would finally be satisfied.

The tragedy is that, during most of this time, Germany was too weak to go to war. If the great democracies had only found the courage to stand up to Hitler, he would have been forced to back down. Instead, he was allowed to gain the strength with which he nearly conquered the world.

When he had fully rearmed his country, Hitler turned to the east. He signed a treaty with the Soviet Union guaranteeing that if he did not attack Russia, Russia would stay out of any war he might begin.* Hitler then felt free to launch a full-scale attack on Poland on September 1, 1939.

At last Britain and France declared war on Germany—but they had waited too long. Poland was overrun in three weeks. Denmark was attacked, and surrendered in two hours. Norway, the Low Countries, and France were rapidly conquered. World War II was only ten months old when Hitler controlled most of Europe.

It was not until two years later that Germany and its ally Japan made their critical mistakes. On December 7, 1941, Japan bombed the American naval base at Pearl Harbor, Hawaii, bringing the United States into the war. That same month, Hitler sent his troops into the U.S.S.R. despite the harsh Russian winter. Like Napoleon some 130 years earlier, Hitler found his army crippled by the combination of Russian bravery and bitter cold.

* Russia was to pay for its cowardice, for two years later Hitler did invade the Soviet Union and Russia suffered more war dead than any other nation.

Gradually the forces of the United States and Russia, along with those of the gallant British army, turned the tide of battle. By the summer of 1944, the Allied victory over the Nazis was only a matter of time. Nevertheless, Hitler refused to surrender, preferring to see his country destroyed than to admit defeat. Only when Russian troops had come within a few blocks of his hideout did he kill himself. Eight days later, on May 8, 1945, the war in Europe was over.

The loss of life in World War II was such as the earth had never seen. At least 15 million soldiers died, and the total of war dead may have reached 40 million.

One group was singled out for slaughter simply because of Hitler's insane hatred. His dream of conquering the world was coupled with the desire of a madman to destroy the entire Jewish people. How close he came to achieving this goal is well known. Here we must tell how the nations of the world permitted him to proceed, almost unopposed, with the most ghastly act of inhumanity that history has ever known.

SUMMARY   *Adolf Hitler announced his plans to conquer the world in his book* Mein Kampf, *but the leaders of other nations refused to take his threats seriously until it was too late. Hitler seized power in Germany during the Great Depression, rearmed the country, and plunged the globe into World War II. Though the war was destructive to many nations and cost many lives, it was disastrous for the Jews, who were singled out by Hitler for mass destruction.*

18

Prelude to Disaster

A Jew named Leo Frank was convicted of strangling a fourteen-year-old girl. The evidence against him was weak—years later his name was cleared of the crime. Nevertheless, a group of men broke into his prison cell, drove him 125 miles to the town where the girl had been born and buried, threw a noose around his neck, and hanged him.

This lynching did not occur in Nazi Germany. It took place in America—near Atlanta, Georgia—in 1915. It was part of a serious wave of anti-Semitism which occurred in the United States at the beginning of World War I.

Anti-Semitism in America

Newspapers were filled with job advertisements saying "For Christians Only" or "Only Christians Need Apply." Banks, insurance companies, and public utilities followed anti-Jewish policies. After the Great Depression began in 1929 and still fewer jobs were available, Jews could hardly find employment.

Jews who applied to college faced special rules and quotas. Only a small number of Jews would be allowed to enter a school, regardless of how many were well qualified to attend. This quota system was most harsh at medical schools, forcing many Jews who wished to become doctors to go to schools in Europe. When they returned home, they found that few Jews were being allowed to serve in hospitals—even hospitals operated by the government.

Teachers had an even harder time. Most college and university jobs were closed to Jews. Men and women who wanted to teach in public schools could rarely find jobs, except in large cities where positions were filled through examinations open to all. Even there, examiners sometimes gave failing marks to Jews for the slightest mistake.

Help Wanted Women—Agencies

NATIONAL

EMPOYMENT EXCHANGE
30 Church St.,- 7th Floor
Hudson Terminal Building

"Specializing in Outstanding Personnel"

INTERVIEWS
Mon.-Fri., 9-2; Sat.. 9-12
appointment for those
now employed

Radio City—42nd St. Area
MULTIg.; kn. mineog.-address, Chr $23
STENO, charge small office, to 27
 years, Christian 5 day week...$20
STENO-Recept; to 26, nice appear.$20
DICT, Op, 2 yr. exp, pleasant off..$20
ASST. Bkpr., Mt. Vernon, Chr...$20'
RECEP-Steno, monitor bd., Chr..$20
STENO, knowl. bkpg, Chr....$18-20
STENO; will teach switchbd, Chr .$18
TYPIST-Clk, bright begin. consid.$70
STENO, knowl. bkpg;beg. cons Prot $17
Lower Manhattan Area
F. C. BKPr, 28-32, knowledge typing,
 West Side, Chr, 5 day week....$30

Many jobs were closed to Jews between the two World Wars, as a wave of anti-Semitism swept across America.

Hatred of our people reached every level of society. One of the most important figures in anti-Jewish activities between the wars was the millionaire founder of the automobile industry, Henry Ford. He used his wealth to begin a magazine, *The Dearborn Independent*, which he filled with anti-Semitic propaganda. Based on the lies he found in the "Protocols of the Elders of Zion" (see Chapter 13), he claimed that an international Jewish conspiracy was seeking to take over the world. Ford also said that Jews were working fiendishly to undermine American traditions.

In time, Ford came to see that what he had published was false. Other Americans, however, continued to spout similar lies. The most notorious was none other than a Catholic priest, Father Charles E. Coughlin. Every week he reached millions of people through a radio program in which he described how Jews were plotting to conquer the world. He blamed the Jewish people for the Great Depression, and defended Nazi violence against Jews. His magazine, laughably called *Social Justice*, reprinted the "Protocols" with Father Coughlin's own vicious commentary.

Charles A. Lindbergh, who became a national hero in 1927 by piloting the first nonstop solo flight across the Atlantic, was another famous anti-Semite. He called Jews a dangerous group trying to push the United States into war. Lindbergh was still making such charges only three months before the Japanese bombed the American naval base at Pearl Harbor.

A severe blow against the Jewish people was also struck by the United States government. This was a law known as the Johnson Act.

The Johnson Act, passed in 1921 and tightened in 1924, reduced immigration from all countries to the United States to a trickle. Not only did the law limit the total number of immigrants each year to 154,000, but it also set quotas strongly favoring immigrants from Northern and Western Europe over those from Mediterranean, Oriental, or Eastern European countries. The Johnson Act was not specifically anti-Semitic; it did not even mention Jews. But since most of world Jewry lived in Eastern Europe, the effect of the law was to shut these people out of the land which had earlier given refuge to so many others. The "golden door" of which Emma Lazarus had written was all but sealed—and remained so even during the darkest days of the Holocaust.

Jewish achievements

Despite all this, the United States offered our people great opportunities. Large numbers of Jews did go to college, and this education helped our people rise in American society faster than any other immigrant group. Jews became cabinet members and Supreme Court justices. Several thousand leaders of European Jewry managed to escape from Nazi Germany and were allowed to enter the United States. The most famous of these was the great scientist Albert Einstein.

Many Americans spoke out against prejudice. In 1921, 119 leading Americans, including President Wilson and former President Taft, signed a statement calling for an end to anti-Semitism. The National Conference of Christians and Jews was created to work for understanding between all religious groups in America.

Jews in America were free to defend their rights. B'NAI B'RITH, a group founded by German immigrants in 1843 for social activities and public service, set up a new agency called the ANTI-DEFAMATION LEAGUE to protect our people from slander in print, broadcasting, and films. The American Jewish Committee, founded in 1906 (see Chapter 16), took a leading role in the fight against anti-Semitism.

Henry Ford, a pioneer in the mass production and mass marketing of automobiles, was also the publisher of vicious slanders against our people.

Louis Marshall led the fight for equal rights for Jews and other minorities.

President of the AJC during the crucial years from 1912 to 1929 was the leading American Jew of the period, Louis Marshall. This son of German immigrants spoke out against injustice of all kinds. He fought the use of anti-Jewish quotas in American colleges. He took part in the successful campaign against Henry Ford's anti-Semitism. In fact, when Ford was finally convinced that the "Protocols" was a book of foolish lies, it was through Louis Marshall that he issued a public apology to the Jewish people.*

* Marshall was a champion of human rights for all peoples. In addition to his work for Jewish causes, he fought legal battles for the Negro community, and was an active member of the National Association for the Advancement of Colored People (NAACP). As a constitutional lawyer, he successfully defended the right of Catholics to send their children to Church schools. Within the Jewish community he was at the same time president of a Reform congregation (Temple Emanu-El of New York) and chairman of a school for Conservative rabbis (the Jewish Theological Seminary).

While the fight against prejudice went on, Jewish religious life in America continued its creative growth. In 1934 a Conservative rabbi, Dr. Mordecai Kaplan, founded a movement which he called RECONSTRUCTIONISM. He taught that Judaism is more than a religion, it is a complete way of life. He called for a rethinking of Jewish philosophy and tradition, and for the creation of new institutions to adapt the best in American culture for Jewish purposes. The rapid growth of Jewish community centers has been due, in part, to Dr. Kaplan's challenge. In addition, the Reconstructionist movement has developed its own synagogues, rabbinical school, and publications.

There was good and bad in American Jewish life between the two world wars. The law guaranteed equal rights to the Jews, but our people found that they had still to fight for those rights in everyday life. But why have we spoken so much about the unpleasant subject of prejudice in America? For two reasons.

First, it is important to realize that even in America, anti-Semitism is by no means unknown—indeed, it continued to affect U.S. actions throughout World War II. Its power was not shattered until Americans learned of the Holocaust and the horrifying results of Jew-hatred.

Second, seeing how anti-Semitism grew in America helps us to understand how Jew-hatred could spread so rapidly and viciously in Europe, where it had a far longer history.

Persecutions in Eastern Europe

The treaties which ended World War I guaranteed justice to all minority groups in Europe. This was in part because of the work of Jewish leaders—including Louis Marshall—who chose to defend the rights of Jews by seeking liberty for all groups. The treaties promised each minority such rights as using its national language in state-supported schools.

Unfortunately, these promises proved to be empty words. The Eastern European countries accepted them merely to please the victorious Western democracies. Poland, newly reborn after so many years as a conquered nation, quickly subjected Jews to pogroms, quotas, and special high taxes. The Polish government took over those industries in which Jews had a leading role—and fired the Jewish workers. For example, at the beginning of the 1920's Poland had 2800 shops where shoes were made by Jews. Within a few years, most of these were closed. Polish Jews were desperate for a new homeland long before Hitler invaded the country.

Things were no better in Rumania. The government soon turned against the Jews. Many were persecuted or imprisoned. Nothing shows the plight of our people better than the case of a Jewish businessman who built and equipped a fine social center as a gift for the local university. The first step taken by the Rumanian officials was to declare the social center off-limits to all Jewish students.

Jewish life in Germany

It may seem strange, in view of what was to happen, but the country on the European continent where Jews lived best was Germany.

Following World War I, the new German government repealed all the country's anti-Jewish laws. German Jews had already helped their country in many ways, but with this new freedom, their achievements reached a new peak. For example, before 1933 thirty-eight Germans received Nobel Prizes. Of these thirty-eight, eleven were Jews or of Jewish descent. By 1924, nearly 16 percent of all German doctors and 26 percent of all German lawyers were Jewish, though Jews were less than 1 percent of the population. Jews also scored notable successes in other professions.

Though the German Jewish community still leaned toward assimilation, there was also a spiritual revival. Original Jewish art and music were created, and there were new and important Jewish thinkers. Two such men became close friends and co-workers.

They were Martin Buber and Franz Rosenzweig.

Martin Buber

Buber grew up under the watchful eye of his scholarly grandfather, but while the older man studied traditional texts, the younger man turned to the study of Ḥasidism. For most German Jews of that time, the ways of the Ḥasidim seemed very foreign and hopelessly outdated. Buber, however, was struck by the deeply personal feeling the Ḥasidim had for each other, and for God. One of his first books (published before World War I) was a marvelous retelling of sayings and stories of Ḥasidic rebbes. The work was a milestone, for it began to bring this important tradition back into the mainstream of Jewish thought.

But Buber did not simply adopt Ḥasidic ideas and practices. He drew from them what seemed meaningful for modern times. He built his own philosophy on the idea of true personal communication. We

Abba Eban Remembers:
Martin Buber

Martin Buber was perhaps the only Israeli philosopher who had a reputation outside the Israeli and the Jewish world. He had a somewhat mystical character and an obscure way of writing. He once came to Washington and was invited to give a lecture in English, which he spoke very well. He insisted, however, on talking in German. When I asked him why, he said, "German is the only language in which I can make myself incomprehensible."

Together with Weizmann, Buber had been one of the earliest Zionist leaders. But later in life he came to feel that the official Zionist leadership was not doing enough to keep in touch with Arab opinion. He therefore devoted his name and prestige to that objective, without ever losing his essential loyalties to Jewish interests.

often think of another person as a "thing," an object we can use for our own needs, said Buber. But this is destructive. We must learn to deal with others as real and valuable people.

In the same way, we must not regard God as a distant and impersonal force. We can best fulfill ourselves by entering into a close personal dialogue with God, as we would with a beloved parent or dear friend. This idea of direct personal communication with God has had great influence both among our own people and among Christian thinkers.

Franz Rosenzweig

Franz Rosenzweig, unlike Buber, was brought up in a wealthy home where he was given little schooling in Judaism. He began to drift toward Protestantism, but before converting he decided to pray one last time as a Jew. The day before his scheduled conversion happened to be Yom Kippur; so it was on the most sacred day of the Jewish year that he wandered into a small Berlin synagogue.

What happened that day changed his life. Sharing the Day of Atonement with Eastern European Jews who felt a deep love for their religion made Rosenzweig realize that Judaism was his true home. He immediately began to study his heritage, but his studies were interrupted by World War I. Serving in the trenches, he wrote his ideas about religion on postcards and scraps of paper which he sent to his mother. She saved them for him, and after the war he used these notes as part of his major book of philosophy, *The Star of Redemption*.

Turning to practical work, Rosenzweig established the Jewish House of Study for adults in Frankfurt. There he taught the classic texts of Judaism in a fresh way, looking at the problems of the present from a traditional Jewish viewpoint. This school served as a model for others throughout Germany. They had particular success in attracting Jews who, like Rosenzweig, had all but lost touch with their religion.

But for Rosenzweig, the study of Judaism was not enough. Only by living as a Jew, he said, can we come to know God, and the way to serve both God and humanity. Rosenzweig made his home completely traditional—not because he believed in blindly obeying Jewish law, but because he wanted to experience Jewish customs firsthand to decide which ones he could truly make his own.

Then, suddenly, he was struck with a terrible paralysis which little by little took over his body. Undaunted, Rosenzweig continued to write, at first using a special typewriter. Gradually he lost his powers of speech and movement, until he could move only one finger—yet he still "dictated" to his wife by pointing to each letter he wished her to record for him. In this slow and painful way he completed a German translation of the poetry of Judah ha-Levi, and began working with Martin Buber on a magnificent new German translation of the Bible.

Doctors said Rosenzweig would soon be dead, but he defied their predictions, surviving the agony of his illness for seven years and living until 1929. Though unable to move, he was a part of all that went on around him, inspiring all those who visited him or who joined in the services which were held in his home.

Buber became the first professor of Judaism in a German university, then escaped from Hitler in 1938 and settled in Palestine. He taught at the Hebrew University and was Israel's leading philosopher of education. He died in 1965 at the age of eighty-seven, revered and admired by Jews and Christians throughout the world.

But for the rest of German Jewry, time had run out.

SUMMARY *The period following World War I was a time of increasing anti-Semitism. In America, this anti-Semitism was part of a pattern of prejudice against foreigners which included the passage of harsh immigration laws. After the war, Eastern European states cruelly and violently oppressed the Jews, despite treaties guaranteeing the rights of all minorities. It was German Jewry which enjoyed the greatest freedom and success in continental Europe, producing such notable thinkers as Martin Buber and Franz Rosenzweig.*

19

The Holocaust

By the time Hitler came to power he was well known as an anti-Semite. Yet some people hoped that as leader of the German government he would become moderate and sensible in his treatment of Jews. Such hopes were soon shattered. In March 1933, just two months after Hitler became chancellor of Germany, bands of Nazis attacked Jewish judges and lawyers in the courthouse of Breslau—less than 200 miles from the German capital, Berlin. In the following weeks, thirty-five Jews were murdered.

This was a warning of the violence that was to come; but during the first years of Nazi rule, most of the outrages against our people were not physical. Actually, the Nazi campaign against the Jews can be divided into three distinct periods.

During the first period, which lasted from 1933 until the outbreak of war in 1939, our people were deprived of all rights as citizens and human beings. The Nazis claimed that the Jews were an inferior race and deserved no rights.

During the second period, from 1939 to 1941, the ghettos and concentration camps were established. Having conquered most of Europe, the Nazis moved Jews into special areas where, cut off from the outside world, our people could be worked—or beaten—to death.

During the third period, from Hitler's invasion of Russia in June 1941 to the end of the war in May 1945, Hitler put into action his "Final Solution" to the "Jewish Problem": the cold-blooded murder of every living Jew.

The unspeakable horrors of the second and third periods—the years known as the HOLOCAUST—have come to overshadow the importance of the first. Yet it was in the less violent years before the war that the German people were being prepared for acts which no moral human being would perform.

And because the rest of the world was silent as rights were taken away from the German Jews, the second two periods of the Nazi terror were made possible.

Phase One—destruction of the spirit

Phase One—the total destruction of the spirit of the Jews in Germany—began in earnest in April 1933. Guards were posted in front of every Jewish business or office, and non-Jewish customers were told not to enter. Laws were passed which made it nearly impossible for Jews to make a living.

At the same time, the Nazis announced that tall, blond, blue-eyed Europeans— whom they called "Aryans"—were the "Master Race" and would soon rule the world.* Non-Aryans, and most specifically the Jews, were to be treated more like animals than like people.

All forms of propaganda were used to teach this obscene doctrine. Newspapers often printed pictures of grinning Nazi youths forcing bearded Jews to clear garbage from German streets by hand. Nazi literature was widely read. Movies

* It never seemed to bother the Germans that none of the important Nazi leaders—least of all Hitler—fit the Aryan pattern.

showed the beauty of the "Aryan type." Street signs carried messages like "Beware of Jews and Pickpockets."

Hitler was even able to find university professors and scientists who were willing to help spread the Nazi lies. A leading physicist set out to "free" science of "Jewish Einstein corruption," on the theory that "science, like every other human product, is racial and conditioned by blood." A Christian Nazi Institute was established to prove that Jesus was not of Jewish origin!

Encouraged and aided by these spineless scholars, Minister of Propaganda Josef Goebbels held a public bonfire where the "Jewish" literature by such great writers as Heinrich Heine and Emile Zola went up in smoke alongside the scientific works of Albert Einstein and Sigmund Freud. Music, theater, the press, radio, films, and museums were all "cleared" of Jews, as were universities and scientific institutions.

Anti-Semitism soon became official government policy. In September 1935, the German parliament passed the so-called "Nuremberg Laws." Jews were no longer

A Jewish boy is forced to cut his grandfather's beard for the amusement of German soldiers.

Warnings to Germans not to buy from Jews were an essential part of Phase One in the Nazi campaign to humiliate our people—a campaign which climaxed with Kristallnacht.

German citizens. They were forbidden to employ Gentile domestic servants, or even to raise the German flag. Marriages between Jews and non-Jews were forbidden.

Moreover, Hitler defined the term "Jew" in a strange new way. Anyone who had two (out of four) Jewish grandparents, or even three (out of eight) great-grandparents, was said to be "Jewish." Thus, Protestants whose grandparents or great-grandparents had given up Judaism for the "safety" of the Christian world suddenly found themselves trapped in the growing web of legalized madness.

Phase One reached its climax on the night of November 9–10, 1938. That evening, Hitler unleashed nationwide riots and almost every synagogue in Germany was destroyed. Jewish homes were smashed, Jewish businesses were looted and burned. At least 30,000 Jews were arrested that night. Then, to bankrupt our people completely, the Nazis forced the Jewish community to pay an enormous fine to cover the cost of the damage!

This event, which became known as KRISTALLNACHT ("Night of Broken Glass"), marked the end of organized Jewish life in Germany.

Phase Two—isolation and terror

Less than ten months later, the Second World War began. Most of the European mainland, except for the Soviet Union, was soon under German control. The Nazis began Phase Two.

Hitler's methods of destroying the Jewish spirit and isolating our people were used in one country after another. Jews were stripped of all legal rights. They were ordered to wear yellow six-pointed stars on their clothing. They were moved to ghettos, newly recreated so that the Jews could be held in complete isolation.

Once ghettoized, they were forced into workshops and factories to produce goods for the Nazis who were oppressing them. Jews in the occupied Western countries—France, Belgium, and the Netherlands—were sent to the east to create a more concentrated pool of slave labor.

The ghettos were dreadful. In the ghetto built in Warsaw, 500,000 persons were herded together into an area where 35,000 had lived. Bread and potatoes were the chief foods, and most people were given no more than 800 calories per day. (A modern book on weight control recommends at least 2000 calories a day.) The whole community was on the verge of starvation. Disease spread rapidly. Yet there was no escape from the terror, for any Jew who tried to leave the ghetto—or who even came too close to the ghetto exit—was shot.

Phase Two moved into high gear in June 1941, when Hitler attacked Russia and immediately began to destroy the Jewish population in the invaded areas. Sometimes the native Christians were incited to massacre Jews. But large-scale murder was more efficiently handled by German troops—though they had to be taken away from the war effort for this purpose.

Soldiers would force Jews to gather together. Whole communities would be crowded into trucks and freight cars, taken to some ravine or ditch, stripped, and then shot—men, women, and children. The countryside became one vast graveyard. Sometimes, as in the case of Babi Yar (near Kiev), the site of these mass executions was not even known until many years later.*

Phase Three—extermination

In January 1942 the Nazis formally began what they hoped would be the total extermination of the Jewish people. In a matter of months, death camps were set up throughout Eastern Europe. Previously

* When the tens of thousands of corpses at Babi Yar were discovered, the Soviet Union refused to raise a monument to their memory. This aroused an international protest, led by non-Jewish Russian intellectuals. At last, the Russian government did put up a memorial. As a final insult, however, the inscription never mentions that most of those who died were Jews.

Polish Jews, under armed guard, await shipment to a Nazi death camp.

Inmates at Buchenwald, a forced labor camp, gaze out from their wooden bunks.

openings in the ceiling. Within three to ten minutes, all were dead. The corpses were stripped of such valuables as gold teeth and false limbs. Their hair was gathered to stuff mattresses, and sometimes the body fat was used to make soap. Any remains were then burned in huge ovens.

It is all but impossible to picture the number of human beings destroyed in these camps. The commander of Auschwitz said this at his postwar trial:

> At least 2,500,000 victims were executed and exterminated there by gassing and burning, and at least another half a million succumbed to starvation and disease, making a total of about 3,000,000. Apart from 20,000 Russian prisoners of war . . . , the victims were Jews from Holland, Belgium, France, Poland, Hungary, Czechoslovakia, Greece, and other countries. We executed about 400,000 Hungarian Jews alone at Auschwitz in the summer of 1944.

Nothing slowed the rate of these massacres except such technical problems as a lack of men to direct them or the shortage of freight cars to transport the victims.

unknown towns became infamous for having camps nearby. Of these, the most notorious was Auschwitz.

Auschwitz was located in a remote, swampy, and disease-ridden region of Poland. Jews sent there were immediately divided into those who were fit for work and those who were not. Each worker was tattooed with a number and sent to one of the nearby factories, which had been built to make use of slave labor. The treatment of these captives was ghastly. They usually lived no more than three months.

Those Jews "unfit for labor" were told they were going to be allowed to wash. They undressed and, with cake of soap in hand, entered a room with what looked like shower heads. A gas which was also used to exterminate bugs and vermin from the camp was then forced through special

The business of mass murder

It is frightening to realize that the murder of Jews became an everyday activity for thousands of Germans. This was horrifyingly obvious in the business world: companies manufactured and sold death equipment as a standard item. One memo to the construction office at Auschwitz from a maker of heating equipment matter-of-factly mentions an order for "five triple furnaces including two electric elevators for raising the corpses."

Industries competed for the chance to profit through this hideous trade. One firm asked for increased business because its earlier work had been of such high quality:

> We are submitting plans for our perfected cremation ovens which operate with coal and which have hitherto given full satisfaction.

> We suggest two crematorial furnaces for the building plant but we advise you to make further inquiries to make sure that two ovens will be sufficient for your requirements.

> We guarantee the effectiveness of the cremation ovens as well as their durability, the use of the best material and our faultless workmanship.

The end of innocence

Until the Holocaust many people felt that no one, however evil, could enjoy making children suffer. The human race can no longer allow itself even this innocent belief. Children who survived the gas chambers because mothers pressed them close to shield them from the poison were thrown by the Nazis into furnaces and burned alive. Special convoys were organized to bring children to the death camps. Those fourteen and older were treated as adults: either killed immediately or forced to work 80 to 100 hours a week at hard labor.

Those children who were imprisoned in the Nazi camp at Terezin, in Czechoslovakia, told their own story in poems and drawings which have survived. Said one:

> *When a new child comes*
> *Everything seems strange to him.*
> *What, on the ground I have to lie?*
> *Eat black potatoes? No! Not I!*
> *I've got to stay? It's dirty here!*
> *The floor—why, look, it's dirt I fear!*
> *And I'm supposed to sleep on it?*
> *I'll get all dirty!*

The unburied dead of Bergen-Belsen. More than 50,000 Jews died in this camp, including Anne Frank (see Chapter 20).

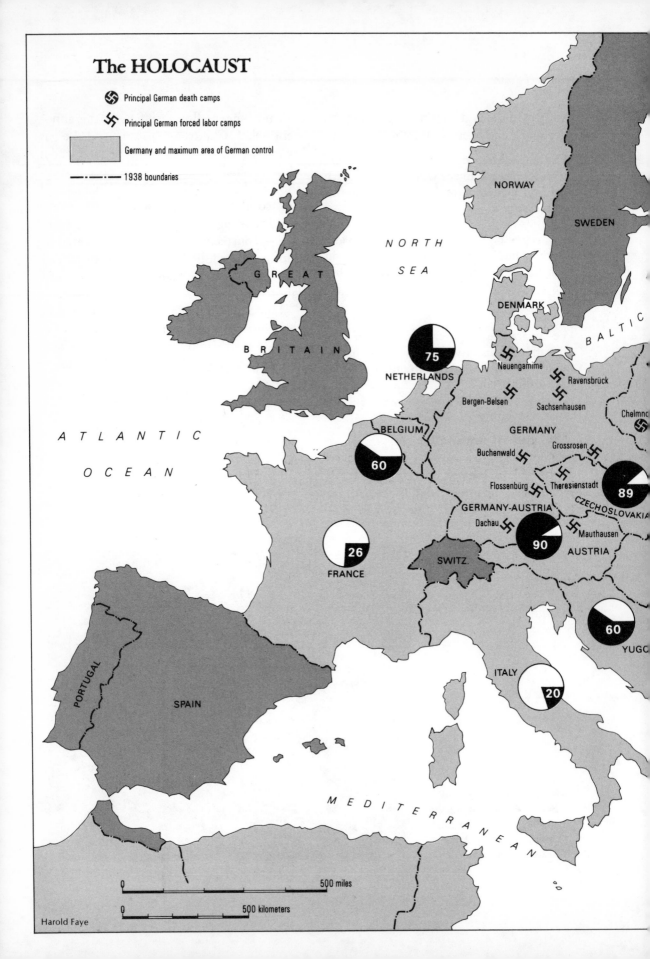

The HOLOCAUST

Principal German death camps

Principal German forced labor camps

Germany and maximum area of German control

1938 boundaries

NORWAY

SWEDEN

NORTH SEA

GREAT BRITAIN

DENMARK

BALTIC

ATLANTIC OCEAN

NETHERLANDS **75**

Neuengamime

Ravensbrück

Bergen-Belsen

Sachsenhausen

Chelmno

GERMANY

BELGIUM **60**

Buchenwald

Grossrosen

Flossenbürg

Theresienstadt

89

GERMANY-AUSTRIA

CZECHOSLOVAKIA

Dachau

Mauthausen

FRANCE **26**

90

AUSTRIA

SWITZ.

60

YUGO

ITALY

PORTUGAL

SPAIN

20

MEDITERRANEAN

| 0 | | | | 500 miles |

| 0 | | | | 500 kilometers |

Harold Faye

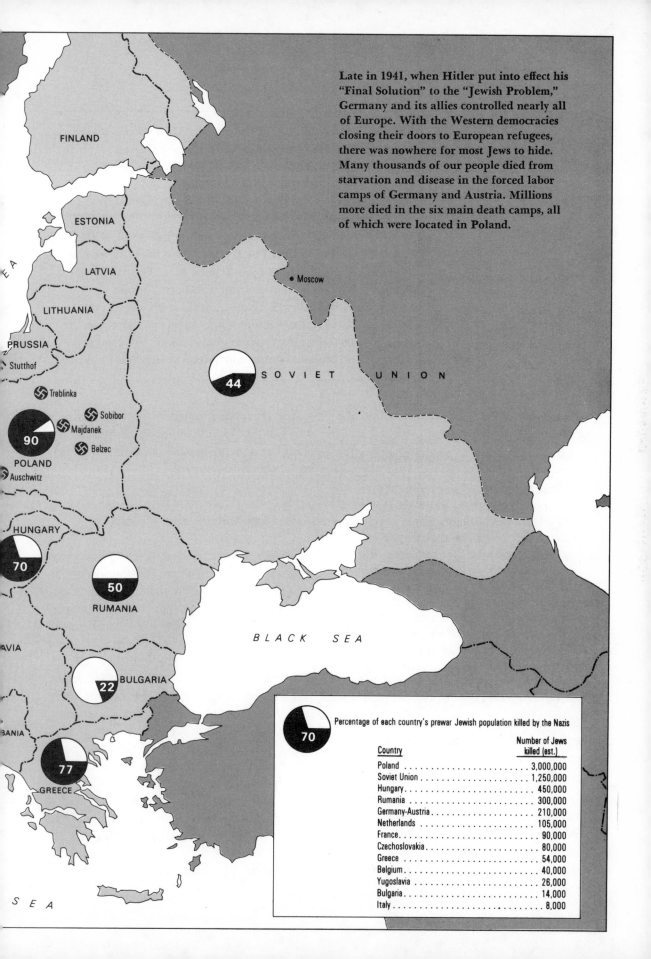

Late in 1941, when Hitler put into effect his "Final Solution" to the "Jewish Problem," Germany and its allies controlled nearly all of Europe. With the Western democracies closing their doors to European refugees, there was nowhere for most Jews to hide. Many thousands of our people died from starvation and disease in the forced labor camps of Germany and Austria. Millions more died in the six main death camps, all of which were located in Poland.

FINLAND

ESTONIA

LATVIA

LITHUANIA

PRUSSIA

Stutthof

Treblinka

Sobibor

Majdanek

Belzec

90

POLAND

Auschwitz

Moscow

44

S O V I E T   U N I O N

HUNGARY

70

50

RUMANIA

B L A C K   S E A

22

BULGARIA

ANIA

77

GREECE

S E A

Percentage of each country's prewar Jewish population killed by the Nazis	
70	
Country	Number of Jews killed (est.)
Poland	3,000,000
Soviet Union	1,250,000
Hungary	450,000
Rumania	300,000
Germany-Austria	210,000
Netherlands	105,000
France	90,000
Czechoslovakia	80,000
Greece	54,000
Belgium	40,000
Yugoslavia	26,000
Bulgaria	14,000
Italy	8,000

*The Other Victims
of the Holocaust*

Millions of people died in the camps. Most of them were Jews, but not all. Hitler murdered many non-Jews who belonged to forbidden social, political, or religious groups. Some Christian Slavs, Czechs, and Poles (all "inferior races" by Aryan standards) were also shipped to the death camps.

Aside from the Jews, no group suffered more at Hitler's hands than the Gypsies. The Gypsies are a nomadic people who may originally have come from India. They reached Persia by the tenth century and Southern Europe about 400 years later. Perhaps 1 million Gypsies were living in Europe when Hitler came to power. Of these, at least 100,000—the entire Gypsy populations of Germany, Austria, and Poland—were murdered during World War II.

Death became a part of everyday life. As one child wrote:

We got used to standing in line at 7 o'clock in the morning, at 12 noon and again at 7 o'clock in the evening. We stood in a long line with a plate in our hand, into which they ladled a little warmed-up water with a salty or a coffee flavor. Or else they gave us a few potatoes. We got used to sleeping without a bed, to saluting every uniform, not to walk on the sidewalks and then again to walk on the sidewalks. We got used to undeserved slaps, blows, and executions. We got accustomed to seeing people die in their own excrement, to seeing piled-up coffins full of corpses, to seeing the sick amidst dirt and filth and to seeing the helpless doctors....

Still, they hoped and prayed. They saw the beauty of nature and dreamed of the future. A twelve-year-old wrote:

*Perhaps it's better—who can say?—
Than watching this, to die today?
No, no, my God, we want to live!
Not watch our numbers melt away.
We want to have a better world,
We want to work—we must not die!*

But the Nazi murder machine ground on. Of the 15,000 children under the age of fifteen who passed through Terezin, only about 100 survived.

Understanding the Holocaust

When the war ended, world Jewry was orphaned. Gone were the hundreds of Jewish communities which had made Eastern Europe the heartland of our people, the source of its vitality. For centuries, the great majority of Judaism's spiritual leaders had either lived or studied there. From Eastern Europe had come the giants of Biblical learning. In Eastern Europe were the great academies of Talmudic studies. Many of the creators of the Zionist idea and the architects of the Zionist movement, the early pioneers, the writers and thinkers, had hailed from Eastern Europe.

One of every three Jews in the world— one of every two Jews in Europe—had been murdered. The total Jewish dead: almost 6 million. Six million! This figure is so familiar, yet almost impossible to under-

Yad Vashem, a national monument and museum in Jerusalem, honors the memory of the 6 million Jews who were martyred by the Nazis.

stand. Imagine the murder of three people each and every morning since the earliest days of recorded history 5000 years ago. Or imagine that everyone in Philadelphia, Detroit, Houston, and Baltimore all died at the same time. Neither total would equal the number of Jews slaughtered by Hitler during World War II.

But more important than understanding the terrible figure of 6 million is to remember that each Jew murdered was a human being—a person who, like each of us, had dreams of happiness, of comfort, of achievement. Yet each was to suffer a horrible death, and for only one reason—belonging to the very people that had given the world these words:

> You shall not murder.
> You shall not hate your brother in your heart.
> You shall love your neighbor as yourself.

SUMMARY *Immediately after coming to power, Hitler began his campaign against the Jews. First, he separated them from society and deprived them of all legal rights. Second, he extended these policies throughout all territories captured by German troops at the beginning of World War II. Third, after his invasion of Russia, he began the relentless extermination of European Jewry. Nearly 6 million Jews were murdered—more than a third of the world Jewish population.*

Resistance to Hitler

The governments of the world knew what was happening to the Jewish people—and they did not care.

In Eastern Europe—an area with a long tradition of anti-Semitism—Hitler's rise to power was greeted not with horror, but with joy. Poland, Lithuania, Latvia, and Rumania passed anti-Jewish laws in 1934, Hungary in 1935. Anti-Semitism became the official policy of these governments well before Eastern Europe was overrun by the Nazis.

Silence in the West

The Western nations knew the fate of Europe's Jews but rarely tried to save them. The administration of the American President Franklin D. Roosevelt, which showed deep feeling for the poor, old, and unemployed during the Great Depression, showed little sympathy when the un-

fortunates were Jewish Europeans. The United States refused to change its immigration laws or open its borders, despite the need of countless men, women, and children to escape from Nazi terror. Not until 1943 did the government set up a committee for victims of war—an action which came too late to save more than a few lives. And American forces in Europe refused to disrupt the Nazi butchery by bombing the rail lines to the death camps.

England did open its doors to some refugees, but not many. When the Nazis wanted to trade the lives of some Hungarian Jews for machinery, they sent a Jew to offer the deal to the British. The British just threw the Jewish agent into prison. And, as we shall see in the next chapter, Great Britain itself was following strongly anti-Jewish policies in Palestine.

The Roman Catholic Pope, Pius XII, did aid and protect a number of Jews, and gave fifteen kilograms of gold (about thirty-three pounds) to help pay a huge ransom which the Nazis demanded of the Jews of Rome in 1943. But, in general, he tried hard not to anger the Germans. Instead of using his full moral authority to oppose Nazism publicly, he carried on his anti-Nazi activities in a quiet and cautious manner.

The French government which came to power after France was taken over by the Nazis helped the Germans in rounding up Jews for the journey to the death camps. The French police isolated the Jews from the rest of the people, making the Nazis' work much easier. Fortunately, "ordinary" French citizens did much to help our people, permitting some of them to escape.

Just how bad things were is shown by the story of two ships filled with Jews who had somehow managed to escape. One was found wandering in the Black Sea in October 1934, unable to land because its 318 Jewish refugees from Poland and Czechoslovakia had no visas. Without visas no country would allow the Jews to enter. The second, which sailed from Europe just three months before the outbreak of World War II, cruised along the American coastline for three weeks with 900 Jews on board. Since no country in the Western Hemisphere would admit them, the ship finally returned them to the massacre in Europe.

All this time, the leaders of the Western democracies were silent. Many did not speak out because they feared that loud protests would only make matters worse for Germany's Jews. (Some people today, unable or unwilling to learn from history, use the same argument to discourage direct action on behalf of Soviet Jewry.) But the fact remains that the nations of the "free world" ignored the persecution of millions

of people, until they suddenly saw that their own liberties were at stake. The results could be foreseen. As early as 1936, Chaim Weizmann said:

> There are six million people doomed to be pent up where they are not wanted and for whom the world is divided into places where they cannot live, and places which they may not enter. Six million!

In less than nine years, the problem was solved. By 1945, these 6 million Jews were dead.

The righteous Gentiles

Though most of the world stood by and watched the slaughter of the Jewish people, a few among the Gentiles came to the aid of their Jewish neighbors. The Italians, though they were allied with the Germans and put many Nazi laws into effect, could not bring themselves to help with mass murder. For several years, Jews from other countries found safety in Italy.

In Holland, the Dutch people tried to resist the Nazis. Many Dutch workmen were killed in protest riots which took place in Amsterdam early in 1941.

In Holland and France, Christian ministers held public prayers for our people. Especially in France, priests showed energy and daring in their efforts to hide and protect Jews.

But the Nazis controlled France and Holland long enough to find and destroy just about the entire native Jewish population. And when the Nazis took control of Italy, one of their first acts was to deport Jews living there to the death camps.

The only truly bright light of this long nightmare shone in Denmark. Though the country was overrun by the Nazis at the very beginning of the war, the Danes

Above, a boat carries Danish Jews to safety in Sweden; below, a woman is helped from her hiding place after her vessel enters a Swedish port.

hardship. At last, in 1943, the Germans decided to round up the Danish Jews to send them to the death camps. Word of this plan leaked out to the Christian community, which rapidly moved into action. When the Nazis set out to make their arrests, they found that almost the entire Jewish population—about 7700 people— had disappeared! The Jews had been hidden by their neighbors and then smuggled across the narrow strait that separates Denmark from Sweden. There, in a country never captured or controlled by the Germans, the Danish Jews remained safe until the end of the war.

Despite the best efforts of the Danes, 464 Jews were captured in Denmark and sent to concentration camps. However, the Danish government showed continuing concern for these prisoners, constantly asking about them. Exasperated, the Germans released the Danish Jews. The result was that only fifty-one Danish Jews died in prison, and of these all but ten were over sixty years of age. In short, 99 percent of the Danish Jewish community was saved from Nazi slaughter because the Danes took action.

Yet even this is not the whole story. During the years that the Jews were in Sweden, their homes in Denmark were kept for them, the rent paid or simply canceled while the Jewish families were absent. Valuables belonging to the Jews were protected by a government bank. The community's Torah scrolls were secretly removed from the synagogue and hidden in a church for safekeeping.

When the Jewish community returned to Denmark after the war, they found their jobs and property waiting there, lovingly preserved by Christian friends and neighbors.

firmly refused to allow the Nazis to carry out any anti-Semitic practices. The Danish king, Christian X, warned the Germans that if Jews were required to wear badges on their clothing, he would proudly wear the same badge himself, and every Dane would follow his example.

Because of the courage of Danish Gentiles, the Nazis allowed the Danish Jews to live for a few years without any special

Jewish rescue efforts

The story of Denmark is unique. For the most part, Jews had to depend on their own people for rescue.

Leading the rescue effort was the American Jewish Joint Distribution Committee (the "Joint"), working together with other organizations. In France, for example, the Joint gave money to any group working to save the lives of Jews. Northern France was conquered by the Germans early in the war. Yet the Joint succeeded in smuggling Jewish children out of northern France into Switzerland. At the same time, more than 11,000 Jews from southern France were also rescued. When southern France was later occupied by the Nazis, the Joint continued its work, supplying food, clothing, and medicine to those in concentration camps, and working underground to help our people.

Lisbon, the capital of Portugal, became the chief transit port for Jews escaping from Europe. The Joint chartered ships to sail for Cuba and America, or bought up all berths on regular passenger ships. Working through local committees or even through German tourist agencies, Joint members met trainloads of Jews coming from Central Europe and cared for the refugees until they could board ships to other lands.

Rescue efforts went on even in the East. During 1939 and 1940, Russia sent 350,000 Jews to a bleak area near the border of Iran. Most of them died of cold and hunger, but the survivors gathered in small frontier towns where they struggled to set up their own communities. A member of the Joint came to their rescue, establishing a relief service for these starving Jews. After the war, most of them escaped from

Through Youth Aliyah, Henrietta Szold helped save the lives of 30,000 children.

Russia, either through Iran or by way of Poland, and made their way to Palestine.

Henrietta Szold and Youth Aliyah

Another agency rescuing Jews was Youth Aliyah. And the story of this group is the story of one woman: Henrietta Szold.

When Hitler came to power, Szold was seventy–three years old, and had behind her a life filled with achievement. Early in the century, she worked at settling Russian immigrants in America, and founded the first night schools for those who wanted to learn English but had daytime jobs. She was secretary of the Jewish Publication Society for twenty-four years, editing and translating works of great importance.

By 1912, Szold was fifty-two and an

ardent Zionist. When she discovered that Palestine was disease-ridden, she dedicated herself to raising the standards of health care in Eretz Yisrael. To this end she founded the Women's Zionist Organization of America, known as HADASSAH, which fifty years later numbered more than 300,000 members, with groups in each of the fifty states and Puerto Rico. Wanting to do more than organize, Szold, at the age of sixty, moved to Palestine to direct the health work personally. Traveling up and down the country by donkey or in old cars, she supervised the building of new hospitals, and gave special attention to creating clinics to teach preventive medicine.

When the Holocaust began, she turned her attention to those children who were allowed to leave Europe even though their parents were forced to stay behind. It was then that she founded and became director of YOUTH ALIYAH, working not only to get the youngsters to safety but also to build a new life for them in Zion. Thanks to her efforts, some 30,000 children were saved from the gas chambers.

In the underground

Within the world of the Holocaust, resistance often meant working with Gentile "underground" movements. Jews were active in every resistance movement they were allowed to join. In France, the proportion of Jews in the underground ran between 15 and 30 percent. Among the many heroes of the resistance was José Abulker, a young Jewish–Algerian medical student who, at the age of twenty-two, made the American landing in Algeria possible. In Russia, Holland, Belgium, and Italy, Jews played a major role in the struggle against the Nazis.

Sometimes, however, the members of a Gentile underground group hated Jews even more than they hated Nazis. Anti-Semitism was particularly strong in the resistance movements of Poland and the Ukraine. In these countries the Jews found themselves with little choice—they had to fight alone. This was a lesson our people learned well. It was in Poland—in the Warsaw Ghetto—that Jewish armed resistance faced its greatest challenge and gained its greatest triumph.

The Warsaw Ghetto uprising

In July 1942 the Nazis began to load the Jews of the Warsaw Ghetto on trains to send them away. Most Jews believed they were being transferred to new quarters. In reality, they were being sent to the gas chambers. By Yom Kippur the Jewish population of Warsaw had been reduced from half a million to 60,000.

Even as the railroad cars filled with Jews began to leave Warsaw, those left behind began preparing for combat. They asked for help from the Polish resistance, but they received little or none. So they began smuggling weapons into the ghetto and training secretly to use them. By December 1942 they were ready for their first battle.

In January 1943, Germans again came to round up Jews for the death camps. Suddenly, they found themselves under attack. Astounded and confused, they fled from the ghetto.

For three months the Germans regrouped their forces. Then, on Passover morning, April 19, 1943, they launched a full-scale assault. Tanks and heavy artillery

The heroic men and women of the Warsaw Ghetto chose to die fighting rather than submit meekly to Nazi terror.

rolled into the ghetto. The Jews fought back with handmade bombs. Though they were up against great odds, the starving ghetto fighters held out against Hitler's war machine for twenty-eight days. Street by street, then house by house, the battle raged. It took the German army longer to destroy the resistance in the Warsaw Ghetto than it had taken to overrun the rest of Poland.

The freedom fighter who led the revolt was twenty-four-year-old Mordecai Anilewicz. Neither he nor any of his comrades had any doubt about the outcome. They knew there was no hope of victory, or even of survival. Yet they were determined to preserve Jewish dignity—to die fighting.

On May 8 the Germans finally captured the headquarters of the revolt, killing Anilewicz in the battle. "The Jews are cowardly," Hitler had said. Yet the Jews of Warsaw had presented Hitler with one of the most difficult military campaigns of his career. Nor could he keep this humiliation a secret. A hundred resistance fighters managed to escape from the ghetto to tell the world of this heroic chapter in Jewish history.

Spiritual resistance

The Jews fought the Nazis in other places—in Vilna, in Tarnow, even in the death camps. But most European Jews did not resist Hitler by violent means. Beaten down by years of persecution and terror, faced with the tremendous power of the German war machine, betrayed by their neighbors, and scarcely able to believe the depths of Nazi cruelty, more often than not they quietly accepted their fate, hoping against hope that they would live to see the Allied armies triumph in Europe.

But they did resist Hitler in a different way: with their minds. Even in the grim ghettos of Poland, the Jews refused to give up their way of life. Artistic and scholarly activities seemed to grow as physical strength faded. Plays were put on as long as there were any Jews alive to perform them. Even though teaching was strictly forbidden, secret schools were set up at all levels. In a remarkable display of scientific courage, a group of doctors made studies of the effects of starvation on themselves and their neighbors—studies which were found and published after the war.

What was true in Poland had also been true of Germany between the time Hitler rose to power and the outbreak of the war. The study of Jewish history and Hebrew soared. Books were published on a wide range of Jewish subjects. Knowledge of Judaism proved to be a powerful weapon in the war of self-preservation. Almost the only people in the ghettos who committed suicide were Jews who, before Hitler, had been so eager to become part of German society that they lost contact with their Jewish heritage.

A portrait of Leo Baeck, spokesman for German Jewry during the Hitler years.

Leo Baeck

Those searching for inner strength had a great leader to help them—a Reform rabbi named Leo Baeck.

Dr. Baeck had been an important figure in German-Jewish life for many years. As early as 1905 he had written a book, *The Essence of Judaism*, in which—with almost prophetic foresight—he stressed the opposition between Judaism, which insists on the freedom of each person, and the demands made by dictators.

When Hitler declared himself dictator of Germany, it was Baeck who became the leader and spokesman of German Jewry. Baeck headed the agencies which directed internal Jewish affairs, and which guided relief efforts for the growing number of

**"In spite of everything I still believe
that people are really good at heart."**
—Anne Frank

poor Jews. As times grew worse, Baeck was invited to come to America. He refused with thanks, saying he would remain with his people while there was a single Jew who needed his help. Later he was sent to a concentration camp where, though nearly seventy, he was put to work pulling a garbage wagon. Undaunted, he continued to inspire his fellow prisoners, teaching them lessons which kept their minds and hearts alive.

By a miracle, he survived the war. The Nazis ordered his execution, but mistakenly canceled it as soon as a Rabbi "Beck" died. When his camp was liberated, he again refused special treatment, choosing instead to remain with his fellow Jews. After the concentration camps were emptied, Baeck did leave Germany, becoming an active leader in the Jewish affairs of

Britain, Israel, and the United States until his death in 1956.

Anne Frank

Perhaps the one Jew whose resistance to Nazism is best known was neither a fighter nor a scholar, but a young girl. Anne Frank escaped with her family from Germany to Holland when Hitler came to power, only to find herself again under Nazi rule when World War II began. Her father arranged for a hiding place over the shop where he had worked, and the Franks lived there with another family, protected by Christian friends. This self-imprisonment lasted for more than two years, as Anne grew from thirteen to fifteen.

Unable to meet new friends, forbidden

even to walk about during the day for fear she would be heard by workmen downstairs, she spent her time writing and keeping a diary of her feelings and thoughts. And in the midst of her complaints and her doubts and her problems, she wrote a paragraph which has been read all over the world:

> It's really a wonder that I haven't dropped all my ideals, because they seem so absurd and impossible to carry out. Yet I keep them, because in spite of everything I still believe that people are really good at heart. I simply can't build up my hopes on a foundation consisting of confusion, misery and death. I see the world gradually being turned into a wilderness, I hear the approaching thunder, which will destroy us too, I can feel the sufferings of millions and yet, if I look up into the heavens, I think that it will all come right, that this cruelty too will end, and that peace and tranquility will return again.

A week after she wrote these words, the hideout was discovered by the Nazis. The Frank family was sent to the concentration camp at Bergen-Belsen, where Anne died. Her diary was found and published after the war.

Through her diary, Anne Frank lives on. Her words tell perfectly the strength of Jewish resistance to the Holocaust—indeed, of all Jewish resistance since the time of Pharaoh. Judaism and Jewish history stand for freedom, for decency, for honesty, for hope and for life—even against the worst the world has offered. Dictators cannot tolerate these ideals of Judaism, but the Jewish spirit will not be crushed. Dictators come and go, yet decent people around the globe still react with joy and hope to the message of a Jewish girl trapped in her pitiful attic in Amsterdam:

> In spite of everything I still believe that people are really good at heart.

SUMMARY *The world turned its back on the plight of the Jews under Nazi rule. With a few exceptions—particularly in Denmark —Western nations ignored the fact that Hitler planned to exterminate the Jewish people. Jews in America and elsewhere organized rescue efforts through such agencies as the American Jewish Joint Distribution Committee and Henrietta Szold's Youth Aliyah. Some Jews in Europe took part in armed resistance against the Nazis, such as in the Warsaw Ghetto uprising. Many who could not fight back with weapons showed great spiritual strength. Two spiritual heroes of the Holocaust were a rabbi, Leo Baeck, and a teen-age girl, Anne Frank.*

21

The Jewish State
Reborn

Swarms of Jewish refugees, threatened with death by Hitler and unwanted in America, looked for safety to the land of Israel. They found it closed to them by the very empire which, through the Balfour Declaration, had promised the Jews a national home in Palestine.

Jews and Arabs

Lord Balfour, who as British foreign secretary issued the declaration which bears his name, was a sincere Zionist. Throughout his life he remained firmly committed to the goal of a Jewish homeland. But why did the English government choose to issue the Balfour Declaration in 1917?

World War I was raging, and England was at war with the Ottoman Turks. Naturally, the British hoped to create as much disorder as possible within the Ottoman Empire. One way to do this was to promise future independence to every group which would work to overthrow the Ottoman sultan. The Zionists formed one such group. The Arabs, who made up more than half the population of the Ottoman Empire, formed another.

The Zionists understood and sympathized with the Arab desire for freedom. Shortly after the Balfour Declaration was issued, Chaim Weizmann traveled to the Middle East to meet one of the leaders of the Arab nationalist movement, the Emir Faisal. Though firm in demanding independence for the Arab countries, Faisal and the other Arab leaders saw that Palestine was unique. It had never been the home of an independent Arab state, and had been under non-Arab rule for more than 800 years.

Weizmann and Faisal were able to agree on the division of lands—it would be Arabia for the Arabs, Judea for the Jews. In December 1918, Faisal made this statement:

The two main branches of the Semitic family, Arabs and Jews, understand one another . . . Arabs are not jealous of Zionist Jews, and intend to give them fair play; and the Zionist Jews have assured the Nationalist Arabs of their intention to see that they, too, have fair play in their respective areas.

Both sides expected to see their dreams of independence come true at the peace conference which followed World War I.

Neither the Zionists nor the Arab nationalists knew that France and England were making a secret deal to divide the Middle East into European colonies. England took Iraq and Palestine, while the French expelled Faisal from Syria and Lebanon. In his anger, Faisal broke his agreement with Weizmann. He and other Arab nationalists, bitterly disappointed, suddenly demanded the liberation of Syria—and its union with Palestine under Arab rule.

Nevertheless, the international community, through the League of Nations, assigned Great Britain the task of turning Palestine into an independent Jewish state. If Britain had done as the League of Nations asked, and if the nations of the world had supported independence for the traditionally Arab areas, many lives might have been saved and war could have been prevented. But this was not to be.

The birth of Transjordan

The first British high commissioner for Palestine—Sir Herbert Samuel—arrived in the country in July 1920. He had a long and distinguished record as a political leader and as a Zionist, and was respected by the Jews in Palestine and throughout the world. Yet Samuel had strict orders from London to do everything possible to make peace with the Arabs, and to do as little as possible about creating a Jewish state. Every year fewer Jews were allowed to enter Palestine, and limits were set on how much land could be bought by Jews. New proposals were made for independence which gave full weight to the existing Arab majority and little or none to Jewish immigrants who were supposed to be coming to Eretz Yisrael.

Then, in 1922, the British government divided the promised Jewish homeland by cutting away the whole region east of the Jordan River, three-quarters of the land area of Palestine. An Arab government was set up to rule this territory, which was called Transjordan.*

Heroism of the ḥalutzim

Even under British rule, the yishuv—the Jewish settlement in Palestine—continued to grow. The tens of thousands of Jews who came to the Holy Land immediately after World War I (the Third Aliyah) included many dedicated pioneers.

These pioneers—called ḤALUTZIM (חֲלוּצִים)—suffered tremendous hardships. Their settlements were small and isolated. Just about every settlement lacked money and medical facilities, and sometimes food. Sometimes the halutzim went hungry so that their cattle might eat. They explained: "We are Zionists, but our cows are not!"

* Transjordan became independent in 1946. (In 1949 it seized a large area west of the Jordan River, and became the Kingdom of Jordan.) During the 1970's, Arabs would claim that Israel had prevented "Palestinian Arabs" from having a state of their own. In fact, the Palestinian Arabs had been given a far larger portion of Palestine than the Palestinian Jews received.

Gradually, swamps were drained, irrigation canals dug, trees planted, and roads built. Bit by bit, the land lost its harshness and became more and more a "land of milk and honey." And while reclaiming the soil, the ḥalutzim built a new type of society, one marked by a deep sense of purpose, strong ideas of justice and equality, and a devotion to democracy at every level.

British hostility, Arab violence

When Herbert Samuel's service as high commissioner ended in 1925, relations were still pleasant between the British and the Zionists. Indeed, Samuel received a friendly farewell. He had built an efficient administration. In the year of his departure 34,000 Jews entered Palestine in order to escape new waves of anti-Semitic persecution in Poland; these immigrants became the Fourth Aliyah. Also in 1925, the Hebrew University of Jerusalem officially opened. The next four years were peaceful, like the calm before the storm.

The calm was shattered in 1929 by Arab riots. One hundred thirty-three Jews were massacred, several hundred wounded, and Jewish property was destroyed on a large scale. The fact that the British did nothing to punish the rioters—or to prevent further outbreaks—made the Arabs even bolder. Riots and attacks against Jews in 1936 amounted to a full-scale Arab revolt, and the next two years saw further violence.

Throughout this period, the answer of the yishuv to Arab rioting was a policy known as HAVLAGAH, הַבְלָגָה (self-restraint). The Jews defended themselves whenever possible, but did not try to "pay back" the attackers by killing Arabs at random. The

In 1936, at the height of the Arab revolt, British officers stopped and searched passersby on the streets of Jerusalem.

reasons for this were partly moral (how could Jews murder innocent people because of the acts of others?) and partly practical (the yishuv wanted to avoid giving the British an excuse to further limit Jewish immigration). Perhaps most of all, the yishuv wanted to show how much Jews wished to live in peace with their Arab neighbors.

Arab terrorism changed the way new Jewish settlements were set up. The task now required special skill and timing. The night before the ḥalutzim took over a piece of land, they would collect all necessary materials in a nearby village. At daybreak, members of the new settlement, with the help of volunteers, would move all the equipment to the chosen site. By sunrise the watchtower would be up, by midday the outer defense wall was standing. In the early afternoon a small farm would be functioning—complete with chickens and cows!

Thus, during the troubled years of the late 1930's, more new Jewish communities were established in Palestine than in any previous period. To the violence of the Arabs and the hostility of the British, the ḥalutzim replied with quickness, hard work, and self-protection.

Then, in May 1939, with the clouds of war gathering in Europe, the British government decided to seek Arab support through a drastic change of policy. England issued a new policy statement, known as a "White Paper." The White Paper said that Jewish immigration to Palestine would be slashed to an average of 15,000 a year for five years, and then shut off entirely. The British administration would be replaced by a local government with a permanent Arab majority. It seemed to the Jews of the yishuv that the White Paper spelled the end of their dream for a Jewish national home.

Before the Zionists could effectively oppose this assault on the Balfour Declaration, World War II had begun.

The yishuv and World War II

The attitude of the Arabs toward the Allies—at least until it became clear that the Allied cause would win—was at best unfriendly, often far worse. Anwar Sadat, who in 1970 would become president of the United Arab Republic (Egypt), was jailed by the British for pro-Nazi activities. In contrast, the Jews of the yishuv were eager from the first to join the battle against Hitler.

The British were embarrassed by the fact that Jewish volunteers vastly outnumbered those of the Arabs. In fact, British officials tried to discourage Jews from signing up, in order to keep the number of Jewish soldiers down to the Arab level. Yet despite low pay and barriers to promotion, Jews continued to demand the right to serve.

In September 1944, the English army finally formed a Jewish Brigade. The Brigade fought bravely in Italy and Central Europe, and made the first contacts with Jewish survivors of the death camps.

But England, even when facing a possible invasion by Hitler, continued to treat Jewish immigration to Palestine as if it were a major threat to the British Empire. The White Paper of 1939 was ruthlessly put into effect. Jewish immigration to Palestine was almost completely stopped. Though millions of Jews were being murdered in Europe, no more than 1500 souls per month were allowed into the Holy Land.

Thus the yishuv was forced to wage not one battle but two: one against Hitler, the other against the British. David Ben-Gurion spoke for all Zionists when he said: "We shall fight the war as if there were no White Paper, and we shall fight the White Paper as if there were no war."

The Zionists tried in every possible way to save Jews from the Holocaust and to smuggle them into Palestine. Some came by foot, taking months to complete the nearly impossible overland journey. Most came by sea, often in old cargo vessels barely able to make the trip.

Since this immigration violated English laws, British forces kept a stern watch along the coast of Palestine. Refugees caught by the English were lucky if they were sent to a detention camp on some island under British control. The less fortunate were sent back to sea. One ship with

Abba Eban Remembers:
David Ben-Gurion

David Ben-Gurion
(1886–1973).

The first fifteen years of Israeli independence were dominated by the figure of David Ben-Gurion. He occupied a larger place in the nation's life than the prime ministership in a democratic country strictly requires. His main gift was his capacity to put the national will to work.

Sometimes he concentrated so hard on a single theme that he became quite absent-minded about anything else. I remember talking to him once at an airport where we were receiving a distinguished foreign visitor. Ben-Gurion turned to me and said suddenly, "What are you doing? Where have you been in the last couple of years?" My reply was: "Prime Minister, for the last three years I have been Minister of Education and Culture in the cabinet over which you preside every week."

Toward the end of his life, he fell out with many of his previous colleagues, developed a kind of despair about some of the unattractive aspects of Israel's political struggle, and even began to doubt whether our nation would survive after his death. This is a common failing of really great leaders. They identify themselves so closely with the history of the nation that they genuinely doubt if it will continue when their own lives come to an end.

Despite some of his weaknesses, Ben-Gurion was a man cast in a heroic mold, and Jewish history will never forget his unique role in bringing Israel out of exile into full statehood.

769 Jews, among them children between the ages of ten and sixteen, was turned back into the Black Sea where it sank, leaving only one survivor.

War against the British

One would like to write that when the war was over—when the shocking results of anti-Semitism were clear to all—the world came to its senses and began to treat our people as human beings. But that would not be true.

Instead, new pogroms broke out, aimed at the helpless survivors of the Holocaust. These homeless Jews begged to be allowed to escape from Europe, but the doors of the West were still closed, and the British remained rigidly opposed to Jewish immigration to Palestine. The homeless were forced to remain on the continent they most feared, a huddled mass of some 300,-000 people grouped together in camps for "displaced persons."

Meanwhile, England was making plans to prevent forever the creation of a Jewish state. Clashes between the Zionists and the British army became more and more severe. Some Palestinian Jews organized an underground resistance movement called the IRGUN (אִרְגוּן). Led by the Polish refugee Menahem Begin, the Irgun declared war on the British, eventually blowing up a section of the British headquarters at the King David Hotel in Jerusalem. At last, in April 1947, the British government realized that it was unable to control Palestine any longer, and handed the matter over to the General Assembly of the new United Nations.

The General Assembly debate

Seven months of hard bargaining followed. The General Assembly, over bitter Arab objections, named a special committee to consider both Palestine and the problem of the displaced persons. At midnight on September 1, eight years from the day World War II began, the committee suggested dividing Palestine into two parts—one state for the Arabs, one

---

Abba Eban Remembers:
Menaḥem Begin

Menaḥem Begin
(1913–   ).

The most extraordinary part of Menaḥem Begin's career is the way it flowered late in life. For twenty-nine years he was an opposition leader, taking his party through eight unsuccessful election campaigns. But once he exchanged the role of opposition orator for that of responsible prime minister, he fully understood that campaign slogans had very little relevance to the real predicaments in which a statesman finds himself.

Thus he gave up more territory and made more concessions than anyone would have believed possible a few months before his accession to power. This, incidentally, is not an uncommon attribute of political leaders. They often tend to take attitudes opposite to those that are expected of them. It is as if they are determined to work against the image that the press and world opinion have fixed upon them.

There was an English historian, Lord Acton, who once said, "Power corrupts." I have never believed this. It very often happens that power ennobles and enlarges the capacities of people beyond what was thought possible before they attained power. There are at least as many cases of power ennobling people as of power corrupting them.

The fact that it was Begin and not a prime minister from the Labor Party who signed our first formal peace treaty with an Arab neighbor must seem ironic to many people, but in a curiously satisfying and appropriate way it testifies to the essential harmony of purpose that flows beneath all the clashes of temperament and political conviction in our national life. When it comes to the great questions of peace and war, we remain at one.

THE EARLY ALIYOT

PERIOD	YEARS	NUMBER OF IMMI-GRANTS	IMPORTANT ASPECTS	FAMOUS SETTLERS (with immigration dates)
First Aliyah	1882–1903	25,000	Individuals and small groups, especially BILU. Settlements supported by Baron Edmond de Rothschild.	Eliezer Ben-Yehudah (1881)
Second Aliyah	1904–1914	40,000	Followed Kishinev pogrom. First kevutzot, labor parties, and self-help organizations formed. Halted by World War I.	David Ben-Gurion (1906)
Third Aliyah	1919–1923	35,000	Followed Balfour Declaration; British rule Palestine. Halutzim; first kibbutzim founded.	Golda Meir (1921) Aḥad Ha-am (1922)
Fourth Aliyah	1924–1928	67,000	Many middle-class Jews, especially from Poland.	Ḥaim Nahman Bialik (1924)

Aliyah did not end in 1928. A Fifth Aliyah (1929–1939) included some 250,000 refugees from European anti-Semitism; most of them arrived after Hitler came to power in Germany in 1933. For the activities of Youth Aliyah during this period, see the previous chapter. The flood of immigrants that began as soon as Israel became independent (see Chapter 23) is sometimes called a "mass aliyah."

state for the Jews. The outline of the future had been set.

Zionists around the world were pleased by the committee report. If it were approved, it would mean that the nations of the world had joined together in order to establish a Jewish state in Palestine. But would it be approved? Much depended on two powerful nations, the United States and the Soviet Union. For six weeks the Zionists fought to win the crucial support of these two world powers. This support was gained in mid-October, but many more votes were also needed. Would the other nations join America and Russia or vote with the Arabs against the Jews?

On November 29, 1947, the key vote was taken by the General Assembly. Should Palestine be divided and a Jewish state approved? If "no," the international community would be saying that the Arabs were to rule wherever they lived—the Jews, nowhere at all. If "no," the Jews, having barely survived the Holocaust, would lose their claim to statehood—perhaps forever.

The United States, the Soviet Union, most European states, many of the Latin

David Ben-Gurion reads Israel's Proclamation of Independence on May 14, 1948.

American countries, and the members of the British Commonwealth voted "yes." All the Arab states said "no." Britain itself abstained. The final total was 33 in favor, 13 opposed, 10 abstentions. The required two-thirds majority of those voting had given its approval.

Fifty years earlier, Theodor Herzl had convened the First Zionist Congress, launching the organized political move-ment to create a Jewish state. Now, after the Holocaust in Europe and because of the heroism of the ḥalutzim, the world had recognized that dream. On May 14, 1948 (the 6th of Iyar 5708), David Ben-Gurion, soon to be the prime minister of the new nation, stood before a picture of Herzl in a crowded room in Tel Aviv to read a Proclamation of Independence.

The State of Israel was born.

SUMMARY   *Hope for lasting peace in the Middle East was badly damaged when the British and French refused to deal fairly with the Zionist and Arab nationalist movements after World War I. Under British rule the Arabs were favored in the historically Jewish land of Palestine. In 1939 the British government issued a White Paper which stated that a permanent Arab majority would rule the Holy Land. During World War II, the British allowed only a trickle of Jewish immigrants, and continued to favor the Arabs (though many Arabs supported the Nazis). After the war, Jewish opposition forced Great Britain to turn to the United Nations, which voted to divide Palestine into two states, one Jewish and one Arab.*

PART SIX

The Nuclear Age

World Jewry Today

My road from London, through Cairo and Jerusalem, to New York and Washington, and then back to Jerusalem has been long and eventful. Many lifetimes have been crowded into a few decades. Those of us who took part in the establishment of the State of Israel have lived more nomadic, unstable, and varied lives than most people usually experience. We seldom knew where we would be or what we would be doing a few years hence.

Even now, Israel is afflicted with many insecurities. Sometimes when you fulfill your goal you feel a sense of emptiness. I remember asking Edmund Hillary, the first man to climb Mt. Everest, exactly what it was like to reach the peak. He told me that his first feeling was one of ecstasy. But then he felt a sense of desolation. Now that

One of the most remarkable features of modern culture
has been the explosion of Jewish activity in the arts.
There have always been Jewish storytellers, poets, and
craftsmen. But for the first time in history, Jewish painters,
sculptors, composers, writers, and performers have gained
a wide audience, among both Jews and non-Jews, for
works on both Jewish and non-Jewish themes. In Israel
and the Diaspora, there are many fine museums that
specialize in the work of Jewish artists. One of these is the
Tel Aviv Museum, the site of the sculpture exhibition
shown on the opposite page.

he had fulfilled his life's ambition, what more could he do? Were
there any Everests left to conquer? In Israel, too, we must find new
Everests, new peaks to reach.

When all is said and done, ours has been an extraordinary enterprise.
We have restored our nation's pride. We have given the Jewish
people a sense of its collective creativity. We have created a home
and sanctuary in which our particular legacy can be preserved and
enlarged. We have taken Jewish history out of provincialism and
caused it to flow once more into the central stream of human
culture. Above all, we have fulfilled our human vocation: we have
redeemed hundreds of thousands of our kinsmen from humiliation
and death, and brought to them a new life and a new hope.

Israel has no cause for apology. Ours is a society inspired by a
positive vision, a nation in which tomorrow is more vivid than
yesterday, a state which would rather build than destroy. We can
only hope that the Jewish people will be ennobled by this
experience of freedom, and will rise byond the sufferings of the past
and the ruins of history to accomplish its unique spiritual mission.

ABBA EBAN

Above, the Jewish Chapel at
Brandeis University, designed by
the architect Max Abramovitz;
upper right, the Bat Sheba dance
group of Tel Aviv; lower right,
"Alamo," a sculpture by Tony
Rosenthal in New York City.

Right, "Jacob's Ladder,"
a huge canvas by
Helen Frankenthaler
(Museum of Modern
Art, New York City);
below, "Third Marble
Doves," a sculpture by
Jacob Epstein (Israel
Museum, Jerusalem).

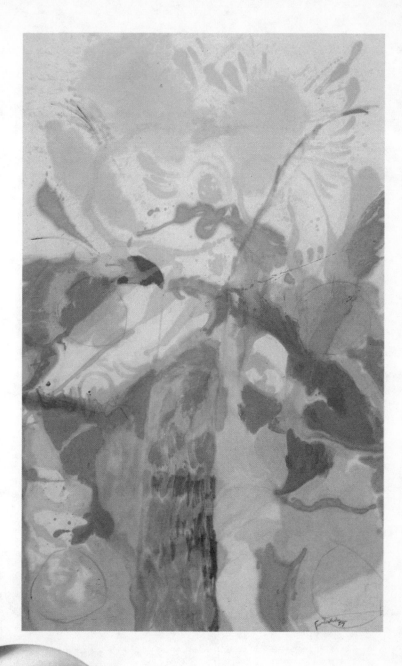

Probably the best-known modern
Jewish artist is Marc Chagall. Chagall
was born in Russia in 1887 but has
lived most of his life in France;
his "Jew with Torah" (above) is on
display at the Tel Aviv Museum.
At right, future Jewish artists develop
their talents at a special studio in
the Israel Museum.

22

INTRODUCTION TO PART SIX:

The Nuclear Age

At 8:15 a.m. on August 6, 1945, the United States exploded an atomic bomb over the Japanese port of Hiroshima, instantly reducing most of the city to rubble. Three days later, a second atomic bomb devastated the city of Nagasaki. On August 14, Japan surrendered to the United States.

World War II was over. The nuclear age had begun.

Hiroshima and Nagasaki were ruins, but most of Japan had not been damaged by the war. Europe, on the other hand, lay beaten and broken. The nations which had controlled most of the world since the nineteenth century were exhausted and shattered by the long conflict. The European empires in Asia and Africa rapidly fell apart. Within four years, nearly half a billion people in India and Indonesia received their independence. In the following decades, more than seventy other nations threw off colonial rule.

Rise of the Third World

This creation of so many new countries made the international scene highly complex. In the first years after World War II, the globe was largely divided between the allies of the United States and the nations controlled by Russian Communism. But many of the new states (and some that were not new) wanted to remain independent of both camps. To do this they formed a loose alliance which became known as the THIRD WORLD.

Some of the Third World nations were large and powerful, but many were tiny and poor.* There were so many of these new states that the Third World could obtain a majority in the United Nations General Assembly, where each nation has

* The five smallest members of the United Nations have a combined population less than that of the city of New Orleans.

Jews and the
Nuclear Age

Albert Einstein, a leading
scientist of the nuclear age.

The nuclear age is perhaps the most exciting—and most terrifying—period in human history. On the one hand, scientists have harnessed the power of the atom to produce electricity, diagnose and treat diseases, and find out the age of the earth. On the other hand, that same power has been used to make ever more dangerous and destructive weapons. The two superpowers, the United States and the Soviet Union, have stockpiled enough bombs to destroy each other and most of the rest of the world. Britain, France, China, and India have also made atomic weapons, and several other nations (including Israel) could make them, and possibly already have.

Jewish scientists played a key role at the dawning of the nuclear age. A Danish Jew, Niels Bohr, did the basic work on atomic structure that made it possible to split the atom. Albert Einstein and Leo Szilard, who together urged the U.S. government to make an atomic bomb, were both Jewish. So was J. Robert Oppenheimer, who headed the Manhattan Project which built the bomb dropped on Hiroshima.

These were all men of genius, who willingly pooled their talents in the hope of building a weapon that would stop Hitler and his allies. And yet, for the most part, they felt little joy in their scientific triumph. Later all of them, in different ways, worked for peace, disarmament, and a slowdown in weapons research. The tragedy of the nuclear age is that the nations of the world were more eager to have the bombs these scientists made possible than to have the peace they loved so much.

---

one vote. But when countries the size of villages could outvote the most powerful nations on earth, the UN became all but useless as a place for serious international debate.

More important, those Third World nations which produce oil were able to join forces to raise the price of the oil they sell to the rest of the world. Since most of these countries are Arab, they were also able to use oil as a powerful political weapon against Israel. In 1973, for example, Arab countries cut off oil shipments to Western nations which supported the Jewish state during the Yom Kippur War (see Chapter 23).

The struggle for freedom

Independence for Third World countries did not always mean independence for those who lived in them. Sometimes the new native leaders were far more brutal than the European rulers they replaced.

The future for freedom seemed no better in other parts of the world. The Soviet Union seized control of a large area of Eastern Europe, separating these nations from the rest of Europe with brick walls and barbed wire, as well as by terror, secrecy, and censorship. The unseen barrier between these Russian–controlled countries and the "free world" was called the "Iron Curtain." Among the Iron Curtain countries were Czechoslovakia, Poland, and Hungary.

When the Czechs, Poles, and Hungarians tried to regain some of their lost freedoms, their rebellions were ruthlessly crushed by the Russian army. Meanwhile, in China, a revolution brought another one-fourth of the world's people under Communist rule.

As more and more of the world came under Communist control, the United States became the leader of the free world. Immediately after World War II, America poured $12 billion of financial aid into the war-torn nations of Europe, saving the battered continent from ruin and helping it return to economic health. When the Soviet Union began a blockade of West Berlin, American planes brought supplies into the former Nazi capital and saved it from the Russians. And when a Communist army attacked South Korea, America was the leading force in a United Nations army which brought an end to the invasion.

American conflicts

It seemed that the free world had learned that dictators—whether Nazi or Communist—had to be stopped. And it seemed best to stop them before they conquered other smaller nations, and before it would be necessary to fight another world war. No longer would the free world back away from the threats of dictators. Threats against free nations would be met, challenged, and defeated.

Unfortunately, world politics refused to stay that simple. In the early 1960's, the United States began sending money, weapons, and soldiers to South Vietnam to keep it from being taken over by the Communists. As the war dragged on, however, it became clear that this was not a heroic fight for freedom—in fact, the United States soon found that it was fighting to save a corrupt government which had little support even among its own people. (Actually, the government of South Vietnam was itself a dictatorship.) In Vietnam, no side was the "right" side. The war itself was long—the longest in American history —and bloody, causing horrible destruction in Asia. At home, the American people were bitterly divided. Some believed the war had to be won at any cost. Some believed that the cost was too high and nothing would be gained even by winning. American forces were finally withdrawn from South Vietnam, which was then overrun by the Communists.

Another major conflict of the 1950's and 1960's involved race. A century had passed since the Civil War, but blacks in the South were still forbidden to attend schools with whites, or to sit in buses if doing so would force whites to stand. Public toilets and drinking fountains carried three labels: Men, Women, and Colored.

The struggle for civil rights—the right of every American to be treated equally by the law—was led by an inspired black

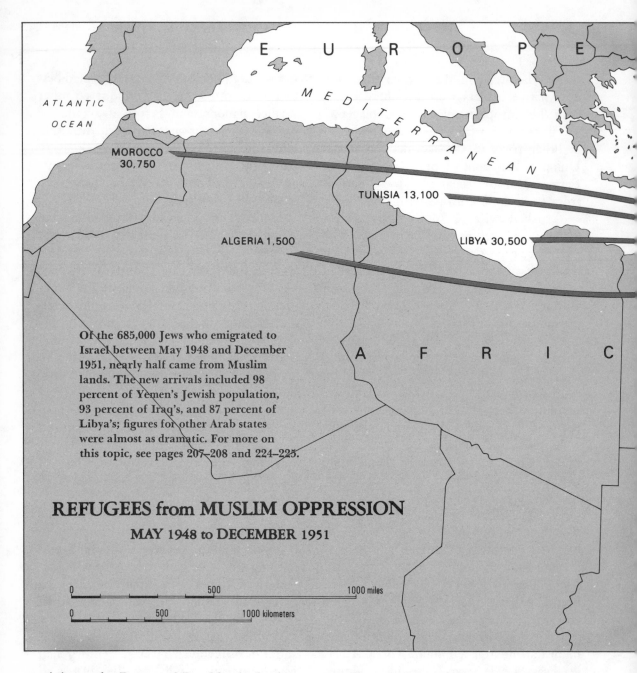

ATLANTIC
OCEAN

E U R O P E

M E D I T E R R A N E A N

MOROCCO
30,750

TUNISIA 13,100

ALGERIA 1,500

LIBYA 30,500

A F R I C A

Of the 685,000 Jews who emigrated to Israel between May 1948 and December 1951, nearly half came from Muslim lands. The new arrivals included 98 percent of Yemen's Jewish population, 93 percent of Iraq's, and 87 percent of Libya's; figures for other Arab states were almost as dramatic. For more on this topic, see pages 207–208 and 224–225.

REFUGEES from MUSLIM OPPRESSION

MAY 1948 to DECEMBER 1951

0   500   1000 miles

0   500   1000 kilometers

minister, the Reverend Dr. Martin Luther King, Jr. Under his bold leadership, blacks and whites marched side-by-side to challenge immoral laws and to boycott segregated institutions. Sometimes all they asked was for blacks and whites to be seated at the same table in a restaurant.

The reaction of traditional Southerners to such peaceful requests was often brutal —Dr. King was eventually murdered. But his followers remained non-violent. Police sent their dogs to attack unarmed men and women whose only crime was wanting to walk together peacefully; but King never allowed his people to damage their cause by imitating the violence of their opponents.

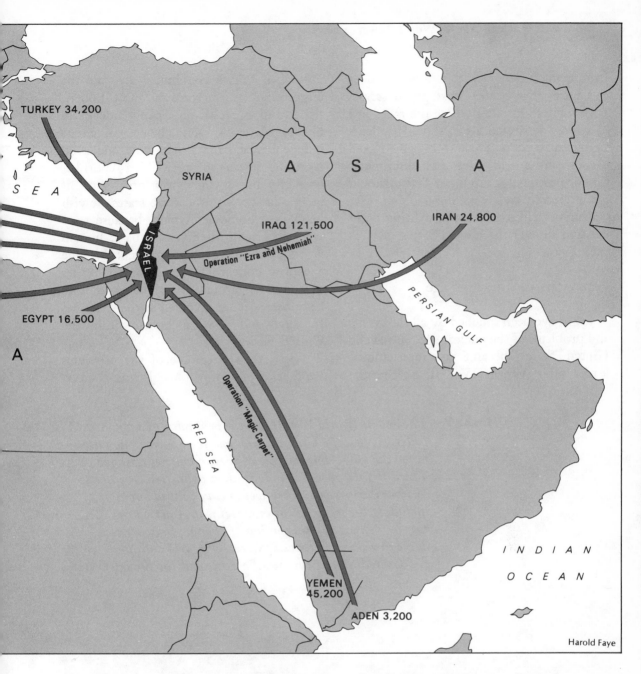

TURKEY 34,200

SYRIA

A S I A

S E A

IRAQ 121,500

Operation "Ezra and Nehemiah"

ISRAEL

IRAN 24,800

PERSIAN GULF

EGYPT 16,500

A

RED SEA

Operation "Magic Carpet"

INDIAN

OCEAN

YEMEN
45,200

ADEN 3,200

Harold Faye

In time, the laws which made blacks second-class citizens fell before the moral justice of the freedom marchers.

The success of the civil rights movement led other groups to organize in defense of their rights. Women, in particular, fought hard for political, social, and economic equality. By the 1970's, the laws of the United States had been changed to prohibit most forms of discrimination.

Yet, just as world politics became more complex after the defeat of Hitler, so the problems of discrimination became more difficult after some of the old unjust laws were struck down. Most Americans now agree that no law should forbid blacks from going to school with whites. But does this mean that blacks *must* go to school with whites? In cities where the races live in widely separated areas, should students be bused to schools where racially mixed classes can be held? Does past discrimination against one group mean that it should get preferred treatment now?

Questions like these are now being hotly debated all over the United States.

Jews in the nuclear age

Jews have been touched by all the events and problems of the nuclear age. Just as the United States became an international leader after World War II, so too the American Jewish community became the largest, most prosperous, and most influential group of Jews on earth—indeed, in history. A Jewish state, Israel, gained its independence from British rule and soon won the respect of the Third World—until the Third World saw greater profit in an alliance with the Arab states. Jewish people in the Soviet Union, because they were so cruelly deprived of basic human rights by the Russian government, became a central concern of Jews—and Gentiles of goodwill—around the globe. And Jews have been deeply involved in the struggles for civil and political rights within the United States.

These, then, are some of the problems we face as part of WORLD JEWRY TODAY.

SUMMARY   *The end of World War II saw the beginning of a new world order. At first the United States and the Soviet Union dominated the globe, but the role of these countries changed as a Third World of newly independent countries developed. Within thirty years, there were many painful conflicts, including the struggle for civil rights in America and the war in Vietnam. In this period of change, Jews became deeply involved in three key areas of world politics: the United States, the Middle East, and the Soviet Union.*

23

The State of Israel

On the platform, David Ben-Gurion stood reading the Proclamation of Independence of the new State of Israel. But it was clear to everyone in that crowded room in Tel Aviv on that humid day in May of 1948, that the struggle for independence and statehood still lay ahead. What the new state needed most was people. Immediately after proclaiming national independence, Ben-Gurion announced the ending of all restrictions on Jewish immigration to the Holy Land. The doors were open to every Jew who wished to return to Eretz Yisrael.

From behind the barbed wire they rushed—men, women, and children. They came from the concentration camps Hitler had hoped would be the end of all Jews. They came from the displaced persons camps of Europe which had been set up to hold these penniless and homeless survivors of the Holocaust until the day some nation would allow them to settle. And they came from the detention camps estab-lished by the British to keep them from entering Palestine as "illegal" immigrants. In only nineteen months, Israel welcomed 340,000 immigrants, almost three times the number that had entered Palestine, legally or illegally, during the last nine years of British rule.

"Operation Magic Carpet"

The refugees from Europe were soon joined by refugees from Muslim oppression. They came from many lands and in large numbers: 34,200 from Turkey, 43,000 from Iran and Afghanistan, more than 30,000 from Morocco, 121,500 from Iraq. During its first forty months, the Jewish state doubled its population through immigration. Israel welcomed the sick and the healthy, the penniless and the prosperous, at a time when the rest of the world said it had "no room" for homeless Jews.

Perhaps the most wonderful tale of immigration to Eretz Yisrael was the story of the 45,200 Jews of Yemen. Yemen is a country in the southwest corner of Arabia, a place where Jews were living at least 300 years before the birth of Muhammad; but for many centuries they had lived under grim persecution. By 1948 life in Yemen had become so unbearable that arrangements were made to fly the Yemenite Jews —all of them—to the new Jewish state.

These Jews were living in such backward conditions that they had never seen an airplane. When they saw the huge aircraft, they believed that they were witnessing a miracle. With these "metal birds" God was keeping the promise made through the prophet Isaiah that the Jewish people would return to Zion "on wings, as eagles." But one group of Yemenites began to light a fire on the floor of their plane when it was time to cook a meal!

Despite such misunderstandings, "Operation Magic Carpet" was a complete success. In just over one year, the entire Jewish community of Yemen was in the Promised Land.

Making a new nation

The sudden flood of immigrants staggered the tiny new country. At the time of independence, there were only 750,000 Jews in Israel. Within only four years, there were 1,500,000. There was no way to provide proper housing, jobs, or health care for so many people in so short a time. The new arrivals could only be jammed into MAABAROT , מַעְבָּרוֹת (tent cities). Telling what the maabarot were like, Israel's fourth prime minister, Golda Meir, wrote:

The man who had lived through years of Nazi slave labor, survived the [displaced persons] camps and braved the trip to Israel and who was, at best, in poor health and, at worst, badly damaged physically and entitled to the best possible conditions found himself and his family (if he still had one) . . . with people with whom he didn't even have a common language. Nine times out of ten, he even regarded his new neighbors as primitive because they had never seen a flush toilet. . . . Or consider the illiterate woman from Libya or Yemen

A "tent city" in 1952. Only six years after this photograph was taken, all the maabarot in Israel had disappeared, and all the new immigrants were properly resettled.

or the caves of the Atlas Mountains who was stuck with her children in a drafty, leaky tent with Polish or Czech Jews who prepared their food differently, ate things that made her feel sick and, by her standards, weren't even Jews at all either because they weren't observant or else because their prayers and rituals were totally unfamiliar to her.

In 1952, when immigration began to slow down (to "only" about sixty a day), the country was able to turn its attention to resettling the new Israelis. By the tenth birthday of the Jewish state, the tent cities had disappeared.

In their place were thriving villages and rich farms. Land which had become desert during centuries of neglect and misuse was again flowing with "milk and honey." One key was the planting of trees—trees whose roots kept soil from eroding, whose trunks provided wood, whose leaves gave shade, whose fruit offered food. By the twenty-fifth birthday of the State of Israel, more than 108 million trees had been planted through the work of the Jewish National Fund.

With the rebirth of the land of Israel came a rebirth of its people. Men and women who had been helpless victims of brutal tyrants were now proud citizens of a free land. Jews who had been deprived of schooling found education available at all levels. Those who arrived as strangers in a sea of languages were quickly taught to speak simple modern Hebrew.

A new generation grew up: young Jews born in a Jewish state. These native-born Israelis were called SABRAS (צַבָּרִים) because they were said to be like the fruit of the Sabra cactus: tough on the outside, but sweet under the skin!

Culture in all forms played an important

The lush landscape of Zikhron Yaakov, in northern Israel. Artificial fish ponds stretch like a patchwork quilt between the Tel Aviv–Jaffa highway (foreground) and the Mediterranean Sea.

role even in such a poor country with so many pressing needs. These were, after all, Jews, with a deep love for the arts, especially for theater, music, and dance. Israel is probably the only country which had a symphony orchestra before it had a government! (Today's Israel Philharmonic was founded in 1936 when it was called the Palestine Orchestra.) A great many museums have been built, including the famous Shrine of the Book, which houses some of the Dead Sea Scrolls—the most ancient existing Hebrew manuscripts.

And the Jewish state has looked after its

non-Jewish citizens, too. All citizens—Jews, Christian, Arabs—have the right to vote. Those Arabs who live in Israel have a high standard of living, and are the only ones in the Middle East to enjoy the freedoms of democracy.

The War of Independence

Caring and providing for new immigrants, building a new nation, reclaiming desert lands to create farmlands, establishing schools and synagogues and courts of law—Israel has done much in a short time. It would be impressive for a nation at peace. It is nothing less than astounding because, for its entire history, Israel has been under siege, threatened with total destruction by its Arab neighbors.

Israel's War of Independence really began in December 1947, just after the United Nations voted to divide Palestine into two countries. But for many months both sides waited. The new Jewish state was barely five minutes old when, just past midnight on the night of May 14–15, 1948, the Arabs launched their first full-scale attack. The Israelis seemed hopelessly outnumbered, yet they scored one victory after another.

For example, early in the war, 45 Arab tanks with more than 150 other armored vehicles came down from the hills of Syria into the Jordan Valley to destroy the kibbutz of Degania. At the same moment, the Israelis were hastily putting together two old howitzers (guns such as those used by the French army in 1870), which had just been rushed to Degania from the port at Haifa. The first Arab tank had already entered the kibbutz when it was hit by a single howitzer shell. The rest of the tank

column, convinced that the Israelis had new heavy weapons, turned and fled. For all practical purposes, this ended the Syrian involvement in the war! *

The War of Independence was not very long—only sixty days of fighting in three spurts between December 1947 and January 1949. Yet in this short war, Israel lost 6000 people, nearly one percent of its small population. The Jewish state also suffered another painful loss: the old city of Jerusalem, including the ancient Jewish Quarter, was held onto by Jordan. For nineteen years it remained under Arab control, and Jews were forbidden to enter it. Jewish holy places, synagogues, and schools were all destroyed. Tombstones were taken from Jewish cemeteries and were used to build roads and toilets.

Despite these losses, the Israeli victory seemed like a miracle. Not only had the Israelis held off the entire Arab world—but for the first time since the days of the Maccabees, the Jews had won a war and were masters of their own homeland.

Unfortunately, the Arab states refused to accept this reality. Although it would have been best if they had joined hands with Israel in developing the Middle East, they preferred to wage war.

The Suez Campaign

The second chapter in this sad story took place in 1956. The dictator of Egypt, Colonel Gamal Abdel Nasser, sent terrorists into Israel to murder civilians. He blocked the lifelines of Israel's sea trade—the Suez Canal and the Straits of Tiran. The Arabs stopped any ship bringing sup-

* The burned out tank can still be seen at Degania, where it is preserved as a war memorial.

The UN PARTITION PLAN 1947

To be under Jewish control

To be under Arab control

⊙ To be under international control

MEDITERRANEAN SEA

Beirut

LEBANON

• Damascus

SYRIA

Jerusalem ⊙

• Amman

Gaza

Beersheba

JORDAN

Suez Canal

• Cairo

Suez

S I N A I

E G Y P T

Gulf of Suez

Gulf of Aqaba

Strait of Tiran

SAUDI ARABIA

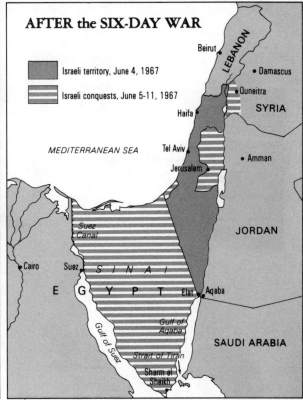

AFTER the SIX-DAY WAR

Israeli territory, June 4, 1967

Israeli conquests, June 5-11, 1967

MEDITERRANEAN SEA

Beirut

LEBANON

• Damascus

Quneitra

Haifa

SYRIA

Tel Aviv

Jerusalem

• Amman

Suez Canal

JORDAN

• Cairo

Suez

S I N A I

E G Y P T

Elat

Aqaba

Gulf of Suez

Gulf of Aqaba

Strait of Tiran

Sharm el Sheikh

SAUDI ARABIA

ISRAEL'S CHANGING BORDERS

When the War of Independence ended, Israel held two areas not included in the UN Partition Plan of 1947: a strip of land in the northwest extending to the Lebanon border, and some territory west of the Jordan, including part of Jerusalem. Israel gave up the territories it captured during the Suez Campaign of 1956. In 1967, however, Israel refused to surrender the regions it won in the Six Day War: the Sinai, Gaza Strip, Golan Heights, and West Bank. The Yom Kippur War in 1973 resulted in a slight Israeli pullback on the Syrian and Egyptian fronts. Much more important changes are likely to come from the peace treaty reached by Israeli Prime Minister Begin and Egyptian President Sadat early in 1979. Under that agreement, Israel will gradually withdraw from the Sinai and will allow the Palestinians of Gaza and the West Bank to move toward self-government.

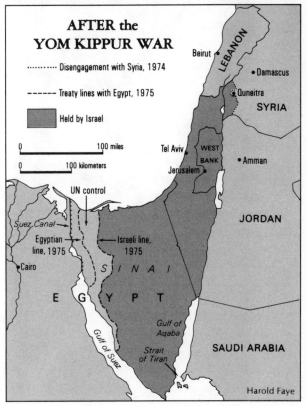

AFTER the YOM KIPPUR WAR

········· Disengagement with Syria, 1974

- - - - - Treaty lines with Egypt, 1975

Held by Israel

Beirut

LEBANON

• Damascus

Quneitra

SYRIA

0   100 miles

0   100 kilometers

Tel Aviv

WEST BANK

• Amman

Jerusalem

UN control

JORDAN

Suez Canal

Egyptian line, 1975

Israeli line, 1975

• Cairo

S I N A I

E G Y P T

Gulf of Aqaba

Gulf of Suez

Strait of Tiran

SAUDI ARABIA

Harold Faye

A Nation Under Siege

Four times, Israelis have had to fight for their freedom: top, heavy action in the Negev during the War of Independence; left, first aid for a wounded soldier during the Suez Campaign; bottom left, a quiet moment on the Golan Heights during the Yom Kippur War; below, the liberation of the Western Wall, the climax of the Six Day War and the most thrilling event in Israel's military history.

plies to the Jewish state. And Nasser announced that he would destroy Israel.

Searching for a way to break out of Nasser's trap, the Jewish state found two unlikely allies: England and France. Only eight years earlier, Israel had been battling England to gain its own independence. France, like England, was quickly losing its colonies and interested only in seeing Europeans keep control of the Suez Canal. Still, fighting for its life, Israel joined with the European nations. The three launched a joint attack on October 29, 1956.

Within 100 hours, the campaign was over. To everyone's surprise, the combined forces of England and France had failed to seize the Suez Canal, but tiny Israel had conquered the entire Sinai Peninsula. Israel later withdrew from the land it had taken, but only after being promised that a United Nations force would guard the Egyptian-Israeli border to prevent future wars.

The next ten years were fairly peaceful. Then Nasser again announced that Egypt would destroy Israel. Again he blockaded the Straits of Tiran. And he ordered the United Nations Emergency Force to leave the Egyptian-Israeli border.

Israel had trusted the United Nations. But now, at the very moment the UN was most needed to prevent war, its troops left the area with extreme speed. Israel had trusted the great democracies. Now not one of them was willing to defy the Egyptian blockade and bring ships into Israel. France, which had been a major supplier of weapons to Israel, even said it would no longer sell arms to the Jewish state.

This was a turning point in Israeli history. Israel discovered that in times of danger it had no friends. The Jews stood completely alone.

The Six Day War

On June 5, 1967, the armies of the Jewish state smashed through the Egyptian lines and plunged into the Sinai Peninsula.

This was the beginning of what would be known as the Six Day War. Actually, the war was won in six hours, when Israeli warplanes destroyed Egypt's entire air force. Most of the Egyptian planes did not even have time to leave the ground.

Syria and Jordan joined the Egyptian attack on Israel. They, too, were quickly defeated. In an effort to save face, Colonel Nasser and King Hussein of Jordan decided to accuse the United States of using its planes to help the Jewish state. But just as Israel's military had been ready for the war, Israel's spies were prepared to do their part. In a spectacular piece of undercover work, the spies recorded the phone conversation between Nasser and Hussein in which the two Arab leaders agreed to spread this lie!

In one week, Israel had turned the threat of extinction to complete military triumph. The world had waited, with fear or hope, to see Israel reduced to ashes. Instead there were pictures of Jewish soldiers swimming in the Suez Canal. The hills overlooking the Sea of Galilee—the Golan Heights, from which Syrians had regularly fired on Jewish farm settlements—were now in Israeli hands. So was the entire area west of the Jordan River (the so-called "West Bank"). Most thrillingly, the old walled city of Jerusalem was captured. For the first time since 1948, Jews could gather for prayer at the Western Wall of the ancient

Temple, the most sacred site of Jewish tradition.

It was difficult for even the most hard-hearted Jew to see the Six Day War as anything less than a miracle.

The Yom Kippur War

For six years there was an uneasy peace. Then, on Yom Kippur 1973, as Jews gathered in synagogues all over the world, Egypt and Syria launched a surprise attack. Israel, caught unprepared, needed three weeks to stop the Arab advance. The number of Israeli casualties was terribly high: 2500 dead, almost 6000 wounded. For such a small country, with such a small population, it was a very high price. Almost every Israeli lost a friend or a relative in the Yom Kippur War.

Yet when the shooting stopped, the Israelis had again performed the impossible. They had crossed the Suez Canal into Egypt, stopping only sixty miles short of Cairo, the Egyptian capital. In doing so, they had surrounded and trapped a large portion of the Egyptian army. At first it seemed that the Israelis had won a fourth victory.

Egypt, however, proud that its armies had not run from battle as they had in earlier wars, behaved as if it had won a great triumph. Even though it was clear to the rest of the world that they had lost the military war, Egypt now made a surprising move by which they won a political victory. The Egyptians proclaimed their friendship for a Jew—American Secretary of State Henry Kissinger—and used him to reach agreements with the Jewish state that they had tried to destroy!

Under pressure from the United States, the Israelis agreed to return the Suez Canal to Egypt, and to withdraw from most of the Sinai Peninsula—giving up the valuable oil wells. They did all this hoping that Egypt would make peace rather than wage war. However, for a long time, the Egyptians did not seem interested in discussing peace—that is, until 1977, when the Egyptian president suddenly accepted an invitation from the prime minister of Israel to come to Jerusalem to speak to the Israeli parliament (the Knesset, כְּנֶסֶת).

The world was stunned. The president of Egypt was Anwar Sadat, the former Nazi sympathizer. The prime minister of Israel was Menahem Begin, the former leader of the extremist Irgun. Yet the two men shook hands like old friends and, standing together in Jerusalem, pledged to the world that there would never again be war between their two countries.

Peace did not come quickly, however. A year and a half passed before Begin and Sadat, helped by American President Jimmy Carter, succeeded in agreeing on the terms of a treaty. And more long bargaining sessions were needed before the ideals spelled out in the treaty could become a reality. The leaders of Israel and Egypt also had to face the fact that other Arab nations opposed the agreement. Instead of welcoming peace, they criticized the treaty and called the Egyptian president a traitor to the Arab cause.

"Palestinians" and the Arab world

The Arabs, unsuccessful against Israel on the battlefield, used other methods against the Jewish state. These included terrorism, political pressure, and the raising of oil prices.

Zionism—the Tasks Ahead

Commemorative coin issued by the State of Israel.

The Zionist movement set out to establish a Jewish state in Palestine and, by so doing, to rekindle the Jewish spirit throughout the Diaspora. In both these aims the Zionists succeeded brilliantly. Can we therefore say that Zionism as a political movement is no longer necessary?

Not if we remember that the Zionist pioneers also had other goals—goals which proved even harder to achieve. The Zionists hoped to create a homeland where our people could live in peace, secure from attack. But unfortunately, after four wars and countless raids by Arab terrorists, Israel is still a dangerous place for a Jew to live.

The Zionists also hoped that the rebirth of the State of Israel would free the Jews from dependence on other nations. That, too, was a false hope. Without emergency help from the United States, Israel might not have survived the Yom Kippur War. During the 1970's, the U.S. government gave more economic and military aid to Israel than to any other country.

The fact that Israel is neither secure nor fully independent does not mean that Zionism is a failure—far from it. But it does mean that the tasks which lie ahead are at least as challenging as the tasks which the Zionist movement has already accomplished.

Israel's most terrible enemies were the so-called PALESTINIANS—those Arabs who deserted Israel during the War of Independence in hopes that the Jewish state would be destroyed.* Through the years, Israel had supported and resettled the Jewish refugees who had come from Arab and European lands. But in the Arab nations, the Muslim leaders left Arab refugees from Israel stranded in tent cities where they had to be supported mainly by aid from America. (Russia gave nothing for the support of these stranded people.)

From 1948 to 1967, no Muslim leader suggested that these "Palestinians" should

* Those Arabs who remained in Israel were and are Israeli citizens.

have a state of their own. Only when the Israelis gained control of the West Bank—an area where Jews had lived for centuries until they were forced out by the Arab riots of the 1930's—did the Arab nations begin to demand that the "Palestinians" be given the region as a homeland.

The "Palestinians" themselves made it clear that their goal was not just the West Bank, but the total destruction of the Jewish state. They began a long series of terrorist attacks. Time and again they invaded Israeli schools and villages, murdering dozens of Jewish schoolchildren. An attack on the Israeli team at the 1972 Olympics left eleven Israeli athletes dead. Bombs were set off in Jerusalem and Tel

Aviv, bringing death to innocent people who happened to be in the streets.

The governments of the world should have spoken out against the terrorist acts of the Palestinians. But they were afraid of losing Arab oil. Still, not speaking out was a serious mistake. Terrorists around the world grew bolder, hijacking airline flights and holding innocent people captive. Even so, the governments of the world powers behaved as if oil were more important than human lives or the safety of their own citizens.

Throughout the 1970's, Arab oil was a powerful weapon. After the Yom Kippur War, the Arab states imposed a five-month ban on oil exports to the United States and other countries they felt had helped Israel. This caused shortages and hardships, especially in Western Europe. When the oil shipments began again, prices were doubled. Moreover, the Arabs refused to trade with companies that also did business with the State of Israel. Company after company, nation after nation gave in to these pressures.

The international surrender to Arab wealth was shown most clearly at the United Nations. In 1974 a leading Arab terrorist, Yasir Arafat, was welcomed to the General Assembly. It was a triumph of evil. Wearing a pistol on his hip, he spoke to the nations of the world—the same nations whose airplanes his people had hijacked! And in 1975, twenty-eight years after voting to create a Jewish state, the UN solemnly declared Zionism to be a form of racism.*

---

* Zionism, of all nationalist movements, has been perhaps the least racist. A vast range of religious groups enjoy full freedom in Israel, as do all races. When Jerusalem was reunified after the Six Day War, all residents of the Old City—most of them Arab—were immediately given Israeli citizenship.

This vote was taken on November 10—the thirty-seventh anniversary of Kristallnacht, the night the Nazis destroyed the synagogues of Germany. It seemed that the United Nations was no longer a place where a democratic state such as Israel could get a fair hearing.

Problems of "Oriental Jews"

In addition to its problems with the Arab world and its search for peace, Israel has problems which divide it from within. Two of these seem the most difficult to solve.

The first is that the Jews of Israel today are divided into two very different groups—those from Eastern Europe and those from Asia and North Africa. The "Founding Fathers" of Israel, such as Chaim Weizmann and David Ben-Gurion, were all from Eastern Europe. So were most of the early settlers and immigrants. But in the first thirty years of statehood, the refugees from Asia and North Africa—called "Oriental Jews"—became a majority of the population. The problem is that they have not gained the political or economic power to match their numbers.

This is not entirely surprising. Most of these Oriental Jews came to Israel knowing little about modern life, and with none of the skills needed for high-level positions in modern government and industry. Many of the founders of Israel are still alive and active, so there has been very little turning over of power to others, regardless of national origin. Yet the younger Jews of European origin know that "their time will come"; the future for the Oriental Jews is much less clear. In the coming years, Israel will need to integrate all Jews into the life of the country.

Russian Jewish immigrants
reach the Promised Land.

The question of religious freedom

Perhaps more difficult is the question of the free practice of Judaism in the Jewish state.

At first, this seems strange. Shouldn't Israel be one country where all Jews are absolutely free to practice their religion? It should be, but it is not.

Most of the halutzim had little interest in religion, but those who were religious were usually Orthodox. Therefore, whenever a question about religion in the young state needed answering, the answer was usually given by the Orthodox pioneers. "Official" Judaism in Eretz Yisrael thus became highly traditional. Now that the country has grown and new generations have been born, more and more of Israel's Jews are seeking a more modern kind of Judaism—more like the Judaism of the American Reform and Conservative movements.

These two movements have been brought to Israel by Israeli Jews searching for religious roots and by American Jews emigrating to Israel who wanted to bring their religious roots with them. But Israel's Orthodox rabbis control marriage, divorce, and conversion, so no Reform and few Conservative rabbis may perform these ceremonies in Israel. The Orthodox also control Jewish cemeteries, which gives them control over Jewish funerals.

The Orthodox, of course, do not limit the practice of Christianity or Islam. So the only people in Israel who do not have full freedom of religion are the Reform and Conservative Jews. Even so, liberal Judaism is growing there.

Four thousand years ago, the Bible tells us, the land of Israel was promised to Abraham and his descendants. The Bible does not suggest that the descendants would en-

"Pray for the peace
of Jerusalem . . ."
(Psalms 122:6)

joy the land without having any problems!

The State of Israel faces enormous challenges. Yet the way it has faced challenges in the past—indeed, the simple fact that it exists—gives all Jews, and many Gentiles, feelings of pride, courage, confidence, determination, and faith.

What Israel's future will bring, no one would be foolish enough to predict. But deep within the hopeful Jewish soul, there remains the dream that, one day . . .

כִּי מִצִּיּוֹן תֵּצֵא תוֹרָה
וּדְבַר־יְהֹוָה מִירוּשָׁלָם

Instruction shall come forth from Zion,
The word of the Lord from Jerusalem.
(Isaiah 2:3)

SUMMARY   *In its first thirty years of existence, the State of Israel took in hundreds of thousands of immigrants from European and Arab nations, reclaimed the land, and built an active cultural life. This was done despite the constant threat from Israel's Arab neighbors. There have been four wars: the War of Independence (1947–1949), the Suez Campaign (1956), the Six Day War (1967), and the Yom Kippur War (1973). The Arabs have also used terrorism and political and economic pressure in attempts to destroy the Jewish state. In addition, the people of Israel face domestic problems which present new challenges for the future.*

24

Many Lands, One People

Jews living in Africa in mud-walled huts.

Jews only 200 miles from the Arctic Circle worshipping in a converted railway station.

Jews in India shaving a child's head and weighing the hair to decide how many coins the family must give to charity.

Jews off the coast of South America entering a synagogue whose floor is covered with sand.

Jews who are not allowed to travel more than two-and-a-half miles from home without special permission from the government.

Jews who are sent to prison for ten years and more just for wanting to emigrate to the State of Israel.

All these are scenes from Jewish life around the world in our own day.

Falashas of Ethiopia

In eastern Africa just north of the equator lies Ethiopia, a country of mountains and rivers, of great physical beauty and dismal poverty. And there, living in primitive mud-walled huts, is a large community of black Jews. In the 1970's their number was generally thought to be between 25,000 and 30,000, though some estimates were much lower.

These people are known as the FALASHAS. We are not certain where they came from or how they got their name. They believe they are descendants of King Solomon and the Queen of Sheba, but some scholars have suggested that the Falashas may actually be descendants of Jewish traders from Yemen, which lies directly across the Red Sea. All agree that this black Jewish community has lived in Ethiopia for more than 2000 years.

For most of this time they lived completely isolated from the outside world—in fact, they believed they were the only Jews on earth! Nevertheless, they held fast to the laws of the Torah, which they interpreted quite literally. (They knew nothing of the Talmud and later works, for these were written long after their community began.) They did not read Hebrew, but studied the Torah from a translation in a local Semitic language called GHEEZ.

Meetings between the Falashas and the rest of the Jewish world began in 1904, when a Polish Jew, Dr. Jacques Faitlovich, learned of their existence. He set out to improve their lives, and to give them the deep knowledge of Judaism which would help them resist missionary pressures to convert to Christianity.

Faitlovich raised funds to build schools for the Falashas. He taught them about their heritage, and about the international Jewish community to which they belonged. He then returned to Europe to tell world Jewry of their brothers and sisters in Ethiopia—black men and women whose ancestors had worshipped the God of Israel when Russia was the home of primitive tribes and Western Europe was ruled by Julius Caesar.

In the 1970's the Falashas were still desperately poor, living largely by selling pottery to tourists. They were also threatened by warfare within Ethiopia. Their hard lives did not, however, weaken their devotion to Judaism. They continued to meet for long services in synagogues covered with thatch or corrugated iron, topped by a Star of David. And they did so with pride.

Trondheim, Norway

Different in almost every way from the Falashas are the Jews of Trondheim, Norway, who claim to have the northernmost synagogue in the world.

Trondheim, Norway's third largest city, began to receive refugees from the Russian pogroms as soon as Norway gave full free-

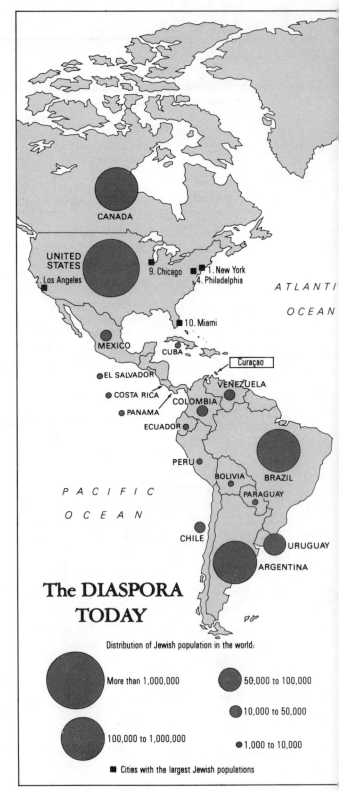

The DIASPORA TODAY

Distribution of Jewish population in the world:

More than 1,000,000

50,000 to 100,000

10,000 to 50,000

100,000 to 1,000,000

1,000 to 10,000

■ Cities with the largest Jewish populations

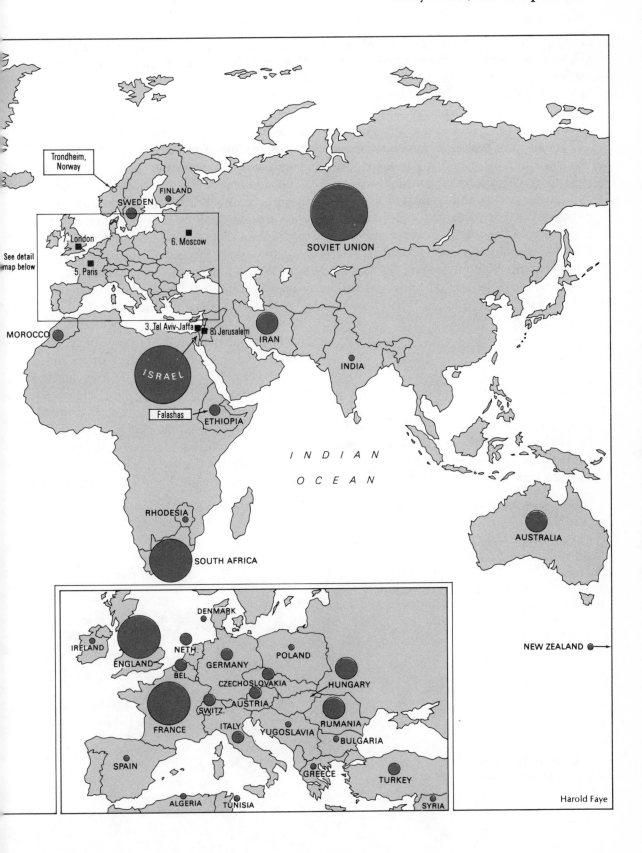

Trondheim, Norway

FINLAND

SWEDEN

See detail
map below

7. London

6. Moscow

5. Paris

SOVIET UNION

MOROCCO

3. Tel Aviv-Jaffa

8. Jerusalem

IRAN

INDIA

ISRAEL

Falashas

ETHIOPIA

INDIAN

OCEAN

AUSTRALIA

RHODESIA

SOUTH AFRICA

NEW ZEALAND

DENMARK

IRELAND

NETH.

ENGLAND

BEL.

GERMANY

POLAND

CZECHOSLOVAKIA

HUNGARY

SWITZ.

AUSTRIA

FRANCE

ITALY

YUGOSLAVIA

RUMANIA

BULGARIA

SPAIN

GREECE

TURKEY

ALGERIA

TUNISIA

SYRIA

Harold Faye

dom to Jews in 1891. Before World War II there were 1500 jews in the country, most of whom were murdered by the Nazis; but by 1975 there were again nearly 1000 Jews in Norway, and 100 in Trondheim.

Though the Jewish community there was tiny, it was surprisingly active. In 1923 the Jews of Trondheim took over an old railway station and converted it into a synagogue. This remained the heart of Jewish life in the 1970's, a center not only for worship but also for several Jewish organizations. Visitors found this Arctic congregation to be one of unity, vitality, and warmth.

India

The story of how there came to be a Jewish community in India is lost as deep in the past as is the origin of the Falashas. The Indian Jews believe it all began when fourteen Jews (seven men and seven women) were shipwrecked on the coast of

* Indian Jews knew nothing of Ḥanukkah until modern times.

India before the time of the Maccabees.* Whatever Jewish things they brought with them were lost at sea, but they preserved what they could remember—the SHEMA, the Sabbath, and circumcision—until a man named Rabbi David arrived from Egypt in the Middle Ages and taught them the Torah and its commandments.

How much of this is history we cannot be sure. Strangely enough, we do know of one very famous Rabbi David who lived in the Middle Ages, sailed east, and was lost in a shipwreck. He was the brother of the most famous Jew of the Golden Age, Moses Maimonides. Some scholars say this was the Rabbi David of Indian fame.

Certainly the community survived with an unusual mixture of traditions. One such tradition was to let a boy's hair grow for several years. The child was then brought to the synagogue in his finest clothes, marching to the sound of fife and drum. Each guest was given the privilege of snipping off a few of his locks, and finally his head (except for the earlocks) was shaved. The hair was weighed and its weight, in gold or silver, was given by his family to the poor or to the synagogue.

A Cochin Jew from southwestern India.

If this sounds strange, don't think of it as the custom of a primitive people. The Indian Jews have been successful business and professional people, and have built magnificent synagogues to serve a community which at one time had over 25,000 members.

In recent years, however, more and more Indian Jews have moved to Israel. While this has been Israel's gain, it has left once bustling Indian synagogues suddenly empty. By 1975 the total Jewish population of India had dwindled to about 8000. Some of the synagogue buildings may survive as museums. What will become of the Indian Jewish community is uncertain.

Curaçao

The oldest synagogue in the Americas is not in the United States, as you might have thought, but is just 800 miles north of the equator. It is on Curaçao, a lovely island off the coast of Venezuela.

Curaçao was under Dutch control in 1653, the year the Portuguese conquered Brazil. Jews who had been living in Brazil fled from the power of the Portuguese Inquisition, and some found a home in the tiny Dutch colony.*

The Jews found a good life in Curaçao, and helped to make the island a major shipping center of the eighteenth century. While today Curaçao is no longer quite so important, our people have continued to prosper, and descendants of the original settlers are still living there among a total Jewish population of about 700.

* Other Jewish refugees were forced by storms and pirates to head north, and landed on another Dutch island colony—New Amsterdam. For more about them, see Chapter 2.

Today they worship in a handsome synagogue built in 1732. (Some of the furnishings are even older. They came from an earlier building on the same site.) All the woodwork is of mahogany, including the many beautiful carvings which decorate the Holy Ark.

The floor of the synagogue is covered with sand. Why this is so, no one knows. It may simply have been a way of muffling the sound of shoes on the tiled floor. A more poetic explanation is that the Jews of Curaçao wanted to remind themselves of the days when Moses and the children of Israel wandered through the sands of the Sinai desert.

The Western world

These small communities are not, of course, typical of most Jews outside the largest centers of world Jewry. More than 1 million Jews in Western Europe, more than one half million in South America, and almost 200,000 in Australia and South Africa live in ways that would seem quite familiar to most of us.

Each community has problems, of course, which may or may not relate to Judaism as such. In South Africa the Jewish community finds itself in a difficult and dangerous position because of the government's policy of strictly separating the ruling white minority and the oppressed black majority. In Argentina an ugly wave of anti-Semitism during the 1970's forced the closing of the American Jewish Committee's office in the capital, Buenos Aires.

But, for now, most Jews in the Western world enjoy prosperity and freedom.

In the Muslim Middle East and, above all, in the Soviet Union, this is not the case.

Portrait of a beautiful Jewess from Tangier, a seaport in Morocco.

Arab lands

For the Jews remaining in Arab lands, life is at best insecure, at worst dreadful. The Koran, the sacred scripture of Islam, calls Jews evil and hypocritical, and Islamic laws require that Jews be treated as second-class citizens. These laws were not always strictly enforced, and during the Golden Age, Jews held positions of great importance in Muslim society. But even the most successful found their lives uprooted by anti-Jewish riots, and in less favorable times Jewish suffering was enormous. It has been estimated that before 1900 there were as many Jewish victims of riot and massacre in the Muslim world as there were in Christian Europe.

It is hardly surprising, then, that the vast majority of the Jews in the Arab world fled to the State of Israel as soon as they could. In 1947, 800,000 Jews lived in Arab lands. By 1977, fewer than 32,000 remained.

Of these, 25,000 lived in Morocco and Tunisia, states which had preserved the civil rights of their Jewish citizens, though not fully protecting them from riot (the Great Synagogue of Tunis was burned in 1967). Some Arab countries had no Jews at all. The once great Jewish communities of Egypt and Iraq now held just a handful—mostly elderly people who were unable or unwilling to begin new lives in the Jewish state.

About 4500 Jews were trapped in Syria under the control of the government's secret police. These officials have dictatorial control over every Jewish life. They control even the issuing of driver's licenses, and can keep a Jew from getting one. As of this writing, Syrian Jews cannot travel more than two-and-a-half miles from their homes without a permit. Almost without exception, they are forbidden to leave the country. Those caught trying to flee have been sentenced to long periods in prison, and their relatives have been brutally tortured.

Meanwhile, they live in the midst of a people being trained in anti-Semitism. Here is a sentence from an official Syrian textbook taught to sixth graders:

> The Jews always and everywhere dislike people living in peace, since their rule and domination over others depends on the existence of anarchy, division, and strife.

International efforts to win freedom for Syrian Jewry have met with very little success.

Iran

The Jews of Iran have been spared this brutal treatment, for although the Iranian government is Muslim, it is not Arab, and does not automatically adopt anti-Jewish policies. Jews have lived there since ancient times, when Iran was called Persia. It is the setting for the Biblical story of Queen Esther.

But from the time the Muslims conquered the country in the seventh century c.e., Jewish life in Persia was much like that of the Jews in Christian Europe: a general picture of misery brightened only on rare occasions. In both areas there were anti-Jewish riots, unfair taxes, and laws requiring Jews to wear special hats or badges at all times. In both areas there were forced conversions, giving Jews little choice but to practice their religion in secret while pretending to be true to another faith. In both areas there was deep longing for a Messiah: through the years Persian Jews believed not only in Shabbetai Zevi, but also in three false Messiahs from their own region! Finally, Jews both in Europe and in Persia fell into grinding poverty and cultural isolation.

The life of Iranian Jewry improved in the twentieth century, thanks to the work of the American Jewish Joint Distribution Committee. The Joint, along with other Jewish groups, set up schools to serve 10,000 students, plus a Jewish hospital and medical service program. Iranian Jews were also able to help each other: a youth center and a home for the aged were set up by the Jews of Tehran, the Iranian capital.

This picture of progress was clouded in 1979 by a revolution that brought Muslim fanatics into power. The new regime lost no time in denouncing Israel, and the 80,000 Jews living in Iran soon began to fear for their freedom.

The Soviet Union

The Jews in the Soviet Union have no illusions about their freedom—or their future.

Despite promises of liberty and equality for the 2,500,000 Soviet Jews, the Communist government has targeted the Jewish community for destruction. There were thousands of synagogues in czarist Russia. In 1976 there were fewer than sixty. Other religions are permitted to train clergymen,

This photograph offers a less glamorous view of Jewish life in Morocco—a lone woman in the Jewish quarter of Rabat.

but the Communists allow no schools for rabbis. Prayer books may not be published, and at times Jews have even been forbidden to make or import matzah. The Yiddish and Hebrew press and all Jewish cultural activities have been destroyed. On a single day in 1952, twenty-four leaders of Yiddish culture were shot.

Those who choose to leave the Soviet Union face new dangers. Some are given exit visas; others are refused time and time again. These "refuseniks" are then demoted or dismissed from their jobs. Their mail is intercepted, their telephone service cut off. They may be drafted into the army, or sent to prison on ridiculous charges—such as being out of work (after having been fired)! In addition to the misery that all prisoners face in Soviet jails, Jews suffer additional punishment from anti-Semitic guards. They live on starvation diets while forced to perform hard labor, and are generally permitted to send no more than one letter a year.

And yet our people continue to apply for exit visas, searching for a way out of the hell which is the life of a committed Jew in the Soviet Union. Their story was told in a letter written by a 12½-year-old Russian boy:

I and my brother, my parents and my grandfathers and grandmothers were born in Russia, but we have only one Motherland. It is Israel. And we want to go there from Russia. We often have troubles because of it. We go for a visa to a special establishment which belongs to the police. We have applied there 24 times for 5 years, and they refused us. But we hope to go soon.

Even the cruel anti-Semitism of the Communist government has not yet destroyed Jewish dreams of a better life, and a better world.

We have looked quickly around the globe. We have found our Jewish relatives in huge communities, in tiny communities, in new lands, in ancient lands, rich, poor, white and brown and black, free and enslaved. We have seen different customs, traditions, ways of life. Yet perhaps the most striking thing is not the differences between these Jews, but their basic similarity. On every continent there are those who know that being a Jew matters. They take pride in being part of the people who first saw the order in the universe, and proclaimed to Israel and all humanity:

יְיָ אֱלֹהֵינוּ, יְיָ אֶחָד.

The Lord our God, the Lord is one.

SUMMARY   *Jews live in widely different communities. Some are small, isolated groups like the Falashas of Ethiopia, while others are in the major centers of the Western world. Many Jews are trapped under dictatorial rule in Arab and Communist lands. But Jews everywhere have shown great dedication to preserving their heritage as part of the Jewish people.*

25

America Since World War II

Wherever Jews have been given freedom, they have made major contributions to the countries in which they lived. But nowhere in the Diaspora has the Jewish contribution been more far-reaching than in the United States. You can see this by imagining a single day in the life of an American—perhaps yourself.

Everyday life in America— the Jewish contribution

You get up in the morning with the happy thought that it is Labor Day; for this extra vacation, you can thank Samuel Gompers, the Jewish union leader who fought for a holiday which would honor American workers.* At breakfast you enjoy a glass of milk—pasteurized because of Nathan Straus, who worked to spread the use of this milk purifying method invented by a Frenchman. You might spend the

---

* Another American holiday has Jewish origins: Thanksgiving was modeled after the harvest festival of Sukkot.

morning listening to radio or watching television, both pioneered by the Jew David Sarnoff. Instead you turn on the phonograph. (The flat disk record was invented by the Jewish scientist Emile Berliner, who also invented the microphone.)

Later you decide to go shopping—perhaps in a department store founded by Jews (see Chapter 8). Looking for children's clothing? Then you owe a debt to Louis Borgenicht, who styled ready-made clothing for children (instead of simply scaling down adult clothes to children's sizes). But if you want a pair of bluejeans—"levis"—you should thank Levi Strauss, who first produced them in 1850 as sturdy pants for California goldminers.

The dollar bills you carry in your pocket are probably not old enough to bear the signature of Henry Morgenthau, Jr., the Jewish secretary of the treasury under Franklin Roosevelt. But the portrait of Lincoln on your pennies was designed by a Jewish sculptor, Victor David

Everyday life in America—how many Jewish personalities and achievements can you identify?

Brenner. This was the first presidential portrait to appear on an American coin. Brenner wanted Lincoln to be on the penny so that every citizen would learn to recognize the Great Emancipator, the man who gave freedom to so many.

It's time for lunch: perhaps a pizza, which some scholars think was first made more than 2000 years ago when Roman soldiers added cheese and olive oil to matzah. If you choose a hamburger or sandwich with a slice of tomato, you can be grateful to Dr. Siccary, the Jewish physician who in 1773 proved that tomatoes were safe to eat. Before his time, people thought that this fruit was pretty —but poisonous!

Now it's time for some entertainment. A baseball game? There have been several great Jewish athletes, including Hank Greenberg, one of only four men ever to hit fifty-eight or more home runs in a season, and Sandy Koufax, the lightning-fast lefthander who refused to pitch a World Series game which fell on Yom Kippur.

Perhaps you check the movie listings. The motion picture industry was largely built by such Jews as Samuel Goldwyn, Louis B. Mayer, and the Warner brothers. The very first talking picture starred a cantor's son, Al Jolson, playing the role of a cantor's son who wanted to enter show business! There have been many other

Jewish movie stars, including Danny Kaye, Barbra Streisand, Kirk Douglas, and the Marx Brothers.

Finally you might decide to see a live show. How about a play by the Pulitzer prize-winning dramatist Arthur Miller? Or a musical like *Show Boat, Oklahoma!, The Sound of Music, My Fair Lady*, or *Fiddler on the Roof*, all composed by Jews?

Heading home you pass a hospital, busily using discoveries of great Jewish physicians. The first doctor to develop children's medicine—pediatrics—as a special field was Abraham Jacobi. The disease of polio was defeated by Jonas Salk, who developed the Salk vaccine. Tuberculosis was largely wiped out when Selman A. Waksman discovered the wonder drug streptomycin.

Still, it's good to know that if you do get hurt, or if an emergency strikes, you can count on the American Red Cross, which was co-founded by a Jew, Adolphus Solomons. (The Red Cross uniform was also designed by a Jew, Henry Dix.) If someone you know needs nursing care, you can call the Visiting Nurse Service, built through the efforts of the Jewish social worker Lillian Wald. (She also pioneered the movement to establish playgrounds for children in American cities.)

Finally, as the day ends and you think back over the things you did, and think gratefully about the country you live in,

Some Jewish American "Firsts"

Justice L. D. Brandeis
(1856–1941).

The first Jew to die for American independence: Francis Salvador of South Carolina, scalped during an Indian raid on July 31, 1776.

The first Jewish Supreme Court Justice: Louis Dembitz Brandeis of Kentucky, served on the High Court from 1916 to 1939 (Brandeis University in Massachusetts is named for him).

The first Jewish cabinet member: Oscar Straus, named Secretary of Commerce and Labor by President Theodore Roosevelt in 1906.

The first Jewish governor: Moses Alexander of Idaho, elected in 1914, reelected in 1917.

The first Jewish American winner of a Nobel Prize: Albert Abraham Michelson of the University of Chicago, winner of the Nobel Prize for Physics in 1907 (he was the first American to win a Nobel Prize in any category).

The first Jewish symphony conductor: Leopold Damrosch, founder of the nation's first symphony orchestra, in New York City in 1873.

---

you find yourself humming the tune "God Bless America"—composed by the great Jewish songwriter Irving Berlin.

Acceptance and self-acceptance

Achievements such as these are ones in which all Jews can take great pride. But in all honesty, we must admit that it was not achievements by Jews which brought an end to the type of American anti-Semitism described in Chapter 18. Rather, it was the Holocaust. When Gentiles throughout the United States saw the results of Nazi Jew-hatred, all major educational, social, and economic barriers against American Jews began to collapse.

For example, in the twenty years after the war, Jewish enrollment in colleges and universities tripled. Four of every five Jewish high school students went to college—double the national average. Fully 10 percent of all teaching positions were held by men and women who had been raised as Jews. And Jewish studies became part of the curriculum at over 200 institutions of higher learning.

Acceptance of Jews was so complete that it became common to speak of Judaism as one of the three great religions of the United States (along with Roman Catholicism and Protestantism), though Jews represent less than 3 percent of the American population.

Not only were Gentiles accepting Jews —Jews were also accepting themselves. Many who had come from Eastern Europe at the beginning of the century, or the children of those immigrants, had been ashamed or afraid of their Jewishness. In their struggle to prove that they were "true Americans," they turned away from their religion. The children and grandchildren of these people, however, felt totally comfortable as citizens of the United

States. In many cases, they returned to their Jewish heritage for identity, for meaning, and for inspiration.

Rediscovering our Jewish heritage

Sometimes they experimented with new forms of study and worship. A group might choose to form a HAVURAH—a small close-knit community of Jews searching together for renewed meaning in Judaism. But more often, Jews turned back to the traditional Jewish institutions.

In 1948, there were some 360 Reform congregations in America—by 1970 there were 700. Even more rapid was the growth of the Conservative movement, which in the same period expanded from 317 to 833 congregations. And during the 1970's it seemed that the Orthodox movement was also flourishing.

New buildings were needed for new congregations, and also for older congregations that moved from decaying inner cities to rapidly growing suburbs. In the twenty years following World War II, some $150 million were spent on synagogue construction.

These congregations were served by an increasing number of rabbis. The rabbinical schools were flooded with applications from young men (and, in the Reform and Reconstructionist movements, young women) eager to become religious leaders. Within synagogues, the right of rabbis to speak out forcefully on current moral and political issues was now accepted as a matter of course. This was the result of long struggles fought by earlier rabbis such as Stephen S. Wise, whose sermons on the problems of the day filled New York's Carnegie Hall each week and were reprinted in major newspapers.

Israel and American Jewry

American Zionists have played a leading role on the world scene. During the United Nations debate over the creation of a Jewish state, the spokesman for world Zionism was an American Reform rabbi, Abba Hillel Silver. It was he who announced to the UN that our people would accept the offer of a tiny portion of Palestine as the basis for a Jewish state. And, he declared proudly, the new state would survive:

> The Jewish people in Palestine is prepared to defend itself. It is not impressed by idle threats. A people that has survived the accumulated fury of the centuries, faced powerful empires in bitter battle for survival, and during the last war saw hundreds of thousands of its sons fighting for freedom in all the liberating armies of the Allied nations while the head of the Palestine Arab Higher Committee was broadcasting Nazi propaganda from Berlin and congratulating Hitler on his African victories over the Allies—such a people will not be intimidated.

On the very day of the final UN vote, he was again called to speak, and delivered an impassioned plea for the partition of Palestine. Only hours later, the UN made its historic decision to create a Jewish state.

By then, the American Jewish community was contributing $100 million a year to the yishuv—a figure dwarfed by later fund-raising efforts, particularly those which followed the Six Day War and Yom Kippur War. The United States government has also given large grants to the Jewish state.

Yet while America has given much to Israel, it has received much in return. Israel has been America's only democratic ally in the Middle East, the one nation in the area which has stood up for democracy and opposed the influence of the Soviet Union.

For American Jewry, the benefits of supporting Israel have been even more dramatic. The cause of Israel and its survival have helped to unify American Jews. The miraculous history of the Jewish state has contributed greatly to the revival of Jewish pride. It has also sparked a growth in Jewish knowledge, and inspired increased study of Hebrew, Hebrew literature, and Jewish history.

The Jewish family—in trouble?

All of this promises much for the future. But American Jewry is also facing important problems.

Jews are grateful to live in a free country where people of all races and religions have the right to meet, work, and study together. We take satisfaction in the fact that Jews are no longer kept out of college because of their religion. However, as Jews and Gentiles spend more and more time with each other, more and more fall in love and marry. The non-Jewish partner may convert to Judaism before or after the marriage, but many do not. And in a home where only one parent is Jewish, the children are less likely to become active members of the Jewish community—if, indeed, they are raised as Jews at all.

Since World War II, the number of mixed marriages has risen with great speed. In the early 1970's, it was estimated that about four out of every ten marriages involving one Jew did not involve a Jewish partner. And the rate was increasing.

At the same time, the average size of Jewish families was shrinking. By the 1960's, the Jewish population was growing at about half the rate of the total American population. By the 1970's, the birthrate was well below the level needed to keep the Jewish population at its present size.

"Zero Population Growth" may be needed to prevent mass starvation in the underdeveloped countries, but it is hard to see how it will help the already small American Jewish community. The combination of mixed marriages and a shrinking birthrate may seriously reduce the number of American Jews, and so limit their ability to help the cause of Soviet and Israeli Jewry. It will certainly mean that fewer and fewer young Jews will have to provide for more and more older people.

Not only do Jews find themselves in smaller families—often they find themselves with no families at all. Many are living as "singles" because they have not yet married, do not wish to marry, or have lost a husband or wife through death or divorce. Traditionally, Jewish institutions have served the needs of couples, particularly those seeking Jewish education for their children. Today, growing numbers of Jews do not fit this pattern.

American Jewry is now working to meet these challenges.

Major efforts are being made to improve Jewish education, in the belief that as young Jews learn more about their heritage they will come to treasure it and live by it. Public attention is being drawn to the issue of the Jewish birthrate, so that Jewish couples will realize that the decisions they make on family size affect the Jewish people as a whole. Jewish institutions are changing their programs to offer more to senior citizens and Jewish singles. In addition, Jewish groups are taking a more active role in finding and bringing back Jews who, for whatever reason, have not been involved in Jewish life.

Abba Eban Remembers:
Henry Kissinger and Arthur Goldberg

Arthur Goldberg
(1908–   ).

In Israel's gravest hours of crisis, in May 1967 and October 1973, the policy of the United States was very largely entrusted to Jewish Americans, Arthur Goldberg and Henry Kissinger. While they acted in accordance with the directives of their presidents and in conformity with American interests, I have no doubt whatever that the depth of their Jewish feeling played a part in helping them to give the American-Israeli relationship an element of human warmth and intensity that might otherwise have been lacking.

In the terrible year 1973, Kissinger was secretary of state. Never before had a Jew been so close to the main center of world power and in such a position to influence the destiny of the Jewish people. In this sense, Kissinger was far more influential than Mordecai at the court of Ahasuerus.

When the cease-fire came in mid-October, Kissinger traveled to Israel. I accompanied him to Yad Vashem, where the memory of the Holocaust is kept alive in a permanent exhibit of documents and pictures. Kissinger was shown an album with the photos and records of the Jews of Fürth in Bavaria, where his family had been. In that book there were about eleven Kissingers who had been destroyed in the Holocaust, as well as other relatives with different names. When I flew with him in a helicopter back to the airport, he didn't say a single word, since he was moved by the traumatic recollections of the Holocaust.

Abba Eban (1915–   ) with Henry Kissinger (1923–   ).

Some Jews have also suggested an active campaign to reach uncommitted Christians who might find value in Judaism, and would benefit by converting to our religion. The effort to attract converts is called PROSELYTISM, and was actively practiced by Jews until it was stopped by the medieval Church.

There will be much discussion in the coming years about whether—and how—we should again attempt to attract significant numbers of converts.

Looking back, looking ahead

History helps us look at our problems more clearly. Seen by themselves, they may appear overwhelming. From the viewpoint of many years, they seem more manageable.

A man who became an American rabbi just after World War I felt that as a Jewish leader he was part of a "holding action." Religion was unstylish in America, both for Jews and Gentiles. Jewish education was at low ebb. It seemed that the most a young rabbi could do was to keep Jewish losses at a minimum, to help Judaism survive till a better day.

In his lifetime, that same rabbi has seen Jewish life changed almost totally. He has seen the Holocaust, the birth of Israel, and the flowering of American Jewry. The "better day" has arrived, one with new problems but with vastly increased opportunities. Thus, it is reasonable to hope and expect that the Jewish people, having created in North America the greatest Jewish community in history, will find ways of coping with the challenges of its current success.

But there is a more basic question that troubles the American Jewish community. It is the question that has been central to Jewish life since the time of Moses Mendelssohn. What does it mean to be a Jew in the modern age? What parts of our tradition are still binding or meaningful? In a world where Jewish ethics have been written into the laws of many nations, in a world where many Gentiles support the existence of the State of Israel and have joined the struggle for human rights in the Soviet Union, what is special about being a Jew?

This is the question we will consider in our final chapter.

SUMMARY   *American Jewry has reached remarkable levels of success in many fields. Since World War II, Jews have been accepted in American life, and have become more comfortable with the fact of their own Jewishness. Synagogues have grown. American Zionists have worked to create and support the State of Israel. Today, American Jewry is facing the problems of mixed marriages and changes in traditional Jewish family life.*

PART SEVEN

And Now?

What does it mean to be a good Jew in today's world?

26

Models for Today

In Volume One we examined the 4000-year-long story of our people. Then, after looking at the full sweep of Jewish history, we asked: "Does all this mean something special? Does our long experience as a people show that Jews have been given a special role in the life of the world?"

Our answer to these questions was: "Unquestionably, yes."

The book you have just read deals with the history of the last two centuries, and so raised very different questions. Even though we believe that Jews as a people play a special role in history, how should we as individuals be part of that history? How should we behave as Jews? On whom can we model our behavior?

In short: What does it mean to be a good Jew in today's world?

The other choice

Of course, we can each choose to avoid this question and simply not worry about being a *good* Jew. We all know people who are Jewish by birth, but whose Judaism—if it exists at all—is limited to the use of a few Yiddish words, a taste for certain foods, or perhaps attendance at services on Yom Kippur.

Such people are cheating themselves of knowledge, wisdom, fulfillment, and fun. They know little or nothing of the drama and excitement of Jewish history. They are deprived of the beauty of Jewish art, literature, music, and ritual. They are untouched by the ideas that have been shared by our people for thousands of years. Saddest of all, they lack roots, a knowledge of how they and their ancestors fit into the scheme of the world.

These are people who are culturally starved. They may be living happily—but then, it is also possible to be happy and live on vitamins, injections, and food pills. Yet just as a person who kept to this diet would miss the true enjoyment of eating, the taste of home-cooked food, and the companionship that can be shared at a good

all the men and women we think of as good Jews—have two crucially important traits in common, traits which distinguish them from "good people" in general.

First, they all have a commitment to the Jewish people. They realize that Jews have the *right* to survive; but beyond that, they believe that Jews *should* survive, *must* survive, for the sake of the world—for the betterment of humanity. Therefore, these "good Jews" are prepared to act in the way they feel will most benefit the Jewish people as a whole.

Second, having committed themselves to the Jewish people, they search for the best way to show that commitment. For some the search is quick—they find one goal and spend their lives working at it. (This was true of Theodor Herzl, who dedicated himself to creating a Jewish state.) Some take pride in spending a lifetime searching for new forms in which to express the timeless ideals of Judaism, varied as the results may be. (The prayer book of the Reform movement offers thanks "for the joy of community, the gift of diversity, and the vision of harmony.") Some remain devoted to the ancient forms of Jewish expression, yet look for the deepest and most meaningful ways to use those forms. (Once a Ḥasidic rabbi was asked what he did before praying. He replied: "I pray that I may be able to pray properly.")

But for all there is the search—the challenge—the adventure.

This has been true of our people throughout history. The Bible describes us as "stiffnecked," ready to argue, to question, to debate with other people or even with God. The pious shtetls of Eastern Europe, which we sometimes think of as filled with Jews who were ready to accept the Divine will, could ring with the cries of a rabbi challenging God Himself:

What do You want of Your people Israel? Why do You afflict Your people Israel? ... There must be an end of this.

And still, through this striving of millions of individuals—people searching, fighting to preserve our heritage, working to bring its truth to the world—we have survived and succeeded, giving proof of the worth of our tradition, and to the value of free thought in action.

The challenge—and the reward

So we do have our model. Not a simple one—not one where we can say, "Oh, all I have to do is be like so-and-so, and I will be a good Jew"—but a truly challenging one. We must be like those who examine, who hunt, who question, who search. We must find in Jewish experience—an experience too great for any one person to grasp entirely—that part we can truly make our own. We must find the role we can best play in the survival of our people, the development of our souls, and the betterment of humanity.

A difficult task? No doubt. But we know the rewards are great. This was told us almost 3000 years ago by the prophet Amos:

דִּרְשׁוּ־טוֹב וְאַל־רָע
לְמַעַן תִּחְיוּ
וִיהִי־כֵן יְהוָה
אֱלֹהֵי־צְבָאוֹת אִתְּכֶם

Seek good and not evil,
That you may live,
And so the Lord God of Hosts shall be
with you.

(Amos 5:14)

Glossary

ALIYAH (pl. ALIYOT) "going up"; especially since 1882, the immigration of Jews to ERETZ YISRAEL.

AMERICAN JEWISH COMMITTEE organization founded in 1906 to protect the rights of Jews in the United States and throughout the world.

AMERICAN JEWISH JOINT DISTRIBUTION COMMITTEE relief and charitable organization founded in 1914; also known as the "Joint" or JDC.

ANTI-DEFAMATION LEAGUE agency founded by B'NAI B'RITH in 1913 to fight ANTI-SEMITISM.

ANTI-SEMITISM hatred of or prejudice against the Jewish people.

BALFOUR DECLARATION letter signed in 1917 by Lord Balfour (1848–1930), the British foreign minister, approving the establishment of a Jewish homeland in Palestine.

BILU from "House of Jacob, come let us go up"; a group of Russian Jewish pioneers who settled in Palestine in 1882, thus beginning the First ALIYAH.

BLOOD LIBEL the lie, invented during the Middle Ages, that Jews murdered Christians in order to use their blood in Passover matzah.

B'NAI B'RITH "Sons of the Covenant"; the world's oldest and largest Jewish service organization, founded in 1843.

CANTONISTS in nineteenth century Russia, Jewish boys who were forced to join the army and were then isolated, mistreated, and often baptized against their will.

CONSERVATIVE JUDAISM branch of modern Judaism which is basically traditional but open to change.

DREYFUSARD during the Dreyfus Affair in modern France, anyone who argued that Captain Alfred Dreyfus (1859–1935) was innocent of the charges against him.

Many other terms not listed here may be found in the Glossary for Volume One.

ERETZ YISRAEL the land of Israel, promised by God to the people of Israel in Biblical times.

FALASHAS black Jews who have been living in Ethiopia for at least 2000 years.

GET a bill of divorce in Jewish law.

GHEEZ the language of the FALASHAS.

HABAD from "wisdom, understanding, knowledge"; the most scholarly branch of HASIDISM; in recent years, Habad has tried in imaginative ways to reintroduce Jews to traditional Jewish practices.

HADASSAH The Women's Zionist Organization of America, founded in 1912 by Henrietta Szold (1860–1945).

HALUTZIM "pioneers"; young Jews who settled in Palestine just after World War I.

HASIDISM "religion of the pious"; Jewish religious sect based on the teachings of the Baal Shem Tov (c. 1700–1760) and stressing joy and devotion rather than study.

HASKALAH "Enlightenment"; especially in nineteenth century Russia, a movement that stressed the need for Jews to take part fully in the general culture.

HAVLAGAH "self-restraint"; policy pursued by Jews in Palestine during the 1930's, avoiding violent response to Arab attacks.

HEDER "room"; traditional Hebrew elementary school, often a one-room schoolhouse.

HOLOCAUST the persecution and eventual murder of millions of European Jews by the NAZIS and their allies.

IRGUN Jewish underground army which rejected HAVLAGAH and violently resisted British rule in Palestine.

JEWISH NATIONAL FUND organization founded in 1901 by the Fifth Zionist Congress, in order to purchase and develop land for Jewish settlement in Palestine.

KETUBAH a marriage contract in Jewish law.

KEVUTZAH   a small collective farm in ERETZ YISRAEL.

KIBBUTZ   in ERETZ YISRAEL, a collective village of any size, including industry as well as farming.

KRISTALLNACHT   "Night of Broken Glass"; in Germany, the night of November 9–10, 1938, when nearly every synagogue was destroyed and at least 30,000 Jews were arrested.

MAABAROT   tent cities used to house new immigrants to Israel during the early years of statehood.

MASKILIM   Jews who supported HASKALAH.

MAY LAWS   in Russia, anti-Jewish laws which took effect in May 1882, during the reign of Czar Alexander III.

MELAMED   teacher in a ḤEDER.

MITNAGDIM   "Opponents"; followers of the Vilna Gaon (1720–1797), the leading opponent of HASIDISM.

MUSAR   "Moral discipline"; traditional Jewish writings on ethics.

NAZIS   members of the National Socialist German Workers' Party, the political party of Adolf Hitler (1889–1945).

NEO-ORTHODOXY   branch of modern Judaism founded by Samson Raphael Hirsch (1808–1888); Neo-Orthodoxy regards the Torah as the source of all moral authority in Jewish life.

ORTHODOXY   generally, in Judaism, the strict observance of Jewish law.

PALE OF SETTLEMENT   during the 1700's and 1800's, the region of Eastern Europe where the Russian government required Jews to live.

PALESTINIANS   residents of Palestine; term now used mainly to refer to those Arabs who fled Israel during the War of Independence (1947–1949).

POGROM   massacre of Jews, especially in Russia and other countries of Eastern Europe.

PROSELYTISM   the attempt to convince members of one religion to convert to another.

PROTOCOLS OF THE ELDERS OF ZION   a book written by anti-Semites to "prove" that Jews are plotting to take over the world.

REBBE   the leader of a Ḥasidic sect (see ḤASIDISM); also called Zaddik.

RECONSTRUCTIONISM   a movement led by Mordecai Kaplan (1881–) which sees Judaism not just as a religion but as a constantly changing way of life.

REFORM   branch of modern Judaism which considers basic Jewish values to be eternal, but which also regards each Jew as the final authority for his or her own beliefs and practices.

SABRA   a native-born Israeli; named for the fruit of the sabra cactus, which is tough on the outside but sweet on the inside.

SCIENCE OF JUDAISM   term coined by Leopold Zunz (1794–1886) to describe his own use of modern research methods in Jewish studies.

SHTADLAN   during the seventeenth and eighteenth centuries, a man who represented a local Jewish community in dealings with the Christian world.

SHTETL (pl. SHTETLACH)   in Eastern Europe, a small Jewish community which might make up all or part of a village; the last remaining shtetlach were destroyed during the HOLOCAUST.

UNITED JEWISH APPEAL   U.S. Jewish fundraising organization founded in 1939.

YISHUV   name applied to the Jewish community in Palestine from the birth of ZIONISM to the establishment of the State of Israel.

YOUTH ALIYAH   organization founded in 1933 to rescue children from hardship and persecution in the Diaspora and raise them in ERETZ YISRAEL.

ZIONISM   in modern times, the movement to establish an independent Jewish state in Palestine.

Index

Entries in italics *refer to* photographs, maps, or illustrations. *To save space, the following abbreviations have been used: b., born; B.C.E., Before the Common Era; c., circa, about; C.E., Common Era; cent., century; d., died; r., reigned. All dates above 100 are C.E. unless otherwise noted.*

The editor and publisher gratefully acknowledge the cooperation of the following sources of photographs for this book:

A.I.C.F., 202; Alliance Israelite Universelle, 68; American Jewish Joint Distribution Committee, 150; Bettmann Archive, 15, 23, 32, 52, 114, 155, 158, 159, 169, 225; Bildarchiv der Österreichische Nationalbibliothek, 87; Brandeis University, 230; C.D.S.C., 173; Central Archives for the History of the Jewish People, Jerusalem, 32; Central Zionist Archives, Jerusalem, 26, 63, 111, 125, 129; Culver Pictures, 45, 162, 224; Danish Information Office (New York City), 180 (two photos); Frank J. Damstaedter, 18, 31, 33, 50, 71, 76, 143, 184; Editorial Photocolor Archives, 39 (Bill Aron).

Also: David Harris, 8; Hebrew Union College–Jewish Institute of Religion, 74; Historical Pictures Service, Inc., Chicago, 26, 32, 42, 104; Historisches Museum, Frankfurt am Main, 63; John Hopf, 73; Israel Consulate General, New York City, 93, 123, 166, 192, 212 (two photos); Israel Government Press Office, Jerusalem, 212; Israel Museum, Jerusalem, 81, 82 (two photos), 83, 199, 200; Israel Office of Information, 191.

Also: Jewish Museum, New York City, 9, 63, 96, 138; Jewish National Fund, 135; Jewish Theological Seminary, 164; Levi Strauss & Co., 77; Magnum, 5 (Erich Lessing), 40 (Paul Fusco, Sepp Seitz; two photos), 110 (Charles Harbutt), 112 (Leonard Freed); Metropolitan Museum of Art, New York City, 2, 5; George Mott, 37 (two photos), 198; Museum of American Jewish History, Philadelphia, 71; Museum of Modern Art, New York City (Gift of Hyman N. Glickstein), 199; Oriental Institute, University of Chicago, 3.

Also: Popperfoto, 62, 63 (two photos); Rapho/Photo Researchers, 109, 110, 198 (Gordon Gahan), 26, 84, 112, 197, 209, 238 (Louis Goldman), 112 (Paolo Koch), 39 (Katrina Thomas), 156 (Gianni Tortoli); Alfred Rubens Collection, 44, 58; Sears, Roebuck & Co., 77; Ann Zane Shanks, 236; Tel Aviv Museum, 153, 200; Union of American Hebrew Congregations, Art and Architecture Library, 37, 82, 83, 84, 198; United Nations, 233; Wide World, 26, 46, 141, 212, 233; YIVO, 56, 105, 155, 171; Zionist Archives and Library, New York City, 122, 189, 208.

On the cover: Babylonian lion, Metropolitan Museum of Art; Spanish synagogue, UAHC Art and Architecture Library; Cardiff rabbi, Magnum (Erich Hartmann); Horb synagogue, Israel Museum, Jerusalem; archaeological dig, Martin S. Rozenberg; Egyptian painting, Metropolitan Museum; Rosh Hashanah plate, Jewish Museum; Arabic medical manuscript, Metropolitan Museum (Rogers Fund, 1913); schoolboys playing soccer, Australian Government Tourist Office; Torah crown, CEDOK.